CONSCIENCE AND COMMUNITY

CONSCIENCE
AND
COMMUNITY

STERLING M. MCMURRIN, OBERT C. TANNER, AND LOWELL L. BENNION

Edited by Robert Alan Goldberg,
L. Jackson Newell, and
Linda King Newell

THE UNIVERSITY OF UTAH PRESS

Salt Lake City

The Defiance House Man colophon is a registered trademark of The University of Utah Press. It is based on a four-foot-tall Ancient Puebloan pictograph (late PIII) near Glen Canyon, Utah.

Printed and bound in the U.S.A.

Library of Congress Cataloging-in-Publication Data

Names: Goldberg, Robert Alan, 1949- editor. | Newell, L. Jackson, 1938- editor. | Newell, Linda King, editor.
Title: Conscience and community : Sterling M. McMurrin, Obert C. Tanner, and Lowell L. Bennion / edited by Robert Alan Goldberg, L. Jackson Newell, and Linda King Newell.
Description: Salt Lake City : The University of Utah Press, [2017] | Includes bibliographical references and index. |
Identifiers: LCCN 2017040686 (print) | LCCN 2017043984 (ebook) | ISBN 9781607816058 () | ISBN 9781607816041 (pbk.)
Subjects: LCSH: McMurrin, Sterling M.--Influence. | Tanner, Obert C. (Obert Clark), 1904-1993--Influence. | Bennion, Lowell L., 1908-1996--Influence. | Church of Jesus Christ of Latter-day Saints--Doctrines. | Mormon Church--Doctrines.
Classification: LCC BX8656 (ebook) | LCC BX8656 .C558 2017 (print) | DDC 289.3092/2792258--dc23

LC record available at https://lccn.loc.gov/2017040686

CONTENTS

PART I

INTRODUCTION
AND
OVERVIEW

1

INTRODUCTION

ROBERT ALAN GOLDBERG

In April 2014, the Tanner Humanities Center at the University of Utah marked its twenty-fifth anniversary with a conference focused on the beliefs, values, and lives of Sterling McMurrin, Obert C. Tanner, and Lowell Bennion. Their lives ran parallel and often entwined. Author Mary Lythgoe Bradford writes that they "grew from the same soil," dipped as infants in Mormon culture and folkways. After education beyond the borders of the Great Basin, McMurrin, Tanner, and Bennion gathered to Utah to begin careers and raise families. In the Zion kingdom they made their marks, and it was within the Mormon community that they faced their greatest challenges.

Sterling McMurrin, a University of Utah professor of philosophy and history, dismissed dogma and doctrine as barriers to a search for moral and spiritual understanding. If heretical in his beliefs, his ideas could not be ignored.

Obert Tanner, also of the university's philosophy department, described himself, first, as a teacher. While he juggled teaching, business, and philanthropy, he sought a world based on Christ's ideals for living.

Many students recall their first encounter with Lowell Bennion as a teacher and director of the LDS Institute of Religion at the University of Utah. A humanitarian, Bennion helped these young men and women to look to and through Mormonism to repair the world.

As important as their academic roles was their influence on the thought and culture of the Church of Jesus Christ of Latter-day Saints. Our conference, "Faith and Reason, Conscience and Conflict," considered how these three men, so tightly bound to their community, sought in Kathleen Flake's words "independence within, not from Mormonism." If they bridled at hierarchy and orthodoxy, they found in Mormonism's teachings and traditions opportunities to confront the pressing social, cultural, and political issues of their time. Their personalities and individual circumstances defined their quests for balance between conscience and community. Sterling McMurrin's dissent was open and direct. Obert Tanner quietly withdrew to practice his own brand of the social gospel without testing church authorities. Lowell Bennion spoke respectfully and without ambiguity in pursuit of mercy and justice but could marshal few advantages to counter his orthodox adversaries.

Context is important for understanding the nature and outcome of these challenges. David O. McKay led the LDS Church when these men brushed most closely with authorities. Mormonism was more isolated than it is today. The church was not so globally ambitious. The personal more often trumped the political; ties of family and friendship with church authorities were telling in the resolution of conflict and the rewarding of merit. In such an environment, with allies in high places and rival factions contending for authority, orthodoxy could be tempered and diversity of thought seemed sustainable. Power could be accommodated and accommodating. This, however, would not guarantee protection or the necessary space for principled dissent.

But Tanner, Bennion, and McMurrin are not simply historical figures whose experiences tell us of a world past. If they touched the issues and events of their times, they continue to speak to us because their concerns continue to haunt us: racial justice, gender equality, and the meaning of integrity and conscience for those enmeshed in community. Their stories expose the tension between faith and reason, conscience and obedience, as they pursued a more enlightened and humane society. Their stories offer lessons for us all, whether authorities, doubters, or those not yet touched by the conflict between freedom and obedience.

They also speak to those outside the Mormon Church for the issues they raised still affect men and women in diverse communities, secular and religious.

Our goal was not a traditional, academic festschrift. Because the focus was on character as well as intellectual contribution, scholars alone could not draw complete portraits. Intentionally, we opted for inclusion of diverse voices. Uniquely, we considered these very public men in the private world of family and friends. Participating were their now-grown children who saw our subjects outside the spotlight in more intimate settings. Combined, these different perspectives complete the picture and suggest the rewards and sacrifices of living open lives.

From our conference has come this book. Participants, now authors, have worked their papers into chapters. Others have joined to add their insights, broadening and deepening our sense of the roles these men played in shaping the past and creating the present. If Mormonism is the context of our effort, issues of conscience, faith, and community know no boundaries and touch us all.

Kathleen Flake begins our discussion by placing Lowell Bennion, Sterling McMurrin, and Obert Tanner within a Mormon intellectual tradition. She describes this tradition as a deep commitment to the love of learning, curiosity, optimism, and originality of thought. Not only did our subjects exemplify these qualities, their lives "teach us about being at once reasonable and religious."

Taking our subjects in turn, each section is composed of three essays. An excellent starting point to frame Sterling McMurrin's contributions is Jack Newell's essay. Newell examines the formative experiences and cultural circumstances that shaped McMurrin in his youth and early adulthood. Tutored by family members and mentors in the LDS Church and at the University of Utah, McMurrin developed the intellectual skills to become, for many, "the conscience of Mormonism." A devout free thinker, he dissented with the hope that the institutions that were dearest to him could maintain their integrity.

To understand Sterling McMurrin's ideas and values, Brian Birch considers the broader American religious context during the first third of the twentieth century. Nationally, liberalism and fundamentalism contested for the religious mind. This drama acted out in Mormonism as well, with the "Old Orthodoxy" challenged by new ideas and values voiced inside as well as outside the church hierarchy. Authorities took sides on such matters as biblical criticism and science's challenge to long-held religious beliefs. It was in this confrontation that McMurrin would find the tools to develop his own intellectual framework.

Boyer Jarvis writes "at close hand" of his longtime friend Sterling McMurrin. He traces McMurrin's career from the LDS Institute of Religion at the University of Arizona, to the University of Utah, to Washington as U.S. commissioner of education during the Kennedy Administration, and back to the University of Utah. Of particular interest are the personal relationships that tied McMurrin to church leaders and that underwrote his role in the federal government.

Bob Goldberg begins the second section by considering the spiritual quest of Obert Tanner. Tanner's vision of a cross-denominational Christianity embraced the world and still enabled him to find comfort in a culturally Mormon home. Mormon culture, so thoroughly instilled by his mother, Annie Clark Tanner, and reinforced by important mentors did not define Tanner, but guided him in the classroom, business world, and philanthropy. As he looked beyond the borders of Mormondom, he never abandoned its church, community, or people.

Education was one of Obert Tanner's highest priorities. Mark Matheson views Tanner's life from this perspective noting the powerful influence of his mother and his father's role modeling as an educator. Obert was a teacher first and understood that education conferred more than knowledge or the benefits of career. It was his "resource against despair." It was Obert Tanner's lever for personal growth, independence, and self-transformation.

Kent Murdock recalls another side of Professor Obert Tanner, his career in the O.C. Tanner Company, a business that sells awards that recognize personal achievement in school and the workplace. Apparent in his business philosophy and relationships with his workers are the small-town Mormon ideals that cultivated self-respect, a strong work ethic, and community. Obert Tanner's business values resonated with his deep spiritual beliefs.

Mary Lythgoe Bradford's essay frames the Lowell Bennion section of this book. Part autobiographical, part academic, her contribution reviews Bennion's life, influence, and activities first as his student and friend, later as his biographer. Bradford guides us though the phases of Bennion's life: the LDS Institute, his academic career at the University of Utah, and the "real world" of community service. Bradford's theme is a question: How does one stay loyal to the community and remain at peace with the soul?

Gregory Prince focuses tightly on Lowell Bennion, Mormon Church president David McKay, and matters of race. The two men were uncomfortable with racial restrictions in the LDS Church and pushed the official boundaries for change. Their effort was cautious and moved less by an intellectual construct than a heartfelt desire to seek justice for the faithful.

In a piece that parallels Boyer Jarvis's essay on McMurrin, Emma Lou Warner Thayne reveals the poet's power in assessing the influence of her mentor, Lowell Bennion. In a final composition before her death, she offered a paean to a teacher and mentor who helped young women and men to understand not only their place in the church and community but themselves. Bennion's message was personal salvation in social action, to heal thyself by healing those who were less fortunate but equally worthy of redemption.

Linda Newell has worked with Bill McMurrin, Carolyn Tanner Irish, and Ellen Bennion Stone to recreate the private worlds of these very public men. Offstage, these men and their families faced the daily challenges, both ordinary and exacting, that would shape not only their immediate families but also generations to come. How they dealt with those close to them in the intimacy of family offers a perspective that compliments their celebrity.

Jack Newell concludes this volume with searching questions. What were the conditions in and around Mormonism in the middle of the last century that prompted the rise and sustained the influence of three such compelling moral and intellectual leaders? Is that fertile ground gone, or might men and women of comparable stature again become widely admired moral authorities? Finally, Newell sheds light on the long and mutually important ties that bound Sterling McMurrin, Obert Tanner, and Lowell Bennion as they each sought to remain loyal to Mormonism while staying faithful to conscience.

2

THE LDS INTELLECTUAL
TRADITION

A Study on Three Lives

KATHLEEN FLAKE

The essays that follow in this volume address more deeply the contributions of Sterling McMurrin, Obert Tanner, and Lowell Bennion.[1] Not only in detail, but also in focus, they provide much that cannot be said here. My essay invites you to think about their religious heritage and philosophical proclivities or, in other words, their place in the Latter-day Saint intellectual tradition.

This tradition has been defined in various ways and sometimes declared not to exist at all. Nearly a century ago, historian Bernard DeVoto—a native of Ogden who spent a year at the University of Utah before finishing at Harvard—once declared, "Civilized life does not exist in Utah...[only] rigorous suppression of individuality, impracticability, skepticism, and all the other qualities of intelligence."[2] He would later apologize, but could not resist adding to it his belief that Mormons were particularly antagonistic to critique. Echoes of his point of view, whether in moderate or extreme form, exist today and invite reflection on the question whether McMurrin, Tanner, and Bennion were part of a larger tradition or *sui generis*. I think it makes them no less admirable and much more understandable if we do see them, each in his distinctive fashion, occupying a place within and contributing to a long history of Mormon intellectuality.

Certainly, if critique is viewed as the *sine qua non* of intellectuality, then DeVoto and others may be right. Not surprisingly, given their lasting experience with prejudice and at times persecution, the Latter-day Saints have been very self-protective, typically limiting themselves to faithful commentary and most attentive to praise. If on the other hand, one allows that intellectual critique and, more, the intellectual cast of mind that produces it derives from deeper commitments—curiosity, originality, love of learning, and optimism about the capacities of human understanding, for example—then the Saints would certainly qualify. Consider that no less an intellectual than the Yale literary critic Harold Bloom once said, "If *intellectual* means what it should mean, then [Joseph] Smith clearly is the most eminent intellectual in Mormon history. He was an authentic visionary, and totally original in mind and spirit—Really a kind of mortal God. I cannot understand why he is not honored more by Americans."[3]

Most of us tend to look for something other than "originality in mind and spirit" when we make our lists of intellectuals. Licensure in a particular academic guild and influence within it tend to be the common markers, but this is a relatively recent phenomenon. Before the entrenchment of those guilds in the contemporary academy, the list of Mormon intellectuals included such explainers or apologists as the brothers Orson and Parley P. Pratt and Eliza R. Snow in the nineteenth century and, later, Brigham H. Roberts, James E. Talmage, and John A. Widtsoe in the early twentieth.

Widtsoe could also be included in the mid-twentieth-century phase of Mormon intellectualism with those then credentialed by some of the world's finest academic institutions, including Harvard, Chicago, and Berkeley. The three men featured in this book, McMurrin, Tanner, and Bennion, graduated with advanced degrees, respectively, from the University of Southern California, Stanford University, and the University of Strasbourg. Thomas Simpson has argued that this educational outmigration from Zion created "extra-ecclesial loyalties [that] would dismantle the ideological framework of Mormon separatism and pave the way for Mormons' voluntary re-immersion into the mainstream of American life."[4] While he may overstate his case, given the complexity of forces in play to accomplish the release of Mormonism from its Great Basin ghetto, Simpson shows a long history of sending Mormonism's best and brightest to receive the Gentile academy's benefits, both direct (intellectual discipline) and indirect (social status).[5] The list of their attainments would be as impossible to catalog as their numbers.

A few examples must suffice. Leonard Arrington was one of the midcentury migrants who returned to Zion and found himself leading a historiographical renaissance.[6] In an article titled "The Intellectual Tradition of the Latter-day Saints," he captures best the spirit of scholarly Mormons during this period:

> No one will deny that our pioneer forebears were worthy builders—that they were adventurous frontiersmen, devoted farmers, and ingenious engineers. But those who tamed the wilderness and made the desert blossom also included poets, artists, teachers, and scholars. Not only did they perfect society with their well-articulated criticisms, but they created symbols and images of lasting value. May our studies establish the relevance of our intellectual heritage for the present, help us in stating more explicitly our aspirations for the future, and propel us to higher levels of achievement in all our endeavors.[7]

These "aspirations" and "endeavors" led mid-twentieth century Mormon intellectuals, no less than their predecessors, to grapple with questions presented by their religion—or any religion for that matter. This instinctive curiosity was present not only among those in the liberal arts, but the sciences as well: theoretical chemist Henry Erying's collection, *The Faith of a Scientist,* being the chief example.[8] "I believe," he wrote, "that many of our young people have impoverished their lives by a thoughtless denial of all aspects of the faith of their fathers in their desire to be what they call scientific and objective."[9] Thus, even if not devoted so completely and explicitly to explaining Mormonism, as were their nineteenth-century predecessors, midcentury Mormon intellectuals seemed drawn to reason about what the life of the mind has to do with a life of the spirit and the demands of faith, however subtly felt. Midcentury intellectuals Sterling McMurrin, Obert Tanner, and Lowell Bennion were no exception. What, we ask, do these men have to teach us about being at once reasonable and religious?

First, a caveat. It is only *reasonable* to begin by admitting that conflicts between reason and faith are not limited to Mormonism, but common to all religions. Indeed, such conflict contributes to the very definition of modernity, and my students of a variety of (religious) stripes wrestle with it. Nevertheless, the conflict takes its shape and form from historically specific cares and aspirations, anxieties, and confidences of the people engaged in such conflicts. Therefore, faithful reasoners or the reasonably faithful have reacted in a variety of ways to them. I would like to consider how McMurrin, Tanner, and Bennion responded to the religious conflicts of their time and place.

Their Lives

Our subjects' lives spanned nearly the entire "American century," as the twentieth century has been called. All arrived within a decade of one another beginning with Obert Tanner's birth in 1904. He was born at a moment of radical change and expansion for the nation certainly, but, no less for Mormonism. The LDS Church was about to recover from the economic costs of the onerous anti-polygamy campaign and had just placed an apostle in the United States Senate. Reed Smoot would represent both church and state for thirty years, rising to the highest levels of political influence.

Thus, our subjects arrived at a time when the church was moving onto the national stage with unprecedented authority and about to follow the American flag abroad with particular force and success.

Obert Clark Tanner was born in Farmington, Utah, the tenth child of plural wife Annie Clark Tanner and her absentee husband. From her memoirs, which her son took pains to publish, we get a glimpse of his life, too: the emotional, moral, economic, and, yes, religious conflicts that were the warp and woof of his formative years. Obert's birth coincided with the beginning of the Smoot hearings in Washington, D.C. He would not have remembered the details, since he was three years old when the hearings ended. But their consequences were lived by him, as he saw the church's diminishing moral and economic support for his family's way of life. His business gave him a degree of wealth that not only spared him repeating his family's poverty, but also susceptibility to the church's fluctuating policies.

Just four years younger than Obert Tanner, Lowell Bennion, too, grew up in this particularly torturous period in Mormon family and ecclesiastical life. He had a much easier time of it, however. His parents had not followed their parents into "the Principle" of polygamy. More influential on their son were their educational aspirations and attainments. Trained at Columbia University, his father Milton was a professional educator who had been named for the great British poet, a sign of his parents' aspirations. In turn, he named his son, Lowell, after the Boston intelligentsia. The son did not disappoint him. Reared in what appears to have been an idyllic setting on the edge of Salt Lake City, he met family expectations for educational excellence and sincere religiosity. Also influential on the young man, however, were early and rewarding experiences with ranching that left Lowell Bennion with great affection for "tent living, cold showers and dawn-to-dusk labor," not unlike the youthful experiences of his later friend and colleague Sterling McMurrin.[10]

McMurrin, like the other two, was a child of the Mormon pioneers and richly connected to LDS leadership. On his mother's side, he had the benefit of connections to the Moss family, founders and later general managers of the Deseret Land and Live Stock Company. Summers working in what he called the "real world" of the ranch seemed to have been for him antidote to the more cultured, even formal environment of his paternal grandparents. He later recalled that a visit from his McMurrin grandfather "was very much like having a visiting church authority in our home."[11] Maybe that was because he was one—holding, as he did, one of the top twenty positions in the LDS hierarchy.[12] Though McMurrin spoke emphatically of his deep love and indebtedness to both grandfathers, later interviews show his mother's family and their ranch made a lasting impression. He was especially impressed that, for grandfather Moss, Mormonism was "simply an inherited property, like the color of his eyes" and, though he was a Mormon bishop and "genuinely devout person," "the Church didn't own him."[13] The same could be said of the grandson. His chief chronicler Jack Newell introduced him as "enviably free."[14]

In each case, these men's families placed them close to church authorities. They were of a generation that inherited a level of familiarity with church hierarchs that made them less high. That would soon end. Church authority was itself changing during these years. Mormonism was modernizing with the rest of America. It was a "progressive era," a time of enthusiasm for professionalization and specialization or, in other words, for higher education and bureaucratic ordering with their rational approaches to any problem. The new generation of church leadership, exemplified by David McKay, James Talmage, Richard Lyman, and John Widtsoe, were college men, not frontiersmen. With them came the ordering of church auxiliaries and quorums according to their specializations and the application of corporate principles and educational curricula.

True to the spirit of the time, our three subjects joined the out-migration of Mormons who sought professional training. After receiving baccalaureate degrees at home from the University of Utah, they roamed far afield. By a mixture of opportunity and talent, as well as their own resolve, they received advanced degrees from some of the world's finest institutions.

Bennion's intellectual aspirations drew him to the German research university, but Nazism drove him across the border to France to complete his academic training. There he produced the first work on Max Weber in English and the first in any language synthesizing the great sociologist's methods. Such accomplishments notwithstanding, he chose to commit the next thirty years of his life to working in the Mormon Church's education system (CES). The LDS Institute of Religion he founded at the University of Utah was his natural home, and he experienced deep satisfaction there. Thirty years later, upon being forced to leave it, he served as the University of Utah's associate dean of students and on its sociology faculty for a decade before retiring. He appeared never to regret dropping his innovative work on Weber or the pursuit of academic distinction. Rather, he chose the career of a public intellectual. As such, in the words of Eugene England, he "helped give rational consistency to Mormon thought...focused it in social morality and service, and opened it to ecumenical dialogue."[15]

Of the three men, Obert Tanner, the benefactor of the Tanner Humanities Center, may be least well known as an intellectual. Though it is not a bad thing to be best known for philanthropy, it is still good to remember that Tanner's philanthropy was an expression of his intellect—his philosophical love of the good, the true, and the beautiful. After receiving a bachelor of arts and a law degree from the University of Utah, he went on for additional studies at Harvard and earned a master's degree and "most of a PhD" in philosophy from Stanford.[16] Before he finished his studies, the tragic death of his and his wife Grace's eldest son made them want to come home to Utah.

Stanford's loss was Utah's gain. For nearly thirty years, Tanner was a professor in the University of Utah's philosophy department, authoring or coauthoring ten books. While on the faculty, he added a *juris doctor* to his credentials, but his interest was always academic; he never practiced law. Much more will be said in the essays that follow, especially about his influence, not only on Utah's cultural community but also in national and international circles. Here, it must suffice to measure this aspect of his work by noting that it earned him the National Medal of Arts and the status of honorary fellow of the British Academy, Oxford University, and Cambridge University.

Sterling McMurrin began his academic career studying history and political science and followed with a master's in philosophy at the University of Utah. He received his doctorate in philosophy from the University of Southern California and was immediately offered a position on its faculty. Twelve years later he, too, returned to the University of Utah, joining Tanner on the philosophy faculty. Over the next forty years McMurrin held many positions: dean of the College of Letters &

Science, academic vice president, provost, dean of the graduate school, and founding member of the Tanner Lectures on Human Values. Many honors followed, including the title E. E. Ericksen Distinguished Professor, the Rosenblatt Prize for Excellence, and, with Tanner, Utah's first Governor's Award for Excellence in the Humanities. McMurrin was the author or editor of twenty-one books and 250 other publications. Midway in his tenure, he was appointed U.S. commissioner of education. Even that could not keep him from Utah. He returned home in less than two years to complete his distinguished career with seven honorary degrees and two professorships named in his honor.

Interestingly, not only Bennion, but also McMurrin and Tanner, began their illustrious careers employed by the LDS CES. Obert Tanner taught in the LDS Institute of Religion at Stanford for five years. Sterling McMurrin labored in Zion's nether regions—Richfield, Utah; Montpellier, Idaho; and finally Tempe and Mesa, Arizona, until he finished his doctoral training. After stellar educations and multiple professional opportunities, each returned to Utah, and, if they left again, it was for a limited purpose and time. All three were, as McMurrin said of himself, "one hundred percent Utahn."[17] This was not simply a matter of place, but culture. They were a product of and became producers of Mormon culture. One can only assume they must have liked it despite all of their struggles within it.

In Utah, their lives intertwined in many ways. All three met during their early years of professional formation. Bennion remembered selling his Oldsmobile to a very young McMurrin in the mid-1930s. Later, McMurrin replaced Bennion at the University of Arizona's LDS Institute of Religion. In a decision that would have repercussions for McMurrin, they traded places again when Bennion asked McMurrin to assume leadership of the "Swearing Elders," comprised of academics at the University of Utah and joined by some daring souls from Brigham Young and Utah State universities.[18] Tanner and McMurrin became "fast friends" in 1938 and office mates in Utah's philosophy department. Meanwhile, the Bennion and Tanner families were neighbors both in the city and, then, as their children grew, in the nearby Millcreek area to which they moved in the mid-1940s. These ties gave them much pleasure but also bound them in times of crisis. When McMurrin was about to be put on trial for his church membership, Tanner made a beeline to his "great and good friend Apostle Adam S. Bennion" who, in turn, went to see LDS Church President David McKay. This led to McKay's famous offer to serve as a witness in McMurrin's defense.[19] As for Bennion, when evicted from his institute position and wondering if his new academic assignment at the University of Utah would satisfy him, he declared, "If not I'll quit and be Obert's gardener."[20] It is not surprising that our three subjects knew each other so early and their paths continued to cross often. Early twentieth-century Mormonism made for a very small town in terms of human relationships, and it was still intact in the 1950s.

Their Conflicts

Not just the normalizing of higher criticism and evolutionary theory, but also the rise of the social sciences and advances in the physical sciences surfaced new challenges, especially to biblical truths. No less destabilizing were challenges to the religious rationalization of racial segregation. Meanwhile, America's churches found common cause in a holy war against godless communism. Religious fundamentalists in diverse denominations were active on any front that offered hope of regaining the cultural authority lost in the 1920s. Mormonism did not escape these broad social forces. The moderate Republican consensus, which had served it so well during the Reed Smoot years, declined under pressure from the anti-intellectualism of Joseph Fielding Smith and anticommunism of Ezra Taft Benson. It was at this historical moment that our three subjects, steeped in the classic liberal arts of rhetoric and reason, reached their professional maturity. Little wonder, then, that they became enmeshed in cultural combat. Two incidents have become symbolically potent for Latter-day Saint intellectuals: the failed effort to excommunicate McMurrin in 1954 and the successful purge of Bennion from the CES in 1962.

Before considering these incidents, it is necessary to understand why Obert Tanner played a marginal role in the collective memory of these events. We know of no occasion when he came into open conflict with LDS Church authorities. This may be because we do not have a comprehensive account of his life; most of what we know comes from others. In their words, he appears, like McMurrin, disinclined to take fundamentalist claims seriously. Moreover, again like McMurrin, his employment in the academy gave him distance from the battle over orthodoxy. Bennion had no such luxury. After all, it was his relinquishing of leadership of the Swearing Elders to McMurrin that provided opportunity to do combat. On the other hand, Tanner seems to have been more like Bennion in his beliefs. Religious experience, not theological principles, mattered to him. In published lectures, he voiced this deep preference: "The argument from religious experience," he said, "is [like friendship]…not a matter of proof but rather of experience, so too is beauty a matter of experience, also love and goodness, and so also is the experience of God. It is a deeper matter explained by the poet: 'Earth's crammed with heaven, and every common bush afire with God: but only he who sees takes off his shoes.'"[21]

Finally, it is important to ask whether Tanner's status as a successful entrepreneur and generous benefactor gave him access to or, as he chose, independence from institutional power. Any of these factors could have placed him at the margins of fundamentalist conflicts. Tanner spoke privately, not publicly, about what concerned him in church affairs. Thus, loyalty, too, played a role. McMurrin summed up his friend's position this way: "In the encounter with scientific knowledge and philosophic wisdom, [Tanner] moved from an early orthodoxy to a naturalistic and humanistic piety, but devotion to his church, its traditions and its people, constantly strengthened rather than weakened."[22]

Unlike Tanner, McMurrin was far less reticent about confronting church authorities. As a result, McMurrin faced the threat of church discipline. Apostles Joseph Fielding Smith and Harold B. Lee, McMurrin's second cousin, were concerned about the Swearing Elders. The group evidently discussed the religiously charged issues of the day frankly and, it appears, critically. Lee asked McMurrin, its leader, if "it be possible at the end of every session for you to summarize the position of the church and simply remind everyone what the beliefs of the church are?" "Utterly impossible," answered his cousin.[23] This answer precipitated a discussion of McMurrin's own beliefs. As he had when a seminary teacher, he responded honestly with his naturalistic views, including a denial of Jesus' divinity and the authenticity of the Book of Mormon.

Afterwards, McMurrin left Utah for a year on a research fellowship. When he returned, he heard rumors of his possible excommunication. He scheduled a meeting with his bishop, who confessed his sense of duty to determine whether an excommunication trial was appropriate. The bishop admitted also that no adverse witnesses could be found. He wondered could McMurrin help? McMurrin promptly gave him the names of "two members who are thoroughly acquainted with the depth of my heresies: Apostles Smith and Lee." [24] It was then that Obert Tanner marshaled David McKay's support, and the matter quietly died.

This story illustrates at least two concerns in the ongoing conversation about anti-intellectualism and freedom of conscience, Mormon-style. The first relates to the range of belief among Latter-day Saints and the permissibility of expressing it. The second concerns administrative anxiety about the Swearing Elders or intellectuals as sources of unbelief. McMurrin cites McKay for liberality with respect to both propositions. To McMurrin's self-effacing statement that "a person of my beliefs does not have any claim on membership in the church," McKay is said to have angrily replied, "Now just what is it that a person is not permitted to believe without being asked to leave this church? Just what is it? Is it evolution? I hope not, because I believe in evolution."[25] McMurrin states also that McKay, pointing in the direction of Smith and Lee's offices, advised him, "If those men...try to get you in a corner again...you just refuse to answer them because what you believe is none of their business."[26] That was something easier said than done, but it apparently did not need to be done. Four years later, in 1957, when the Ohio State University asked the church to recommend a lecturer on Mormonism, McMurrin was called, and by Harold B. Lee. "One of the major strengths in Mormon theology is its concern for reasonableness in religion," McMurrin once declared.[27] He certainly made it sound so in *The Philosophical Foundations of Mormon Theology*.

McMurrin remained, as he said of himself, a giver of "in-house criticism." His preferred self-description was "a good, well-rounded heretic." [28] This label was not only apt, but also served to create a useful boundary, marking his independence within, not from Mormonism. Lack of such independence was his chief criticism of his people.

Whenever asked, he lamented that "the intellectual life of the church—in terms of openness and free discussion—has been going downhill since the deaths of B. H. Roberts and James E. Talmage in 1933." [29] Note this is the year McMurrin turned nineteen. Today we are hard-pressed to think Talmage a freethinker or Roberts part of a free discussion. So, McMurrin's nostalgia for those days may be just nostalgia—even a reflection on a loss of innocence from the days when, with his father, he would read these men's writings. Nevertheless, as late as 1981, he told an interviewer, "We are going through a stage of intense indoctrination in the church that robs the individual of intellectual freedom." [30] And he was right, at least about the first half of that assertion. The last twenty years of the twentieth century was a time when LDS Church organization was fully bureaucratized and dogmatism dominated its official discourse. Those at midcentury, including McMurrin at times, who believed McKay was the exception and had a moderating affect, must admit he never publicly used his considerable authority to speak against dogmatism. This was even the case when McKay believed others were doctrinally in error—a situation that proved especially fateful for Lowell Bennion.

Bennion's story is more complicated and without a happy ending. He was known for his liberal views. But, in his sanctuary and supervised by church pragmatists, he had avoided conflict. This period of grace ended in the 1950s, when the CES was reorganized and newly appointed Brigham Young University (BYU) President Ernest L. Wilkinson was called to lead it. Wilkinson wanted to replace LDS Institutes of Religion adjacent to universities with junior colleges to facilitate later enrollment at BYU. Through a number of strategies that will be discussed in detail later in this volume, Wilkinson ultimately forced Bennion from his position. Bennion hoped President McKay would intercede, but he did not. After twenty-seven years, Bennion lost his sanctuary.

Many years later, Obert Tanner recalled his dismay at the firing. While his friend was caught in a power struggle with church fundamentalists, Tanner gave a speech entitled "Truth and Myth as Competitors for the Mind." "A culture of greatness," he said, "whether it be in politics, religion, or economics, should constantly read out truth-claiming myths....It is better to disband power structures for possibly better ones than to preserve them by the aid of myths."[32] Though he could have been more specific,he could not have been clearer.

In response to the uproar of appalled friends and students, Bennion would only say, "I managed not to please somebody, so we go on to other things."[33] Friend and high ecclesiastical official Marion D. Hanks recollected, "It had to hurt him and badly...[But] he took it better than his defenders and protagonists who wanted to cause a stir. He put that down."[34] Bennion took the advice he had consistently given his students: focus on the gospel message, not matters on its periphery. "My satisfactions lie in creation, service, and trying to keep my integrity," he said.[35] The ethical life and loving service were the core, everything else was secondary.[36] He turned to other institutions, some of which he created, like the Teton Valley Boys Ranch; others he led, such as the Salt Lake Community Services Council, where he served for seventeen years. As significant, however, were his innumerable acts of individual kindness— and even rescue. Happily, these are memorialized in the University of Utah's Bennion Community Service Center, which encourages students to go and do likewise.

Their Truths

Consider whether there are lessons for us in the way these men responded to the enduring conflict between faith and reason. I say "lessons" in the plural not only because of the instructive complexity of their differing responses to the conflicts they experienced between church and conscience. Especially instructive is their shared refusal to choose between one or the other of two loves—one of the mind, the other of the spirit.

My list of lessons begins with Obert Tanner's advice about the academy and the church: know the difference. He declared, "It is no wonder that universities find religion a difficult problem, for it seems to defy or escape our intellectual categories. It is, therefore, also inevitable that universities are unable to deal with more than [the] fringe [of] religion— the ideas about religion, not the personal and private experience of religion. It is no wonder that churches and free universities are respectful but reserved toward each other."[37] We should likewise be respectful and reserved toward each.

Lowell Bennion modeled sensitivity to another difference between the gospel and the church. "The church," he said, "is the instrument, the vehicle, to inculcate the Gospel into the lives of men and women. It was established by Christ...'to perfect the Saints'.... The church is both divine and human."[38] Elsewhere, he explained the significance of this distinction by borrowing a phrase from Montague: "We who can honestly believe in God... [believe also] 'the things that matter most are not ultimately at the mercy of things that matter least.'"[39] This was for Bennion an article of faith and a basis of the hope that enabled him to act so charitably.

The lesson from Sterling McMurrin's life is, not surprisingly, more complex. It comes from a statement he made about himself, beginning with his days teaching seminary. "I had a genuine love for the church as an institution and its people...I was devoted to the church, really was, and am right now. I've always considered myself as Mormon as these Orthodox Mormons, though I have been a confirmed heretic."[40] There is some truth here about the relationship of love to criticism and self-knowledge; something that goes to the heart of the difference between heresy and apostasy, between loyal opposition and just plain opposition. McMurrin may represent the truth that some things cannot be competently critiqued, unless they are loved also.

In each of these three lessons, I believe there is wisdom for any day, not just in their own. Another faithful intellectual, Bonner Ritchie, is reputed to have said you cannot make institutions safe for people, only people safe for institutions.[41] The wisdom of these three men can make people safe for institutions, even churches and, ultimately, this is what we should remember: not the offenses that they received, but the truths they taught. I think they, too, would have it that way.

NOTES

1. Erin Schill provided valuable assistance in the preparation of the original version of these remarks as the 2014 Sterling McMurrin Lecture on Religion and Culture.

2. Bernard DeVoto, "Utah," *American Mercury* 7 (1926): 322, and "A Revaluation," *Rocky Mountain Review* 10 (Autumn 1945): 8–10, as quoted in Leonard Arrington, "The Intellectual Tradition of the Latter-day Saints," *Dialogue: A Journal of Mormon Thought* 4 (1969): 13–26. For resistance to critique, see "The orthodox Mormon mind cannot tolerate any objective treatment of Mormon history whatever," ibid.

3. Harold Bloom to Henry L. Miles (May 24, 1995) in Henry L. Miles, "An Old Mormon Writes to Harold Bloom," *Dialogue: A Journal of Mormon Thought* 40 (Winter 2007): 166.

4. Thomas W. Simpson, "The Death of Mormon Separatism in American Universities, 1877–1896," *Religion and American Culture: A Journal of Interpretation* 22, no. 2 (2012): 163–201.

5. Simpson's research identified approximately fifty Latter-day Saints who studied "abroad" before 1890. After this date, the numbers "increased so much that it is virtually impossible to know exactly how many there were between 1890 and 1896," ibid., 186 n.6. His dissertation extends this analysis to 1940. See, Thomas W. Simpson, "Mormons Study Abroad: Latter-day Saints in American Higher Education, 1870–1940" (PhD diss., University of Virginia, 2005).

6. Called the "New Mormon History," this movement among a young generation of academically trained historians contextualized Mormon history within larger sociocultural developments and subjected it to humanistic interpretation. See, for example, Arrington's essay "The Search for Truth and Meaning in Mormon History," *Dialogue: A Journal of Mormon Thought* 3 (Summer 1968): 56–65.

7. Arrington, "Intellectual Tradition," 26.

8. Henry Eyring, *The Faith of a Scientist* (Salt Lake City: Bookcraft [1967] 2007).

9. Ibid., 31.

10. Mary Lythgoe Bradford, *Lowell L. Bennion: Teacher, Counselor, Humanitarian* (Salt Lake City: Dialogue Foundation, 1995), 20.

11. Sterling McMurrin and L. Jackson Newell, *Matters of Conscience: Conversations with Sterling McMurrin on Philosophy, Education, and Religion* (Salt Lake City: Signature Books, 1996), 5.

12. Joseph W. McMurrin was one of the seven presidents of the LDS Church's First Quorum of the Seventy.

13. McMurrin and Newell, *Matters of Conscience,* 8.

14. Ibid., xiii.

15. Eugene England, "Lowell L. Bennion," in *Utah History Encyclopedia,* ed. Allan Kent Powell (Salt Lake City: University of Utah Press, 1994). See www.uen.org/utah_history_encyclopedia/b/BENNION_LOWELL.html, (accessed April 15, 2015).

16. McMurrin and Newell, *Matters of Conscience,* 235.

17. Ibid., 23.

18. Ibid., 181.

19. Ibid., 197.

20. Bradford, *Bennion,* 183.

21. Obert Tanner, *One Man's Search* (Salt Lake City: University of Utah Press, 1989), 151.

22. Sterling McMurrin, Foreword to *One Man's Search,* xii.

23. McMurrin and Newell, *Matters of Conscience,* 192.

24. Ibid., 195.

25. Ibid., 198.

26. Ibid., 199.

27. Ibid., 112.

28. Ibid., 114.

29. Ibid., 209. See also the Seventh East Press interview. Blake Ostler, "An Interview with Sterling McMurrin," *Dialogue: A Journal of Mormon Thought* 17 (Spring 1984): 18–43. It was from his father, McMurrin said, that he received the "church writings" that were "far superior…to most of what comes out today." In addition to Roberts and Talmage, he admired Orson F. Whitney, and Adam S. Bennion. McMurrin and Newell, *Matters of Conscience,* 17.

30. Ostler, "Interview," 21.

31. Bradford, *Bennion,* 165.

32. Tanner, *One Man's Search,* 109.

33. Bradford, *Bennion,* 181.

34. Ibid.

35. Ibid., 183.

36. Ibid., 132.

37. Tanner, *One Man's Search,* 151.

38. Bradford, *Bennion,* 182

39. Lowell L. Bennion, *The Things That Matter Most* (Salt Lake City: Publishers Press, 1978), 59.

40. McMurrin and Newell, *Matters of Conscience*, 114.

41. J. Bonner Ritchie is professor emeritus of organizational behavior at the Brigham Young University Marriott School of Management and a scholar in residence at Utah Valley University.

PART II

STERLING MCMURRIN

3

THE ESSENTIAL MCMURRIN

Formation of Character and Courage

L. JACKSON NEWELL

Sterling Moss McMurrin was a scholar, leader, and raconteur. He cut a wide swath across his native Mormonism and Utah's academic and cultural institutions, and he left a distinctive mark on the intellectual life of the nation. Having learned of McMurrin's success in leading summer seminars for U.S. government cabinet officers and corporate leaders in the early years of the Aspen Institute in Colorado, President Dwight Eisenhower called McMurrin to serve as U.S. envoy to Iran (for five months in 1958). Later, President John F. Kennedy appointed him U.S. commissioner of education.

McMurrin returned from Washington, D.C. in 1963 to resume his career as a professor of philosophy and history at the University of Utah. He would earn high respect as a scholar, lecturer, dean, and vice president, while also serving occasionally on federal commissions and corporate boards. He turned down offers of several university presidencies because that role would have compromised his freedom to think and act as he chose. In the end, his prickly but devoted relationships with the Mormon Church, Mormon culture, and the state of Utah became his hallmark. It was the "loyal opposition" facet of his character—his independence from bureaucracies, insistence on truth telling, and comfort with heresy—that defined his life, intrigues us today, and constitutes his importance beyond his time. Two decades after his death, we still know more about what he believed and how he acted than we do about what shaped his character. It is the formative experiences during the first three decades of Sterling McMurrin's life that I explore here—the crucible in which his thinking and values were forged. He entered adult life at a propitious time in his culture's development.

McMurrin's grandfathers provided him with two powerful but contrasting models of success. Joseph W. McMurrin was a prominent Mormon general authority, one of seven presidents of the First Quorum of the Seventy, at a time when that group regarded itself as possessing authority equal to the Quorum of the Twelve Apostles. At the least, this body provided much of the intellectual strength and most of the independent thinking within the church hierarchy. This quorum's other six leaders included historian Brigham H. Roberts and the irrepressible former mule driver and original Swearing Elder J. Golden Kimball. Joseph McMurrin directed the European missions of the LDS Church for a time, but lived in southern California and presided over church affairs there when Sterling was growing up.

A captivating orator at the height of his powers, Joseph McMurrin had earned distinction as a young man for having taken three bullets in a celebrated 1885 gun battle with U.S. Marshal Henry Collins. He was a bodyguard for Mormon Church President John Taylor, who was hiding from federal authorities for preaching and practicing polygamy. "From a kid's perspective," McMurrin remembered, "it's a story about a federal marshal trying to kill your grandfather because of his religion." He continued, "This tends to give you certain impressions about both the government and your religion."[1] Joseph McMurrin, was a man of the cloth who represented both courage as a daring young man and eloquence in his mature public life. Possessing a mammoth personal library of classics that impressed his studious grandson, he was urban and urbane.

Maternal grandfather William Moss cofounded (with his father) the Deseret Land and Live Stock Company in 1891. An immense sheep and cattle operation spreading across a quarter-million acres in northeastern Utah, it grazed as many as 80,000 sheep on this home ranch and, in the winter, on a million acres of federal grazing allotments on Utah's western desert.[2] A man of affairs with an aura of power, in midlife he accepted a church call to serve a mission in England—a common practice at the time. The experience proved distasteful. He returned with nothing positive to say about proselyting or city living. Still, he agreed to serve as bishop of his local congregation after he returned home to his life as a rancher, banker, and business leader[3]

From the age of nine, Sterling and his three brothers, two older and one younger, worked as ordinary ranch hands for William Moss on the Deseret Ranch. Like the townspeople in nearby Evanston, Wyoming (who reportedly stepped back on the sidewalks when Moss ambled by), they held him in awe. To this man of action, with whom he formed especially close bonds, the young McMurrin owed many of his distinctive qualities—his independent spirit, passion for horses, and love of the West's open landscapes. When Sterling McMurrin served as marshal for University of Utah commencement exercises late in his career, with scepter in hand, I knew where he got that authoritative swagger.

McMurrin described his father, Joseph Jr., a Utah schoolteacher who became a Los Angeles parole officer, as "a misplaced college professor."[4] He encouraged Sterling as a youth to read Darwin and Plato and often conversed with him about serious books. Having received a stronger dose of religion from his parents than he could stomach, Joseph Jr. remained devoted to Mormonism, but he was no toady. He encouraged his sons to question church doctrines and pronouncements, but later wondered if he had gone too far. When McMurrin graduated from college, his father remarked wistfully, "Well, it looks to me like you don't believe anything."[5]

His mother, Gertrude Moss, was a "completely open-minded and approachable" person whose company he said "I always delighted in."[6] From her, and from his McMurrin grandmother, he absorbed social graces that served him well when his career blossomed on larger stages. Even so, this gentle and religious woman could be direct, asking her sons occasionally, "Do you believe all that stuff about the *Book of Mormon*?"[7] When he was fifty years old, McMurrin dedicated to his mother what would become his most enduring book, *The Theological Foundations of the Mormon Religion*.[8]

Reared and schooled primarily in Los Angeles, but working long summers on the range, Sterling and his brothers learned both intellectual and practical skills. All pursued productive careers. Blaine helped direct the return of U.S. military personnel from Europe after WWII and then settled into the Los Angeles business community. Keith spent his career with the U.S. Postal Service. Harold became a New York actor, sometimes on Broadway. He remarked privately on several occasions that from an early age there was something about Sterling—his intellect and his presence—that set him apart. His grandfather Moss, his parents, and his brother, Keith, all acknowledged this phenomenon. His achievements as a student did nothing to discourage their hopes, while adding to his ample self-confidence. Rather than feeling the burden of high expectations, Sterling seemed to go to college assuming, in a positive way, that he had nothing to prove.

Ignoring prompts from local ecclesiastical officials to prepare for and serve a mission for his church, which his father and two older brothers had done, McMurrin enrolled at the University of California, Los Angeles (UCLA) in the autumn of 1931. However, he suddenly fell victim to bronchial asthma attacks. A year that began with academic promise and even the hope of running on the track team ended frighteningly with his mother occasionally driving him, as he gasped for breath, to the clearer air of the San Gabrielle Mountains—or administering morphine to ease his frenzied condition.

Another summer on the Deseret Ranch proved liberating, and his asthma cleared. Emboldened, he rejected his grandfather's persistent counsel to transfer to the University of Utah "where you belong anyway." Sterling started another year at UCLA, but recurring health problems caused him to transfer to the University of Utah in the autumn of 1933.

At the time McMurrin enrolled, the university resembled a modern liberal arts college. With about 3,500 students, almost all undergraduates, its faculty was a close-knit body, focused on teaching and abuzz with energy generated by issues swirling around Mormonism, Utah, and the nation. The institution had been jolted into modernity eighteen years earlier when the newly formed American Association of University

Professors (AAUP) chose the University of Utah for its first investigation of breaches of academic freedom.[9]

Without offering reasons for his actions, President Joseph T. Kingsbury had refused to renew the contracts of four recently arrived, outspoken, and popular non-Mormon professors in February 1915. Met with vigorous protests, he repelled objections and ignored calls for appeal. The Board of Regents rallied behind him, claiming it could govern the university as it (and its appointed representative) saw fit, echoing assertions by the Brigham Young University president and board when they purged three progressive professors four years earlier.[10]

This tempest had been brewing for many months, triggered by the June 1914 valedictory remarks of student Milton Sevy. Sevy had lambasted the regents and state legislature for their "ultraconservatism" that suppressed the spirits "of young, progressive men" on campus. "We cannot grow as we should under such a policy," this Mormon graduate proclaimed, rather "we must have a broader and bigger outlook."[11] President Kingsbury had taken the bait and accused the faculty of having aided and abetted Sevy's impertinence—which, he charged, risked legislative support of the university.

Kingsbury's attempt to rid the university of four vulnerable professors met stout resistance from other faculty, seventeen of whom resigned in protest (constituting nearly one-third of the teaching staff). Student body officers also protested vigorously, as did the alumni association, and prominent women's literary groups in Salt Lake City. Kingsbury, the regents, and the governor dug in, resulting in an ugly standoff. The *Deseret News* and *Salt Lake Tribune* took opposing sides, and the eastern press weighed in as the controversy drew national attention.

The newly formed AAUP took note, activated its Committee A (for academic freedom), and dispatched a team of well-known scholars to investigate. Johns Hopkins University philosopher Arthur O. Lovejoy led the delegation that spent four days in Salt Lake City. They commanded such respect that the board of regents agreed to meet with Professor Lovejoy to discuss the imbroglio. AAUP president John Dewey, then at the peak of his fame at Columbia University, examined the evidence and crafted the association's blunt eighty-two-page report. The University of Utah was found wanting in its recognition of faculty rights, intellectual freedom, and procedures for adjudicating academic and personnel disputes. "The Board denied [defined] the limits of freedom of speech in the university in such a way as to justify any member of the faculty in resigning forthwith," concluded the AAUP's Committee of Inquiry.[12]

It was now President Kingsbury's turn to resign, under heavy criticism. The regents were also forced to grant new protections for academic freedom and faculty rights. With these developments, some of the professors who had resigned over Kingsbury's actions rejoined the faculty—which was then organizing its first academic senate to assert self-governing powers.[13]

This story became a legend. Repeated for years around the state, it had villains and heroes aplenty. One of the strongest voices for academic freedom had been David W. Evans, from a prominent Mormon family.[14] Most important, the University of Utah had survived a rite of passage through which its identity would shift from a tame Mormon school to an emerging national institution. The University of Utah became what Thomas Jefferson had hoped to see realized in his University of Virginia: "This institution will be based on the illimitable freedom of the human mind," he wrote, "for here we are not afraid to follow truth wherever it may lead, nor to tolerate any error so long as reason is left free to combat it."[15] Sterling McMurrin was reared with stories of the Kingsbury debacle. He would expect nothing less than a Jeffersonian university when he enrolled in 1933.

The university's escape from orthodox Mormon control, however, was still not complete. John A. Widtsoe followed Kingsbury as president. He vacated the post in 1921 to become a member of the Quorum of the Twelve Apostles in the LDS Church. Succeeding Widtsoe, Professor George Thomas brought a new quality of academic independence and worldly experience. He had grown up as a Mormon boy under rough family circumstances near Logan, Utah, gained admission to and graduated from Harvard University, and earned his PhD in economics in 1903 from Germany's Martin Luther University of Halle-Wittenberg. Coming home, he distinguished himself as a professor at Utah State University and as a public school reformer and civic leader in Logan. Moving to Berkeley, California, he directed the Federal Land Bank for a term.[16] But Thomas resigned that post to join the University of Utah faculty, and within several years the Board of Regents chose him to lead the institution.

President Thomas served for twenty years, but he shaped the university chiefly during his first decade. Philosophy professor Ephraim E. Ericksen, who had preceded Thomas's arrival, helped the new president attract other notable scholar-teachers in the late 1920s and early 1930s. Roughly in order of their appointments, they included major figures such as geologist Frederick Pack, sociologist Arthur Beeley, historian Sydney Angleman, English and Judaic Studies professor Louis Zucker, English scholar Brewster Ghiselin, and botanist Walter Cottam.[17] Waldemar P. Read, who would become an important influence on McMurrin, joined the faculty after earning his PhD at the University of Chicago—beginning his illustrious four-decade career as professor of philosophy and champion of intellectual freedom within a culture that he famously accused of "a stifling sameness of belief."[18] Mostly Latter-day Saints, these scholars embraced science and the new Biblical criticism with open minds and curiosity. They formed the nucleus of the awakening institution. As a new student, Sterling McMurrin sought these men out and took classes from most of them.

Professor E. E. Ericksen immediately struck a chord with the young McMurrin and became his mentor and friend. Ericksen had risen from Mormon roots, earned his bachelor's degree at the University of Utah and his PhD at the University of Chicago. Under his influence, and that of the newly arriving professors, the university became a haven for big and audacious ideas. From their perch on the hill east of the city, these scholars tested the limits of Mormon orthodoxy. Some of them did so from within the fold.

Downtown, the LDS Church was confronted with emerging knowledge that challenged its historic claims about the origin and nature of the Book of Mormon, the age of the Earth, and the efficacy of its own organization. For example, Brigham H. Roberts, the career-long contemporary of

McMurrin's grandfather as a president of the First Quorum of Seventy, was fearlessly researching the historicity of the Book of Mormon and warning other church leaders of the problems he uncovered. Church authorities reeled in response to such challenges, often resisting or denying the implications of new evidence about the length of geological time, the evolution of species, and the implications of sociologist Max Weber's insights concerning the nature of complex organizations (which the church was rapidly becoming).

The seriousness of the clash between old ways and new knowledge—and between the Mormon leadership and the university—comes into sharp focus when we consider that the LDS Church was still nearly two decades away from having its first college-educated president.[19] Further, the Great Depression had destabilized the nation's economic, political, and social landscape, feeding reactionary instincts as fully as it spawned countervailing progressive forces in Utah and across America. Sterling McMurrin's undergraduate years occurred in the midst of a double upheaval, one spiritual and another material. He arrived wired to engage the first battle, seemingly less concerned about the other one.

He soon felt that his legs had been knocked from beneath him. His McMurrin grandfather had died the previous October, and now, during his first term at the University of Utah, he suffered the passing of his beloved grandfather Moss.[20] Sterling packed everything he had taken to Utah when he went home for the winter holiday break—intending to close ranks with his grieving family and resume his studies at UCLA. His asthma flared up again, however, so he returned to Salt Lake City in January. He would now settle into the rhythms of a place that would nourish and test him for the rest of his life.

As they savored their freedom to think and write freely, some of the university's most notable professors were also engaged as lay persons leading LDS Church education policy boards, writing curriculum materials, and serving in other leadership capacities. As members of the general board of one of the LDS Church's youth organizations (the Young Men's Mutual Improvement Association), two of these scholars, E. E. Ericksen and Arthur Beeley, pushed for teaching manuals and pedagogy that emphasized thinking and reasoning skills. But during McMurrin's first year as a student, Apostle John Widtsoe (recall that he was also the university's immediate past president), resolved to rid the general board of progressive educators Ericksen and Beeley. When the two did not take his suggestion to resign, he dissolved the board, and then reconstituted it with the same membership, but without the two professors.[21] A harbinger of things to come, this was an early shot across the progressives' bow.

Following these events closely, President Thomas, whom McMurrin described as "a kind of crusty character," remarked within his hearing: "They burned down the whole barn to get rid of a couple of rats."[22] Ericksen and Thomas rose in McMurrin's esteem and he soon found himself working part time in the president's office—assigned to assemble materials for a history of the University of Utah.[23] McMurrin's ties with the institution's leaders continued to grow. He remembered with special savor his conversations with Professor Louis Zucker on Judaism, Christianity, and Mormonism that expanded his interest in theology. But that was not all.

Natalie Cotterel passed Sterling on the narrow east steps of the Cowles Building when they were both juniors. It was love at first sight "at least on my end," he claimed. An Idaho farm girl, Natalie was reared as an Evangelical Protestant. Her family worshipped at the local Baptist church. She had moved to Salt Lake City to attend East High School and live with her highly educated, loving, and "intensely anti-Mormon" aunt and uncle. She and Sterling met at the university library a few days after they had passed in the stairwell. She was majoring in Spanish and psychology, he in political science with an interest in philosophy. Their courtship flourished over the next year and they planned to marry after they received their bachelors' degrees in 1936. When that time came, however, they could not afford that luxury because of the persistent economic depression. Natalie moved back to Idaho and taught school for two years while McMurrin remained behind to earn his master's degree in history in 1937. They continued their romance by correspondence.

Professors E. E. Ericksen and Waldemar Read, and President George Thomas, had a plan for McMurrin. He should go to the University of Chicago to earn his PhD in philosophy, as Ericksen and Read had done, and return to teach at the University of Utah. Enthusiastic about such a prospect, McMurrin was accepted at Chicago, but the Great Depression again altered his course. No graduate fellowships were available. Lacking the means to continue without such help, he tacked in another direction. He would find a job so that he and Natalie could marry.

Two progressive educators still presided over the LDS Church Educational System (CES), Frank West as commissioner and Lynn Bennion as supervisor of seminaries and institutes—programs of religious instruction designed as adjuncts to students' secular studies in high school and college. These men also had their eyes on McMurrin, so when they discovered that he was looking for a job, they pounced. In an interview that resulted in an offer, they grilled him about his knowledge of the arts and humanities and explored "my attitudes toward religion and the church, but never raised questions regarding my religious orthodoxy."[24] Waldemar Read had begun his career as a seminary instructor and encouraged McMurrin to accept a seminary position in Richfield, Utah. McMurrin later reflected: "Those of us who went into seminary and institute teaching in those days were really led to believe that the Church wanted genuinely honest scholarship, and I think that for the most part it did."[25]

McMurrin was frank about his liberal views on Mormonism and Christianity with townspeople and church leaders in this rural Utah community. He did not hide his doubts about the divinity of Jesus or the miraculous origins of the Book of Mormon. Nevertheless, they liked and accepted him because his teaching proved superior. The Hansen family from whom he rented his room "thought he walked on water."[26] When the church offered him a contract to teach a second year, he and Natalie resolved to marry. She had converted to Mormonism a year earlier, but McMurrin always admired her Protestant training. She knew a great deal about the Bible, he said, "and had a good religious upbringing. She has always been very devout in a way that I like."[27]

Apostle David O. McKay, already a member of the LDS Church's governing First Presidency, performed their marriage in the Salt Lake Temple on June 8, 1938. Their friendship with McKay remained close and occasionally propitious until he died thirty-two years later.

Even so, Sterling and Natalie never wished to return to the inside of an LDS temple.

Over time, church officials in Richfield grew less tolerant of McMurrin's unorthodox views, so Bennion transferred him to a high school seminary in Montpelier, Idaho. His teaching continued to shine and a year later he was transferred to the Mormon seminary in Mesa, Arizona. The following year, however, he secured a simultaneous appointment in Tempe, Arizona, with the Philosophy Department at Arizona State College (now Arizona State University). In both venues his reputation as a teacher-scholar soared as students and onlookers crowded into his classrooms and public lectures. Lynn Bennion, his supervisor, explained the reason: "No theological claim was too sacred to be challenged in McMurrin's classes, and no idea was too wild to merit consideration. But Sterling knew more about Mormon theology, and the whole history of Christianity, than anyone in church education before or since."[28] He brought ideas alive, "savoring every exchange and being completely at ease in any situation with his distinctive manner of speaking."[29] In 1943, McMurrin was appointed director of the LDS Institute of Religion at the University of Arizona.

It was during his church employment that many of Sterling and Natalie's lifelong friendships began. They drew close not only to Frank West and Lynn Bennion (Lowell's older brother), but also to Stewart Udall, Boyer Jarvis, Obert Tanner, and Lowell Bennion, as well as their wives and families. All were about to be tested in the fiery furnace of resurgent church orthodoxy.

At the behest of former U.S. diplomat and LDS apostle J. Reuben Clark, seminary and institute teachers throughout the CES assembled at Aspen Grove in a Provo Canyon camp environment for two months in the summer of 1938. Clark and fellow apostles Joseph Fielding Smith and John A. Widtsoe admonished them repeatedly to teach the fundamental doctrines laid down by church leaders. Progressive pedagogy and any exploration of the meaning or implications of doctrines had no place in the system, Clark declared. With vast experience (and infamous racist opinions) in foreign policy, he now retrenched to parochialism in religion. He stoutly defended the church practice of denying men of African descent ordination to the Mormon priesthood and discouraged any questions about it.

At the same conference, Joseph Fielding Smith demanded adherence to the belief that the Earth was created by God essentially as we know it only about six thousand years ago.[30] With B. H. Roberts now dead for six years, Smith resolved to bury the disquieting questions Roberts had raised about the origins and nature of the Book of Mormon. Obedience to the dictates of authority ruled the encampment, even as other perspectives were occasionally voiced. One of those was a speech Sterling McMurrin was invited to give, the substance of which does not survive.[31] Regardless of this opportunity, the experience stunned McMurrin while also defining his position on the modernist side of the divide with the fundamentalists.

If he needed a prompt to continue his formal study of philosophy, he received it from those summer events. McMurrin commenced doctoral work in philosophy at the University of Southern California, first during his summer vacations, then on a year's leave from the institute, and finally in full-time study. He received his PhD in May 1946.

His dissertation, "Positivism and the Logical Meaning of Normative Value Judgments," began with this preface: "The moral crisis that characterizes our time is...the wide disparity...between man's technical attainment in the control of his environment and the effectiveness of his moral and spiritual idealism. It is increasingly imperative that the conduct of men and nations be brought under the dominion of a moral ideal."[32] If his first thirty-two years, which had not only seen the Great Depression, the Holocaust, and World War II, but also his own experiences with ideological rigidity, had taught him anything, it was that modern bureaucracies posed serious new threats to personal freedom and moral responsibility.

Sterling McMurrin's mantra was now clear. His would become a clarion voice calling institutions of all kinds—religious, educational, and political—to live by their highest ideals. His dissertation preface continued, "As a practical issue, this [task of adhering to a moral ideal] is...a responsibility of religion, education, and politics. But the integration of fact and value, necessary to both personal and social character, demands a theoretical foundation which will give meaning and direction to practical effort."[33] He would strive throughout his life to provide such a theoretical foundation for the Mormon religion, the University of Utah, and the federal role in public education.

For reasons McMurrin ascribed chiefly to his persistent asthma, but that probably had more to do with affinity for his native state and culture, he turned down an offer to join the USC faculty and accepted appointment as professor of philosophy at the University of Utah. There, he joined the professors who had inspired him as an undergraduate—Ericksen, Read, and others—and soon became their leader as dean of the College of Letters and Science. It was from this platform that he rose to national service as a roundtable leader at the Aspen Institute, presidential envoy to Iran, and U.S. commissioner of education. These exploits were behind him at the age of forty-eight, when he returned to the University of Utah. With occasional stints at other universities, and more forays into the university's administrative machinery than he admitted to liking "except for the assistance provided by truly able staff members," McMurrin settled into the role he enjoyed most: truth teller. His prominence on the national stage added power to the voice that he raised at home. It reverberated far afield.

McMurrin's growing mystique owed its existence to a powerful set of paradoxical qualities. He was at once a towering intellect with a photographic memory and a man who never broke a sweat. He did not seem to work hard or long on anything, partly because he could do almost everything easily. McMurrin was known as a consummate scholar, yet his landmark publications were delivered from the lectern—a forum in which his astonishing memory, command of language, and charismatic bearing (that tousled hair and persistent fiddling with his noisy metal watchband) converged to create a stimulating and challenging experience for any serious audience.

There is not a major philosophical work on his resume. The closest is a 1955 revision of the two-volume *A History of Philosophy* by B. A. G. Fuller, one of his aging mentors.[34] At the same time, some of McMurrin's major addresses, for example his 1968 speech at a meeting of the Salt Lake chapter of the NAACP about the rights of black citizens in Mormon Utah, left no room for equivocation—though there was plenty of criticism, especially from LDS Church authorities.

Such landmark speeches peppered McMurrin's long career. These are readily available because his best-known books are collections of these addresses. Prime among these volumes, *The Philosophical Foundations of Mormon Theology* is a long essay published as a booklet by the University of Utah Press in 1959.[35] It originated as a lecture McMurrin gave during the winter of 1957–58 on four major campuses in Utah: the University of Utah, Utah State University, Brigham Young University, and Weber State College.

After McMurrin returned from his service as U.S. commissioner of education in Washington in 1963, he gave a series of five lectures at the University of Utah on key facets of Mormon belief. These lectures became the five chapters in *The Theological Foundations of the Mormon Religion*, published in 1965. Thus, the year 2015 marked the fiftieth anniversary of the University of Utah Press's publication of this book—for years its best-selling work. It remains in print as a second edition by Signature Books, which includes the earlier and briefer *The Philosophical Foundations of Mormon Theology.*

McMurrin's other paradoxes included the delight he took in proclaiming himself a heretic, which he matched with ferocious defenses of his church and its culture when outsiders attacked either. Similarly, his forbidding public countenance (he wrote in paragraph-long sentences) contrasted utterly with his impish playfulness when among friends. He relished telling ironic or absurd stories about religious beliefs. One of his favorite tales was of a man who came up to him after a lecture in Arizona and said that he had figured out that the Gulf of Mexico occupies the depression left when God took the city of Enoch up into heaven. McMurrin asked: "That must have been a pretty big city, don't you think?" Shrugging his shoulders, the man replied with his own question, "Well, what else do you think could have made that great big hole?"

Two poignant incidents illustrate McMurrin's paradoxes. When he met with LDS Apostles Joseph Fielding Smith and Harold B. Lee (his cousin) in the summer of 1952, and flatly rejected his religion's major tenets, he walked home with what he described as the most free and joyous feeling of his life. He had found peace in simple honesty. From that time forward, McMurrin defined himself, publicly and privately, as a "good heretic." He would say, "A heretic does not believe the tenets of his religion, but I'm not against the church, I'm for it. That's why I'm a *good* heretic."[36] Decades later, he would weep unexpectedly when recalling the death of Joseph Fielding Smith, explaining that this apostle, as fundamentally as they had disagreed, always expressed his convictions with dignity and respected those with whom he battled. Others who criticized McMurrin less severely—Apostles Harold Lee or Mark Peterson for example—did not earn that same level of respect.

When I asked McMurrin in one of our early conversations for *Matters of Conscience* what had caused him to become disillusioned with Mormonism, he looked surprised and said, "Oh, I was never illusioned!" We argued over this point on several occasions, my point being that his integrity and intellectual honesty were legendary, so he *must* have believed what he taught at least when he began his career as a church educator. His reply, repeated along the same lines every time we revisited this issue: "I can't remember a time when I didn't have doubts...about the authenticity of the Book of Mormon, which I have never accepted as a genuine historical document or scripture, or of the divinity of Christ, or the factual truth of much that is in the Bible. So I have never gone through any kind of religious crisis—either in my attitudes or my beliefs."[37]

After examining McMurrin's upbringing and education, and considering the state of the LDS Church when he joined its educational system in 1937, I believe I understand his answer. Those who hired him that summer were more concerned about the brilliance of his mind and the goodness of his instincts than the orthodoxy of his views. And he believed that he could do something of value for his students and church.

I was asked recently, "Why didn't Sterling McMurrin leave the church?" I asked him that too—and he responded with a quizzical look, "To go where?" He happily embraced his role as Mormonism's most eloquent and prominent spokesperson when the national press sought a candid perspective on issues affecting the faith. Besides, he said on many occasions, "What could be more entertaining than to watch all the foolishness the apostles [and he always pronounced the "t" in apostle] engage in while trying to defend some of their indefensible positions. Like keeping the priesthood from blacks."[38] Toward the end of his life he would substitute "women" at the end of that sentence. For all of his lighthearted independence, he did not like being labeled "the loyal opposition" (a description I used above with trepidation) because it sounded to him like an "oxyMormon."

McMurrin eschewed labels, but he did not object when I described him as an existentialist without the angst. He saw no reason to believe that a divine hand guided human affairs or saved us from our recklessness. But I would defend the proposition that McMurrin was a Christian existentialist—in that he understood, consciously respected, and lived the broad ethics of Jesus throughout his life. He believed in the essential goodness of Christian principles and of his native Mormonism, but that was very different from believing they were true.

In writing about the potential of religion to enrich human lives, he observed that "religion should bring consecration to life and direction to human endeavor, inspire men and women with faith in themselves, dedicate them to high moral, preserve their natural piety in the presences of success, and give them strength to live through their failures with nobility and face with high courage their supreme tragedies."[39]

About a year before he died, McMurrin concluded a formal lecture at the University of Utah by entertaining questions. "Are you an atheist, and if not, why not?" came the first query. Unfazed, he noted that philosopher Bertrand Russell once responded to the same question, saying that he "leaned toward atheism." McMurrin went on: "I'm on that knife edge with Russell, but I lean toward theism." Religion, he stated, is felt, not thought. It has little to do with theology and is rarely a rational choice. Always leaving room to play with his conclusions, McMurrin remarked to his faculty colleague and fellow skeptic, Brigham Madsen, as they strolled across the campus one gorgeous spring morning, "Brig, maybe we're wrong!"[40]

Through thirty years of growing up and attaining an excellent education, benefitting from principled, caring, and courageous mentors along his path, Sterling McMurrin learned to live well—free from anger (but not of righteous indignation), free of hypocrisy (but not of paradoxes and his cherished ironies), and free to be who he was and to say what he believed (and did not believe). Yet he served three great institutions with distinction throughout his life: the LDS Church, the federal government, and the University of Utah. His secret was the uniqueness of his perspective: He loved the *principles* for which these institutions stood, not the institutions per se. When their leaders acted in conformity with those underlying ideals, they gained his profound respect. When they violated those ideals, he let them (and, if appropriate, the world) know. McMurrin was never a servant of institutions; he was a trustee of their highest values. As a result, he never found himself in the position of defending the inevitable mistakes that organizations and their leaders make, nor of rationalizing positions that violated his conscience. This was the source of McMurrin's integrity, and his power.

Sterling McMurrin carried mysteries to his grave. Having rejected all of the important theological claims of Mormonism, and not visiting a Mormon temple since the day he married Natalie six decades earlier, he chose to be laid to rest in his Mormon temple clothes and ceremonial apron. Tucked in his coffin, too, was the trademark resin-encased scorpion bolo tie that still rests on his chest. To the end, Sterling Moss McMurrin reveled in baffling his friends and detractors.

Summing up his life as perfectly as he could, McMurrin opined in a private conversation shortly before his death that the existence of suffering and evil in human experience had so outweighed joy, especially in the twentieth century, that it might have been better if human life had never appeared on earth. "But Sterling," I interjected, "no one enjoys life more than you." "Well, as long as we are here," he said with a wink, "we should make the most of it."[41] I believe he did.

Sterling McMurrin with a favorite horse at the family cabin near Zion National Park, early 1980s. Courtesy of Laurie McMurrin Reed.

Sterling and Natalie McMurrin with poet Carl Sandburg at the Salt Lake City airport, circa 1959. Courtesy of Laurie McMurrin Reed.

The McMurrin family, summer 1963. Left to right: Joe, Melanie (in front), Sterling, Natalie, Laurie, and Jim. Not shown: oldest daughter, Trudy. Courtesy of Laurie McMurrin Reed.

Sterling McMurrin offering the first Sterling M. McMurrin Lecture on Religion and Culture, autumn, 1992. Courtesy of Laurie McMurrin Reed.

NOTES

1. Sterling M. McMurrin and L. Jackson Newell, *Matters of Conscience: Conversations with Sterling M. McMurrin on Philosophy, Education, and Religion* (Salt Lake City: Signature Books 1996), xviii.
2. Jean Ann McMurrin, *The Deseret Land and Live Stock Company: A Brief History, 1891–1991* (Woodruff, UT: Deseret Land and Live Stock Company, 1991), 1–11. The Church of Jesus Christ of Latter-day Saints bought the ranch in 1983.
3. McMurrin and Newell, *Matters of Conscience*, 8.
4. Ibid., 15.
5. Ibid., 19, and Brigham D. Madsen, "Sterling M. McMurrin: A Heretic but Not an Apostate," in *Mormon Mavericks: Essays on Dissenters*, ed. John Sillitoe and Susan Staker (Salt Lake City: Signature Books, 2001), 295.
6. McMurrin and Newell, *Matters of Conscience*, xviii.
7. Ibid., 13.
8. Sterling M. McMurrin, *The Theological Foundations of the Mormon Religion* (Salt Lake City: Signature Books, 2000). This second edition of the book also contains McMurrin's *The Philosophical Foundations of Mormon Theology* and a "Biographical Introduction" by L. Jackson Newell.
9. Craig H. Bowen, "Academic Freedom and the Utah Controversies of 1911 and 1915" (Salt Lake City: University of Utah, 1995). This is a spiral-bound report of 112 pages.
10. For details, see Brian Birch's chapter of this book.
11. Bowen, "Academic Freedom," 19.
12. Ibid., 67.
13. See Allyson Mower and Paul Mogren, *When Rights Clash: Origins of the University of Utah Academic Senate* (Salt Lake City: J. Willard Marriott Library, University of Utah, 2014).
14. Ibid., 24. David W. Evans' respect for academic scholarship led his family to establish the prestigious David W. and Beatrice C. Evans Biography Award in 1983, and then to remove it from the control of Brigham Young University a few years later because religious tests were suggested for judgment of candidates' books. The Evans family transferred administration of the award to Utah State University.
15. Thomas Jefferson to William Roscoe, posted from Monticello, Virginia, December 27, 1820.
16. Ralph V. Chamberlin, *The University of Utah: A History of Its First Hundred Years, 1850 to 1950* (Salt Lake City: University of Utah Press, 1960), 372–73.

17. Ibid., 478.
18. Gregory A. Prince and William Robert Wright, *David O. McKay and the Rise of Modern Mormonism* (Salt Lake City: University of Utah Press, 2005), 42.
19. David O. McKay's ascension to the presidency in 1951 marked the beginning of the new era of college-educated Mormon prophets.
20. Coincidentally, Brigham H. Roberts, whose intellect and courage McMurrin admired, died on September 27 that year.
21. McMurrin and Newell, *Matters of Conscience*, 54–55.
22. Ibid., 55.
23. For the rest of his life, McMurrin took satisfaction from being the university's first official historian.
24. McMurrin and Newell, *Matters of Conscience*, 105.
25. Blake Ostler, "An Interview with Sterling M. McMurrin," *Dialogue: A Journal of Mormon Thought* 17 (Spring 1984): 20.
26. William McMurrin. Personal conversation with the author, April 10, 2015.
27. McMurrin and Newell, *Matters of Conscience*, 92.
28. Ibid., xix.
29. J. Boyer Jarvis, personal conversation with the author, March 2, 2016.
30. Joseph Fielding Smith, *Man, His Origin and Destiny* (Salt Lake City: Deseret Book Company, 1954).
31. McMurrin probably did not write out his remarks, judging by his career-long pattern of speaking from sparse notes at most, so it is not surprising that no record can be found of what he said.
32. Sterling M. McMurrin, "Positivism and the Logical Meaning of Normative Value Judgments" (PhD diss., University of Southern California, May, 1946), 1.
33. Ibid.
34. B.A.G. Fuller, *A History of Philosophy*, and *A History of Modern Philosophy*, 2d ed., rev. Sterling McMurrin (New York: H. Holt and Company, 1955). A third edition came out in 1962.
35. Sterling M. McMurrin, *The Philosophical Foundations of Mormon Theology* (Salt Lake City: University of Utah Press, 1959).
36. I remember McMurrin expressing this point in precisely these words, but he conveyed the idea in similar ways on many other occasions. McMurrin and Newell, *Matters of Conscience*, 372.
37. Ibid., 368.
38. Sterling M. McMurrin, *Religion, Reason, and Truth: Historical Essays in the Philosophy of Religion* (Salt Lake City: University of Utah Press, 1982), 112.
39. J. Boyer Jarvis told this story to the author, March 26, 2015.
40. McMurrin and Newell, *Matters of Conscience*, 374.

4

THE "OLD ORTHODOXY"

Sterling McMurrin and the Development of Mormon Thought

BRIAN D. BIRCH

In his 1965 review of Sterling McMurrin's *The Theological Foundations of the Mormon Religion*, Robert McAfee Brown stated that the work "is not an exposition of Mormon religion in isolated splendor, but an exposition of Mormon religion in relation to the *living* options that confront both Mormons and non-Mormons today."[1] Brown's words aptly describe the kind of project McMurrin understood himself to be doing. In the fifty-plus years that have passed since the book's publication, the "living options" he referenced are still very much in play within Mormon discourse, though in different forms and in connection to different interlocutors.

A key feature of McMurrin's well-known book is his repeated reference to an ominous dogmatism he observed creeping into Mormon theology. In various places he referred to this approach as the "old orthodoxy," which took various shapes depending on the subject at hand. The two primary forms include a Christian anthropology that embraces human depravity and helplessness in the face of sin and a form of authoritarianism that rejects rational inquiry in favor of biblical literalism and an uncritical view of religious history. This essay aims to situate McMurrin's perspective in Mormon thought by addressing key episodes in Mormon history that bear on these themes.

McMurrin and the Modernist Project

Perhaps the best articulation of McMurrin's outlook on religion is a lecture he delivered at the University of Utah in 1954 entitled "The Patterns of Our Religious Faiths."[2] Here he laid out a scheme for religious life that offers insight into his theological vision. McMurrin described liberal religion as featuring a caring and interactive God in relation to a human family bound by a common moral project. This includes the "total affirmation of life" and the embrace of optimism in mortality and the life to come.[3] The last few pages of his essay are a credo for theological liberalism:

> The only religion which can fully satisfy today's ideal is a religion that is committed sincerely to the search for truth, that refuses to ground faith on naive credulity, that refuses to prostitute learning for the defense of belief, that encourages rather than condemns genuine and uncensored scholarship, that is not afraid of what men may learn in their quest for knowledge.[4]

McMurrin presented this essay in the face of a resurgence of negative elements in Christian theology: "Today religion is moving once more toward the twin evils of irrationalism and authoritarianism, and only those who set themselves firmly against these corruptions are faithful to the high estate to which humanity has finally come."[5]

Though he readily acknowledged that each of the Abrahamic religions contains both fundamentalist and liberal elements, he placed Mormonism alongside other liberal movements, including those of Hillel, Socrates, Maimonides, Arminius, Hegel, and William James. "Mormonism, which exhibits its nineteenth-century American origins, is in substantial agreement with typical fundamentalist Protestantism, as for instance its biblical literalism, dispensation theory of history, and eschatology. It has, nevertheless, a positive conception of human nature and a generally life-affirming quality that gives it a pronounced liberal character."[6]

These tensions motivated McMurrin's project and remained a central theme in his works on Mormonism—which at times moved elegantly between the philosophical and the homiletic. The moral dimensions of his writings express urgency in the face of neo-orthodox theological movements that threatened to overtake American Christian thought and that influenced twentieth-century Mormon sensibilities. To see this, we must return to the opening decades of the twentieth century.

The American Context

In 1909, a group of wealthy Christians enlisted Baptist Pastor A. C. Dixon to compile a defense of traditional Christian teachings. The series that emerged in 1915 was entitled *The Fundamentals: A Testimony to the Truth*, and it would alter the direction for the generations that followed. Compiled in twelve volumes, *The Fundamentals* became the gold standard for traditionalist belief in American churches and provided the name for the movement that rallied around it, namely fundamentalism. Millions of copies were distributed to churches, missions, and divinity schools.

The Fundamentals were published in the heart of one of the most religiously fractious periods in American history. The ensuing debates splintered traditional Protestant denominations and, in many respects, continue to define the American Christian landscape. The issues in play concerned the central features of Protestant thought, which were distilled into the "Five Points": the inerrancy of the Bible, the virgin birth, atonement theology, the resurrection, and the role of miracles. These points were affirmed at the 1910 Presbyterian General Assembly and were required of candidates for ordination to its ministry.

The need to shore up the fundamentals of evangelical belief came as a result of the rise in the nineteenth century of higher criticism, psychoanalysis, and natural selection. The advance of these intellectual trends placed increasing strain on traditional approaches to biblical authority and original sin. Attempts to reconcile biblical narratives with naturalistic methodologies led American Christianity toward a dramatic split known as the fundamentalist-modernist controversy.

A key moment in these debates came in 1922. Harry Emerson Fosdick, the leading liberal theologian of his day, stood before the First Presbyterian Church of New York to deliver one of the most famous sermons in American history, "Shall the Fundamentalists Win?" In reference to the flood of new scholarship, Fosdick declared: "Now, there are multitudes of reverent Christians who have been unable to keep this new knowledge in one compartment of their minds and the Christian faith in another. They have been sure that all truth comes from the one God and is His revelation."[7]

As divisions hardened, the debates came to be understood as a battle for nothing less than the integrity of the Christian faith. For J. Gresham Machen, the issue was quite simple: "Christianity is founded upon the Bible;" liberalism, on the other hand, "is founded upon the shifting emotion of sinful men."[8] For many fundamentalists like Machen, fellowship with liberal Christians became increasingly difficult. The tensions became so pronounced that legions of congregations separated from established denominations and formed their own seminaries, missions, and churches. In an important sense, however, the modernists had won. By the end of the 1920s, faculty sympathetic to a more open approach dominated most major seminaries. Princeton Theological Seminary, for example, long held to be a guardian of conservatism, had undergone its own battle resulting in faculty resignations and the establishment of a rival seminary under Machen's leadership. The schism became so deep that the *Christian Century* opined that "the God of the fundamentalist is one God; the God of the modernist is another."[9] Though many had hoped for a grand bargain, there would be no reconciliation.

In the aftermath, a new theological movement emerged that was equally critical of liberalism and fundamentalism. Championed by Karl Barth, Emil Brunner, and the American theologian Reinhold Niebuhr, neo-orthodoxy rejected both the optimism of liberal theology and the anti-intellectual elements of fundamentalism. Their attempts to recover the essence of Reformation thought led them to reinforce and amplify the categories of faith, grace, and the transcendence of God. At the same time, however, they rejected biblical literalism and embraced forms of higher criticism.[10] The Bible was not to be understood as an alternative explanation of scientific realities, but rather as an instrument through which God calls human beings to recognize their helplessness.

McMurrin's Inheritance

It was in this environment that McMurrin entered graduate study in history and religion. After completing his doctoral work at the University of Southern California, he pursued postdoctoral studies at both Princeton University and Union Theological Seminary—notably the two key institutions in the fundamentalist-modernist controversies. His writings demonstrate a keen understanding of the contours of the debate and how they informed American theological trends.

Though the LDS Church had distanced itself from other Christian denominations, key aspects of its discourse mirrored the broader Protestant community. This was the case most notably in the areas of evolution and higher criticism of the Bible. In 1911, Brigham Young University found itself in the midst of a modernist crisis of its own. The university had recruited faculty with advanced degrees from institutions such as Harvard; the University of California, Berkeley; and the University of Chicago. These young professors were dynamic and popular, and they brought with them progressive ideas that resulted in a crisis for the institution and, by extension, the broader church.

LDS Commissioner of Education Horace Cummings had received complaints from ecclesiastical leaders regarding the teaching of evolution and higher criticism. Cummings responded with a visit to the university that included interviews with faculty, administrators, and students. He reported that the curriculum in question treated the Bible as "a collection of myths, folklore, dramas, literary production and some inspiration."[11] Cummings concluded that responsibility rested on "four or five" professors and recommended their immediate reassignment. BYU President George Brimhall agreed and noted, "It seemed that they were more determined than ever to teach theology according to their own ideas and theories, instead of according to the revealed truth."[12] As a result, three professors faced a choice between resignation or conformity.[13]

A year earlier, in 1910, Joseph Fielding Smith had been called to serve as a member of the Quorum of the Twelve Apostles. Smith was the grandson of Joseph Smith's brother Hyrum and son of Joseph F. Smith, who served as president of the LDS Church from 1901 to 1918. Though he had little formal training in higher education, Smith would become one of the most influential forces in the LDS Church on matters of education, historical studies, and doctrinal interpretation. At the time of his appointment, the quorum had witnessed internal debates regarding both evolution and higher criticism of the Bible. A handful of publications were in circulation that attempted to synthesize evolution with LDS theology, and that enjoyed various forms of support and encouragement from some high church leaders.[14]

For several years, the leadership of the church was split on the issue of evolution and there was a growing need for an official statement. This came in a 1909 document entitled "The Origin of Man" that coincided with the centennial of Darwin's birth and the fiftieth anniversary of the publication of *The Origin of Species*. In carefully worded sections, biological evolution was treated with caution, but was not categorically rejected:

> It is held by some that Adam was not the first man upon this earth and that the original human being was a development from lower orders of the animal creation. These, however, are theories of men. . . . Never, unaided, will he discover the truth about the beginning of human life. The Lord must reveal Himself or remain unrevealed. [15]

The best-known episode of this period was a long-running debate about the writings of B. H. Roberts, whose magnum opus, *The Truth, the Way, and the Life*, ignited further controversy regarding life on earth prior to Adam. In his attempt to reconcile scriptural accounts with contemporary science, Roberts proposed that "pre-Adamites" lived before Adam and Eve, but were destroyed prior to the account of creation recorded in Genesis. A vocal Joseph Fielding Smith roundly rejected Roberts' views and went public with his case.

That both men were within the highest circles of leadership posed an unwelcome challenge. The matter was referred to a subcommittee of apostles who reviewed the texts in question and made recommendations to the First Presidency. The committee responded by deeming Roberts's views as "objectionable doctrines" that appeared to be "out of harmony with the revelations of the Lord and the fundamental teachings of the Church."[16]

Attempts to persuade Roberts to remove these sections proved unsuccessful. He threatened to publish the book independently if he could not obtain church approval. On the other side, Smith proved to be a powerful and doctrinaire voice. As a self-designated champion of orthodoxy, he did not shy away from public debate and referred to theories of evolution as "false as their author who lives in hell."[17]

After much deliberation, the First Presidency did not side definitively with either man. Instead, it instructed all general authorities to "leave Geology, Biology, Archaeology, and Anthropology, no one of which has to do with the salvation of souls of mankind, to scientific research, while we magnify our calling in the realm of the Church."[18] The episode proved to be pivotal in the way the LDS Church handled subsequent theological disagreements.

This was borne out in the aftermath of a 1931 address by fellow apostle James Talmage, who expressed views contrary to those of Smith. Though hesitant to perpetuate controversy, Talmage recorded in his private journal a growing desire that something should be said "to make plain that the Church does not refuse to recognize the discoveries and demonstrations of science."[19] The *Church News* eventually published the speech, but it marked a turning point in ecclesiastical practice. The publications of the church became increasingly centralized and more tightly monitored.

Once again, however, LDS educational leaders experimented with secular graduate studies among its educators. This effort began in the 1930s with LDS Commissioner of Education Joseph Merrill, who invited eleven students to attend the University of Chicago Divinity School. The offer came with a stipend and the promise of employment upon return to Utah—assuming continued faithfulness to the church. As a result, a number of students completed their studies and returned west to fill positions in the Church Educational System (CES). Others, however, pursued secular academic posts. Though most participants considered it a success, church leaders were mixed. The University of Chicago was an intriguing choice in light of previous debates. On the theological spectrum, it was

decidedly modernist in orientation and had a reputation as one of the
most progressive institutions in the country. It was also one of the few
schools sufficiently inclusive to accept Mormons.[20]

Aspen Grove

A critical turning point for both Sterling McMurrin and the LDS Church
occurred in the summer of 1938. As part of a CES summer program, he
attended a six-week camp in Aspen Grove intended to provide training
for LDS seminary and institute teachers. Upon his arrival, McMurrin
reported that we "divided ourselves up pretty quickly into liberal and
conservative camps, and I landed among the liberals."[21]

J. Reuben Clark, a member of the First Presidency, was among the guest
speakers. His address dramatically altered the direction and culture of Mormon education. In a speech titled "The Charted Course of the Church in
Education," Clark took the occasion to lay down the proverbial law regarding the goals and orientation of CES curriculum. Key elements of the talk
included the proscription against secular theories and perspectives:

> You are to teach this gospel, using as your sources and authorities
> the standard works of the Church and the words of those whom
> God has called to lead his people in these last days. You are not,
> whether high or low, to intrude into your work your own peculiar
> philosophy, no matter what its source or how pleasing or rational
> it seems to you to be. [22]

With the Chicago experiment clearly in mind, Clark stated that "on
one or more occasion our Church members have gone to other places
for special training in particular lines. They have had the training that
was supposedly the last word, the most modern view . . . then they have
brought it back and dosed it upon us without any thought as to whether
we needed it or not."[23] Regarding the manner of teaching, he declared that
young Latter-day Saints were hungry for spiritual truth in a clear, simple
and "undiluted" form. This emphasis on simplicity and a common sense

approach to scripture resonated with fundamentalist discourse and was consistently amplified by both Clark and Smith. The purpose of church education is simply to build faith. All other aims are secondary and, in many cases, detrimental: "These students are prepared to believe and understand that all these things are matters of faith, not to be explained or understood by any process of human reason."[24]

Afterward, McMurrin recalled quite a bit of energy and discussion around the campfire. A veteran teacher offered his immediate resignation while others wondered how deep the impact would be. They did not have to wait long. In the following months, Clark wrote to the LDS commissioner of education laying out specific protocols for church instruction. "Teachers will do well to give up indoctrinating themselves in the sectarianism of the modern 'Divinity School Theology.'" "If they do not, they will be no longer useful in our system."[25] Having concluded that the Chicago program brought, at best, mixed results, Clark and Smith were determined to rid church education of any modernist aspirations.

The culture that resulted, and against which McMurrin railed, was one in which church curricula became self-contained, aimed exclusively at cultivating spiritual responses, and eschewed contemporary scholarship. While Clark was active in operationalizing his vision, it was uncertain how much support he had among his colleagues in the quorum. The evidence suggests that church leadership remained divided on applying contemporary scholarship to LDS history, scripture, and theology.

This became manifest again in the challenges McMurrin's friend Heber Snell faced when his book *Ancient Israel: Its Story and Meaning* ignited another round of controversy in 1948. Snell had graduated from the Chicago Divinity School in 1941 while serving as a CES institute director in Pocatello, Idaho. Snell undertook the project with the encouragement of LDS Church CES Commissioner Franklin L. West and he aimed to develop a credible and academically relevant textbook for LDS college students. The book proved to be a critical success in the broader scholarly community. McMurrin wrote a positive review in *The Personalist,* and the work was praised in the *Journal of Religion* as "first rank source material for the church school teacher."[26] However, a number of LDS educators were publicly critical, resulting in a heresy trial prompted by the church's board of education.

Among the points of contention were Snell's claims regarding the nature of biblical revelation and the interpretation of key passages. In lengthy exchanges, he and Joseph Fielding Smith differed over the degree of deference due to traditional LDS interpretations of scripture. Smith maintained that, in spite of textual evidence to the contrary, "sacred writings cannot be interpreted by men who are uninspired by the light of the Spirit of the Lord."[27]

Snell was caught between competing factions at church headquarters. In consultation with Franklin West, he was encouraged to reply to the charges, and West offered to deliver the document to the board's executive committee. Snell was exonerated, but did not escape the scrutiny of Joseph Fielding Smith, who took steps to ban the book from BYU and the Institutes of Religion. Other apostles, however, including John Widtsoe and Joseph Merrill, praised the book. For his part, McMurrin joined Snell in meetings with Smith and wrote a lengthy response to public criticisms of the book.

The Challenge of History

Six years after Snell was cleared of heresy charges, Sterling McMurrin presented a paper at the University of Utah entitled "Religion and the Denial of History." In this work, he proposed a division of labor between science and religion: "For while the natural sciences tell us a great deal about the planetary motions, the structure of atoms, the nature of protoplasm, or the function of glands, they tell us nothing about God or the ultimate meaning of life."[28] Though he acknowledged that scientific discoveries have produced "major disturbances" in the history of religion, the relationship between the two is at its heart a "philosophic issue."

> The humane disciplines and arts rather than the natural sciences are religion's chief intellectual challenge. But more than that, and this is the crux of the matter, it is the study of religion itself that

occasions the most difficult and discomposing questions. It is when religion is studied and discussed seriously by rational and informed persons with open minds and honest intentions that it encounters its most severe testing.[29]

Further, the real challenges to faith do not lie in contemplating religion in its abstract and ideal forms, but in its concrete messiness as people have attempted to work out and apply the implications of scientific discovery, historical investigation, and textual criticism. He also maintained that the study of history can produce a "liberalizing power" that frees a person from the limitations of culture and the "blinders imposed by his own time and place." The price for this freedom, however, is awareness of historical development in religion and in the very areas that produce resistance. Religion "can be and often is the motive for the intentional distortion of history, especially of its own history."[30] Of course, there are a variety of reactions to this phenomenon. One may feel liberated and persist in faith, aware of new possibilities for growth and development. Or people may "abandon their religious beliefs because of the intellectual or moral disillusionment experienced as a consequence of their encountering historical facts which they cannot accommodate to their faith."[31]

Though the essay did not mention Mormonism specifically, its implications were clear for any tradition with an inherent interest in its own history. In the case of the Latter-day Saints, the stakes are very high indeed. It has been commonplace in Mormonism to assign to its founding stories a functional authority similar to that of dogma in traditional Christianity. In this situation, McMurrin warned that the protectors of the faith may "disguise themselves as historians, make history an appendage to theology, and write theology which the trusting reader believes is history."[32] This conflation of theology and history increases the temptation to subject history to censorship, proof-texting, and strained forms of exegesis. With Snell as a case in point, historians attempting to analyze and contextualize religious history are periodically accused of deliberately, and in some cases perniciously, making the sacred profane.

As a form of the "old orthodoxy," McMurrin contended that the denial of history allows for a perpetual confusion of history and myth. This, in turn, can lead to jarring anachronisms in the attempt to sustain theological consistency across historical epochs. McMurrin understood this to be one of the greatest dangers to genuine devotion, which is to "take history seriously and yet find it possible to accept religion.[33]

Theological Foundations

Two years after he delivered this important lecture, McMurrin's interests turned to the philosophy of religion and theology. In 1957, Elder Harold B. Lee asked McMurrin if he would fill a request from The Ohio State University for a presentation on Mormonism. He repeated this lecture at Utah's major universities and colleges, and it formed the basis for an essay in 1959 entitled *The Philosophical Foundations of Mormon Theology*. Here, McMurrin outlined his major positions and called the reader's attention to the philosophical schools of thought most resonant with Mormonism. This was an opportunity to place his tradition on the intellectual grid and situate it relative to the major alternatives. A primary aim of the essay was to identify Mormonism with a pluralist metaphysics that focuses on dynamism, change, pluralism, and "becoming" over and against the tradition of "being"— which had a strong influence on classical Christian theism. "Nowhere is this pluralism more evident than in the doctrine of God, for instance, where not only is the Godhead defined as three independently real persons . . . but where also there is the idea that for the total universe there is a multiplicity of personal deities who are genuinely real as individuals."[34]

McMurrin also addressed Mormonism's rejection of creation *ex nihilo* along with its metaphysical and ethical implications for the relationship between God and humanity. Rather than standing apart from history, God is understood to be a temporal being who is situated *within* a metaphysical reality and who works to advance humanity toward divinity.

The essay was a welcome contribution given the paucity of publications that dealt carefully with Mormonism in comparative contexts. In his interviews with Jack Newell, McMurrin reported that University of Utah President A. Ray Olpin sent copies to LDS general authorities and received a warm reply from LDS President David O. McKay—with a reassuring word that he held McMurrin's name in "high regard." However, J. Reuben Clark was not as receptive, commenting that "there is a great deal of difference of opinion regarding [McMurrin's] address and its usefulness to us."[35]

After his stint as commissioner of education in the Kennedy administration, McMurrin returned to the University of Utah. As Jack Newell points out, "McMurrin might have written more on Mormon thought at the time, but his life was consumed by larger issues."[36] When he returned to Utah in 1964 as the E. E. Ericksen Distinguished Professor of Philosophy, McMurrin was asked to deliver additional lectures on Mormon theology. These formed the basis for his book-length treatment *The Theological Foundations of the Mormon Religion*. The work was intended to be the first in a series on different religious traditions, but the project was never completed.

Relative to other works of its kind, *Theological Foundations* stood alone for a generation as the only substantial attempt to bring Mormon thought into comparative alignment with the Christian theological tradition. Though far from exhaustive, it is penetrating and provocative, written with the kind of flair one would expect from McMurrin. In its pages, Mormonism is cast as a challenging alternative to traditional orthodoxies. The book is also unapologetic in its heterodoxy and revels in the association of Mormonism with various Christian heresies. Though overdrawn at times, these associations are important in understanding not only the relationship between Mormonism and the Christian community, but also the relationship between historical and contemporary Mormonism. Among the many possibilities, McMurrin chose to focus on the concept of God and the theology of human beings. He opens the book thus: "The most interesting thing about Mormon theology is that it incorporates a liberal doctrine of man and a radically unorthodox concept of God within the general framework of historic Christian fundamentalism."[37]

Though he claimed to engage in mere "exposition," McMurrin was decided in his theological tastes.[38] He preferred the spirit of Joseph Smith's Nauvoo sermons, John Widtsoe's *Rational Theology*, and B. H. Roberts's *The Mormon Doctrine of Deity*, each of which emphasized a progressive, optimistic, and radically perfectionist view of human nature. To the extent he was doing constructive theology, McMurrin attempted to highlight the *distinctive* elements of Mormon thought, and especially those that resonated with the liberal movements in the Christian tradition. In fact, he went so far as to write that to depart from this fundamental liberalism was to miss the "authentic spirit of the Mormon religion."[39]

From a stylistic standpoint, McMurrin wrote *Theological Foundations* in the spirit of the history of ideas. Characteristic of this approach is the effort to paint major intellectual themes with a broad brush. This fit McMurrin's temperament. He did not enjoy technical theological distinctions so much as the application of philosophic themes to religious thought and practice—a theme present in his lectures and publications.

McMurrin's high public profile and the production of a book-length work made him the subject of both scholarly and ecclesiastical scrutiny. Though the book has proven to be a major contribution to Mormon studies, there was vibrant discussion of its merits in the aftermath of its 1965 publication. The newly launched journal *Dialogue* published a roundtable discussion of the book, which included a variety of voices, including David Bennett from the University of Utah; Richard Lloyd Anderson from BYU; and Robert McAfee Brown, the famed American liberation theologian. The roundtable was important for gauging the different audiences to which the book might appeal.

The introduction to the roundtable notes that McMurrin's book is "unique in its attempt to describe Mormon theology in relation to traditional categories of Western thought and which is attracting unusual interest both in the Mormon community and among others."[40] Brown's comments are of particular interest given his stature in the global theological community. He was among the Protestant invitees to participate as an observer at the Second Vatican Council and taught at Stanford University when Eugene England and Wesley Johnson founded *Dialogue* and solicited his participation. Brown characterized McMurrin's book as an illustration of the "concern to *relate* the Mormon religion to classical and liberal Christianity."[41] As someone who personified American liberal theology, Brown was certainly in a position to recognize McMurrin's orientation and sensibilities.

Louis Midgley's response was far less sanguine, and he pounced on what Brown and others observed as key omissions in the text. Midgley, a longtime BYU professor and associate editor of the *FARMS Review of Books*, had been among the most active apologetic voices in Mormonism. His concerns return us quickly to the key theme of this essay, namely the question of the "old orthodoxy" and its application both inside and outside Mormonism. Midgley immediately rejected McMurrin's alignment of Mormonism with the liberal theological tradition. He objected most strongly to McMurrin's humanistic bent as it relates to LDS concepts of grace, arguing that "humanism is radically inconsistent with the doctrinal content of the Mormon scriptures."[42]

Though Midgley studied under McMurrin and had real affection for his former professor, he was dogged in defending LDS orthodoxy as he understood it. The rub between Midgley and McMurrin was one of the key points of emphasis for *Theological Foundations*, namely McMurrin's belief that the old orthodoxy robbed Mormonism of its distinctiveness, moral strength, and overall vitality. Yet this was precisely what Midgley advocated. For him, Mormonism had *finally* recognized that the Book of Mormon contains a robust redemption theology and was working to align itself with the full implications of these insights.

This intellectual divide fostered a serious and sustained disagreement between McMurrin and his critics. When pressed, McMurrin reaffirmed his commitment to human rationality, perfectibility, and innate moral goodness. He conscientiously connected Mormonism with the fourth-century heresy of Pelagianism precisely to emphasize Mormonism's metaphysical commitment to libertarian free will. For Pelagius, the command of God to avoid sin *implies* that the ability to do so is present (ought implies can). Thus, only an unjust God would give a command that was impossible to obey. This emphasis on human freedom and the ability to develop spiritually led to the accusation that Pelagius denied the fundamental role of divine grace. For this reason, the Synod of Carthage (418 CE) and the Council of Ephesus (431 CE) condemned his works as heresies.

Historically, Latter-day Saints have strongly emphasized human agency. This has manifested itself in narratives and metaphors that imply a form of "works righteousness." From this view, because agency is metaphysically necessary, grace has been seen as supplementary. McMurrin was quick to point out that "Mormon theological essays abound with the terminology of 'merit.' Such terms as 'good works,' 'deserve,' 'reward,' and 'achievement' are common in the discussion of salvation."[43] Though he has been rightly criticized for ignoring the grace-saturated passages in the Book of Mormon, McMurrin puts his finger on the movement afoot in Mormon theology and predicts its direction.

A fitting example is found in his discussion of the fall, wherein he makes a remarkably prescient comment about the general direction of Mormon sensibilities. Speaking of spiritual death, McMurrin opines that it has been

> difficult for Mormon theologians to define and they have usually passed over it casually. Yet it needs their careful attention, for it is just here that a bit of the old orthodoxy threatens to rear its head in the form of something not totally different from original sin. The eventual treatment of this issue may determine much of the character of Mormon theology in the future.[44]

This brings us back to the beginning of this essay. It has been fifty years since the publication of *Theological Foundations*, and forms of this "old orthodoxy" are still very much part of contemporary LDS discourse. It is indeed one of the "living options" that confronts Mormonism in its quest to be true to its history, texts, and best moral self. Due in part to Sterling McMurrin's persistent attention to each of these areas, Mormonism is in a much better position to understand itself, relate to other Christian religions, and absorb the implications of its perspective.

NOTES

1. "Roundtable: The Theological Foundations of the Mormon Religion," *Dialogue: A Journal of Mormon Thought* 1 (Spring 1966): 108–9.
2. The essay was later published in McMurrin's collection of essays under the title"The Primary Forms of Religion in Judeo-Christian Culture." See Sterling M. McMurrin, *Religion, Reason, and Truth: Historical Essays in the Philosophy of Religion* (SaltLake City: University of Utah Press, 1982), 83–112.
3. McMurrin, "Primary Forms,"89.
4. Ibid., 112.
5. Ibid.,111.
6. Ibid., 91.
7. Harry Emerson Fosdick,"Shall the Fundamentalists Win?" First Presbyterian Church of New York City, May 21,1922.
8. J. Gresham Machen, *Christianity and Liberalism* (Grand Rapids, MI: Wm. B Eerdmans, 1923), 79. Machen was an influential and pivotal figure in this period,and his fortunes reflected the push and pull of the broader debates.
9. "Fundamentalism and Modernism: Two Religions," *Christian Century* 41 (January 3, 1924): 5, 6. See also Matthew Avery Sutton, *American Apocalypse: A History ofModern Evangelicalism* (Cambridge, MA: Belknap Press of Harvard University Press, 2014), 79–109.
10. For a full treatment of Mormon connections to, and entanglements with, neo-orthodox theologies, see O. Kendall White, *Mormon Neo-Orthodoxy: A Crisis Theology* (Salt Lake City: Signature Books Utah, 1987).
11. J. Marinus Jensen, et al., *History of Brigham Young University* (1942), L. Tom Perry Special Collections, Harold B. Lee Library, Brigham Young University, Provo, UT.
12. Ernest Wilkinson, ed. *Brigham Young University: The First One Hundred Years* (Provo, UT: BYU Press, 1975), 1:426. See also Richard Sherlock, "Campus in Crisis: BYU's earliest conflict between secular knowledge and religious belief," *Sunstone* (May, 1985): 32; Gary James Bergera, "The 1911 Evolution Controversy at Brigham Young University," in *The Search for Harmony: Essays on Science Mormonism, ed. Gene A. Sessions and Craig J. Oberg* (Salt Lake City: Signature Books, 1993), 23–41; and Thomas Alexander, *Mormonism in Transition: A History of the Latter-day Saints 1890–1930* (Urbana: University of Illinois Press, 1996), 171–4.
13. Three professors eventually resigned or were dismissed, including Ralph Chamberlin (biology) and brothers Joseph Peterson (education) and

Henry Peterson (psychology). William Chamberlin, Ralph's brother, was recruited at the same time and advocated similar methodologies. Though pressured, he was initially spared, but resigned five years later.

14. Important examples include Nels Nelson, *Scientific Aspects of Mormonism or Religion in Terms of Life* (New York: G. P. Putnam's Sons, 1904); Charles W. Penrose, "The Age and Destiny of the Earth," *Improvement Era* 12 (May 1909); and John Widtsoe, *Joseph Smith as Scientist: A Contribution to Mormon Philosophy* (Salt Lake City: Young Men's Mutual Improvement Association, 1908).

15. First Presidency of the Church, "The Origin of Man," *Improvement Era* 13 (November 1909): 81.

16. George Albert Smith to Rudger Clawson, October 10, 1929, Rudger Clawson Papers, J. Willard Marriott Library, University of Utah, Salt Lake City. See also Richard Sherlock, "We Can See No Advantage to a Continuation of the Discussion: The Roberts/Smith/Talmage Affair," *Dialogue: A Journal of Mormon Thought* 13 (Fall 1980): 67–68.

17. Joseph Fielding Smith to President Rudger Clawson, addressed for the Quorum of the Twelve Apostles, January 21, 1931, Rudger Clawson Papers, J. Willard Marriott Library, University of Utah, Salt Lake City. See Sherlock, "We Can See No Advantage," op 69. Smith regularly used the arguments and rhetoric of fundamentalist authors and maintained regular correspondence with George McReady Price, the leading fundamentalist proponent of "Catastrophism." See Ronald L. Numbers, *The Creationists: From Scientific Creationism to Intelligent Design* (Cambridge, MA: Harvard University Press, 2006), 339–45; and Philip L. Barlow, *Mormons and the Bible: The Place of the Latter-day Saints in American Religion* (New York: Oxford University Press, 2013), 133–40.

18. "First Presidency Minutes," April 7, 1931, quoted in William Evenson, "Evolution," in *The Encyclopedia of Mormonism*, ed. Daniel H. Ludlow (New York: Macmillan, 1992), 1: 478.

19. James A. Talmage, Journal November 21, 1931. L. Tom Perry Special Collections, Harold B. Lee Library, Brigham Young University, Provo. Also see James P. Harris, ed., *The Essential Talmage* (Salt Lake City: Signature Books, 1997), 239.

20. See Casey Paul Griffiths, "The Chicago Experiment: Finding the Voice and Charting the Course of Religious Education," *BYU Studies* 49 (2010): 91–130; "Russel Swenson, "Mormons at the University of Chicago Divinity School: A Personal Reminiscence," *Dialogue: A Journal of Mormon Thought* 7 (Summer, 1972), 37–47; Armand L. Mauss, *Shifting Borders and a Tattered Passport: Intellectual Journeys of a Mormon Academic* (Salt Lake City: University of Utah Press, 2012), 144–45.

21. Sterling M. McMurrin and L. Jackson Newell, *Matters of Conscience: Conversations with Sterling McMurrin on Philosophy, Education, and Religion* (Salt Lake City: Signature Books, 1996), 115.

22. J. Reuben Clark, "The Charted Course of the Church in Education," 10. See www.lds.org/bc/content/shared/content/english/pdf/language-materials/32709_eng.pdf?lang=eng, (accessed October 11, 2016.)

23. Ibid., 8.

24. Ibid., 5.

25. Scott Esplin, "Charting the Course: President Clark's Charge to Religious Educators, *The Religious Educator* 7 (2006), 112. Another young CES employee at the time, Boyd K. Packer, came to like the address so much that in a 1993 address to church educators he declared, "It is revelation; it is as much revelation as that which you find if you open the standard works." At the time of the address, Packer was the senior apostle overseeing the CES. Boyd K. Packer, "The Great Plan of Happiness") address to religious educators, August 10, 1993), 3. Jeffrey Holland echoed this during his tenure as dean of BYU Religious Education: "Read it carefully and ponder it. For by applying the definition the Lord Himself gave, this instruction may comfortably be referred to as scripture." Earlier in 1981, President Packer delivered another landmark address with similar themes, entitled "The Mantle Is Far, Far Greater Than the Intellect."

26. William A. Irwin, review of *"Ancient Israel: Its Story and Its Meaning,* by Heber Cyrus Snell," *Journal of Religion* 29 (1949): 240–41. For McMurrin's review, see *The Personalist* 30 (1949): 318. See Richard Sherlock, "Faith and History: The Snell Controversy" *Dialogue: A Journal of Mormon Thought* 12 (Spring: 1979) 27–41; Barlow, *Mormons and the Bible*, 153–54; and Armand L. Mauss, *The Angel and the Beehive: The Mormon Struggle with Assimilation* (Urbana: University of Illinois Press, 1994), 95–99.

27. Joseph Fielding Smith to Heber Snell, May 27, 1949. See Sherlock, ""Faith and History," 33.

28. Sterling M. McMurrin, "Religion and the Denial of History," *Sunstone* 3 (March/April 1982): 46. The original paper was presented at the Great Issues Forum at the University of Utah on March 23, 1955. It was revised and reprinted in McMurrin, *Religion, Reason, and Truth*, 133–44.

29. Ibid., 46–47.

30. Ibid., 47

31. Ibid.

32. Ibid., 48.

33. Ibid., 32.

34. Sterling McMurrin, *The Philosophical Foundations of Mormon Theology* (Salt Lake City: University of Utah Press, 1959), 8.

35. McMurrin and Newell, *Matters of Conscience*, 354.

36. L. Jackson Newell, "Introductory Essay" to *The Theological Foundations of the Mormon Religion*, 2nd ed. (Salt Lake City: University of Utah Press, 1965; repr., Signature Books, 2000), vi.

37. *McMurrin, foreword to Theological Foundations, i.*

38. In his response to reviewers of the *Theological Foundations*, McMurrin states that his motive was "simply to describe comparatively the distinctive character of Mormon theology, though I hoped in doing so to show that Mormonism has more intellectual strength than most of its critics suppose and that most of its adherents seem willing to admit." Joseph Jeppson, "Notes and Comments," *Dialogue: A Journal of Mormon Thought* 1 (Summer, 1966), 135.

39. McMurrin, *Theological Foundations*, 111.

40. *Dialogue: A Journal of Mormon Thought* 1 (Spring, 1966): 107.

41. Robert McAfee Brown, "A New Step in Understanding," *Dialogue: A Journal of Mormon Thought* 1 (Fall 1966): 108–9. See *BYU Studies* 9 (1969), 103–9.

42. Louis Midgley, letter to the editor, *Dialogue: A Journal of Mormon Thought* 1 (Fall, 1966): 6–8.

43. McMurrin, *Theological Foundations*, 75.

44. Ibid., 71.

5

FERTILE GROUND, FRUITFUL HARVESTS

Sterling McMurrin in Arizona and Washington, D.C.

J. BOYER JARVIS

The story of Sterling McMurrin's early career years in Mesa and Tucson, Arizona, involved an auspicious convergence of remarkable Latter-day Saints who, along with him, would play significant roles in shaping Mormon, Great Basin, and American culture in the decades following World War II. Lowell Bennion was one of them, but this little circle also included future United States cabinet secretaries, a future university president, several who would become celebrated educators and public intellectuals, and two future LDS Church presidents. Southern Arizona was fertile ground for talented Mormons in the 1940s. Those who took root there established connections that served them and their institutions well throughout their productive lives.

Around Labor Day in 1940, a very attractive young couple, Sterling and Natalie McMurrin, arrived in Mesa, Arizona, where he had been assigned to take charge of the LDS seminary adjacent to Mesa Union High School. The leaders of the Maricopa Stake welcomed them warmly, and McMurrin was soon appointed to the sunday school Board. Invitations to speak at various church meetings followed, and after someone learned that Natalie possessed a fine singing voice, she was frequently asked to favor the congregation with a vocal solo.

A classmate persuaded me to go with him to the first evening meeting of a weekly seminary class offered by McMurrin. I went and I never returned. Even his teaching was not enough to offset my bias against church instruction.

According to his assignment, McMurrin dedicated one half of his time to the high school-level Mesa Seminary and the other half to an interdenominational religious studies program at Arizona State Teachers College (now Arizona State University) in nearby Tempe. During the summer, Sterling and Natalie went to Los Angeles where he continued graduate study in philosophy at the University of Southern California (USC).

Although I had shunned seminary in high school, I showed up one day in January, 1943, at the LDS Institute of Religion when I entered the University of Arizona. At that time, the institute director, Daryl Chase, was anticipating his transfer to the much larger institute in Logan (which led eventually to his presidency of Utah State University). When he departed at the end of the semester, he knew that his replacement in Tucson would be Sterling McMurrin. On March 29, 1943, Dr. Chase wrote a detailed letter to McMurrin to orient him to the job he was about to undertake. It read in part:

> I know that you will enjoy living in Tucson where you will advance the work of the Church and leave a living monument to yourself— brother you already have a following here. Next to Jesus, and the Prophet Joseph, you are at present quoted more often by LDS students than all the other worthies, both modern and ancient.[1]

When the McMurrins arrived in Tucson in September, they received a warm welcome, not only from the institute students and the local Latter-day Saints, but also from University of Arizona officials. That positive reception rested not only on his impressive academic credentials and growing reputation but also upon the solid academic accomplishments of his two predecessors. Lowell L. Bennion, the founding director of the institute at the University of Arizona in 1937, had earned his doctorate at the University of Strasbourg, and Daryl Chase, his successor in 1939, held a PhD in religion from the University of Chicago.

McMurrin's Arizona years roughly coincided with World War II. Like all patriotic Americans, he wanted to serve in the military, but his chronic bronchial asthma resulted in a 4-F draft classification (unfit for service). Undeterred, he made several attempts to obtain a chaplain's commission in the army and navy. Both branches rejected him.

Like Bennion, Chase, and their families who preceded them, Sterling and Natalie were assigned to live in a small upstairs apartment at the back of the institute building. While that arrangement afforded them little privacy, he could perform all of his teaching, administrative, and custodial duties without leaving the premises. In addition to the director's apartment and office, the building housed a chapel, recreation hall, library, classroom, lounge, and study areas.

The institute was a social gathering place, not only for LDS students attending the university, but also for Mormon service men stationed in or near Tucson. The long-standing friendship of William Mulder and Sterling McMurrin began when Mulder visited the institute while he was enrolled in a naval officers training program at the University of Arizona. Mulder later served for many years as a distinguished professor of English at the University of Utah.

Under McMurrin's leadership, the high point of the week at the institute was Sunday school. We assembled in the chapel at 9:30 a.m. to listen to the CBS radio broadcast of *Music and the Spoken Word*, featuring the Mormon Tabernacle Choir, and then listened to Sterling's always morally uplifting, intellectually stimulating, and thoroughly original lessons. I acted as his Sunday school superintendent for a time, being succeeded by Stewart Udall who would later become U.S. secretary of the interior under Presidents John F. Kennedy and Lyndon B. Johnson from 1961 to 1969.

McMurrin served on the Southern Arizona Stake high council and enjoyed cordial relationships with its president, Alonzo Ballentine, a son-in-law of apostle Joseph F. Merrill, and Gordon Kimball, the bishop of the Tucson Ward and a brother of Spencer W. Kimball (whose eventual presidency of the LDS Church will surface importantly later in this essay).

From time to time the McMurrins hosted official visitors from Salt Lake City. One of my favorite recollections is Sterling's report of Apostle John A. Widtsoe's parting admonition as they stood on the front steps of the institute at the end of his visit: "Preach the Gospel, sugar coated when necessary."

The following letter from recently appointed Apostle Harold B. Lee (who later served as LDS Church president) reflects the quality of hospitality that the McMurrins typically provided their guests:

> Dear Sterling and Natalie:
> I have just returned home and take this opportunity to again express my deep appreciation for your many kindnesses extended to me during my stay in Tucson. I enjoyed greatly the lovely spirit and sweet humility you both express and could only wish that my own girls were under your influence. The care you gave me both as to my clothes and other personal kindnesses could hardly have been extended more lovingly by my own mother. I should only hope for the time to have you drawn closer to us here and elsewhere.
>
> With kindest regards, I am sincerely and affectionately yours,
> Harold B. Lee.[2]

Sterling McMurrin was similarly held in high esteem, but for different reasons, at the University of Arizona. There the non-Mormon head of the Department of Philosophy and Psychology sought to appoint him to his faculty.

One of my classmates at the University of Arizona was Irmalee Webb, who later married Stewart Udall. At the beginning of autumn semester, 1945, she told me she was planning to take a comparative economics course and, if I would join her, we could study together. I readily agreed. One December evening we were studying in the institute classroom when

Sterling looked in to say goodbye since he and his family were leaving for the winter holidays in Los Angeles. After he left, Irmalee and I disagreed over McMurrin's belief in Mormon doctrine. To settle our argument, we decided that I should ask him. Sterling's prompt reply to my letter came on USC. Department of Philosophy stationery:

> Dear Boyer:
>> Yea and/or Nay
>>> S.[3]

McMurrin finished his PhD in May 1946, and immediately accepted a regular appointment to the USC faculty effective that fall. Just two years later, he became professor of philosophy at the University of Utah.

During the 1950s Professor McMurrin served as dean of the University of Utah's College of Letters and Science, and then as vice president for academic affairs. In the summers, he gave lectures and led seminars at the Aspen Institute for Humanistic Studies in the Colorado Rockies.

One midweek evening, a few days before the inauguration of President John F. Kennedy on January 20, 1961, Sterling invited Waldemar Read and me to join him for lime flips at Dan Johnson's Ice Cream Parlor on the corner of Ninth East and Seventh South in Salt Lake City. Waldemar had been a teacher and mentor to McMurrin during his undergraduate years at the University of Utah, and they remained fast friends. As we slurped our lime flips, Sterling asked us if he should leave the University of Utah and take a job in Washington D.C.—a job from which the current occupant was about to be released. "Tell us more," Waldemar and I responded almost simultaneously.

McMurrin then told us that Alvin Eurich, president of the Fund for the Advancement of Education, had called to ask if he would accept appointment as United States commissioner of education—if the job were offered to him. As we talked, Waldemar and I recognized that the call from Al Eurich suggested to McMurrin the possibility of service to his country that had been denied him during World War II.

McMurrin was suddenly entering new territory. A day or two after President Kennedy's inauguration, he flew to Washington, D.C. to meet with Abraham Ribicoff, the new secretary of the Department of Health, Education and Welfare. The two developed an immediate respect and liking for each other. Before McMurrin departed for his flight back to Salt Lake City, Secretary Ribicoff told him that he would ask the president to appoint him to the position of United States commissioner of education.

The secretary's recommendation was received favorably at the White House, but before the appointment could be announced, political protocol required clearance from Senator Frank Moss and other Utah Democratic Party officials. With that formality accomplished, on January 31, 1961, President Kennedy announced his nomination of Sterling M. McMurrin to be the new United States commissioner of education.

As commissioner-designate, McMurrin continued to perform his duties as academic vice president at the University of Utah. During February and March, he commuted frequently between Salt Lake City and Washington while he negotiated with President A. Ray Olpin for a leave of absence from the university and conferred with staff members in the U.S. Office of Education. Meanwhile, he waited for the Senate to confirm his appointment.

To most of the leaders of national educational organizations, as well as to many political pundits in the nation's capital, President Kennedy's selection of a philosophy professor as U.S. commissioner of education was a surprise. Unlike his predecessor, he had never been a member of the National Education Association (NEA) or of any local teachers' association, nor had he any experience as a public school administrator. For as long as most interested people could remember, the influence of the NEA had been strongly felt in the U.S. Office of Education.

While some people wondered what an unknown professor of philosophy from Utah could do in Washington, those who knew Sterling McMurrin hastened to congratulate him. LDS Church President David O. McKay wrote on him February 1, 1961:

Dear Dr. McMurrin:

Among the many thousands who are happy over your appointment as United States Commissioner of Education, I take this opportunity to express appreciation of President Kennedy's good judgment in choosing you for this high and responsible position, and to assure you of my affectionate regard, confidence, and heartfelt wishes for your unbounded success…Sister McKay joins in every good wish for you and Sister McMurrin in your service to the Nation.

Affectionately,

David O. McKay[4]

After the formal committee hearings at which Utah's senators from both sides of the aisle, Republican Wallace Bennett and Democrat Frank Moss, strongly endorsed his appointment, McMurrin received unanimous confirmation at the end of March.

Secretary Ribicoff conducted the swearing-in ceremony on April 4, 1961. Following the ceremony, the NEA staged a reception for the new commissioner in its elegant headquarters building. Among the hundreds of people attending, the one person, other than the honoree and Mrs. McMurrin, who attracted the most attention, was Sterling and Natalie's good friend, Walter Reuther, president of the United Auto Workers Union. Their friendship had begun when Reuther attended one of McMurrin's Aspen Institute seminars.

William Carr, executive secretary of the NEA, thanked Commissioner McMurrin for bringing Reuther to the NEA headquarters and confided that for years the NEA's effort to entice the renowned labor leader to visit its office had been unsuccessful.

With a staff of approximately 1,200 civil service employees in the U.S. Office of Education, the commissioner was allowed to have two non–civil service assistants. McMurrin invited me to be one of them. By June of 1961 we had settled our families within a mile of each other in nearby Arlington, Virginia. Most days we rode to and from the office together. Twelve-to-fourteen-hour days, plus another six or more hours on Saturdays, was our normal work schedule.

Invitations rapidly accumulated from across the country for Commissioner McMurrin to speak at conferences, conventions, and commencements. To the amazement of his staff, he wrote his own speeches or spoke extemporaneously. Among his themes were the need to raise standards at all levels of the educational process. He advocated increasing the compensation for public school teachers, particularly in inner-city schools. He also proposed substantial increases in federal aid to education, and maintained that such support could be made available without infringing upon the treasured American tradition of local control of public schools.

Commissioner McMurrin presented with compelling clarity the challenge confronting the United States in its competition with totalitarian states that sought to extend their influence around the world. He caught the attention of members of Congress and of high officials in many federal government agencies outside the Department of Health, Education and Welfare. Soon he was engaged in conversations with representatives of the Department of State and the National Science Foundation regarding ways to enhance the quality and availability of education for the protection of individual freedom and national sovereignty.

Representatives of the United States Chamber of Commerce, who had long regarded the U.S. Office of Education as a mere extension of the NEA, welcomed the opportunity to have their views considered by a different kind of U.S. commissioner, one who recognized that business has legitimate interests in shaping federal educational policies.

McMurrin's advocacy for greatly increased federal expenditures in support of education was not universally approved. Senator Barry Goldwater of Arizona, who in 1961 was anticipating his 1964 campaign for the presidency, suggested in his newspaper column that massive federal aid to education would inevitably undermine the authority of local school boards and result in tyrannical central control of the nation's schools. Likewise, the Maryland State Teachers Association, reacting to Commissioner McMurrin's call for elevating standards for preparing future teachers, passed a resolution "vigorously denouncing" the commissioner for questioning "the quality of all teacher education programs throughout the United States."[5]

At the same time, Sister Mary Josetta, R.S.M., president of Saint Xavier College in Chicago, wrote President Kennedy to express the appreciation of many educational leaders for Commissioner McMurrin's contributions to constructive educational policy changes:

> Dear Mr. President,
>
> During his months in office we have watched and listened, first with interest, then with admiration, to Mr. Sterling McMurrin, Commissioner of Education. While we have not had occasion to welcome him to our campus, we have been deeply conscious of his presence. Never in my twenty years in higher education has there been so able and articulate a representative of education in the government. Mr. McMurrin's statement before the Appropriations Subcommittee of the House of Representatives last May 8, "The Present Condition of American Education," was one of the clearest, most cogent arguments for the value of liberal education I have read. Having spent the past fifteen years in the development and implementation of liberal education on all levels, it is a source of hope, encouragement, and, I think, progress to see the enduring goals in the education of free men hold first place in the minds of our country's leaders. Mr. McMurrin's extraordinary capabilities are recognized and deeply appreciated by those of us who share his work.
>
> Respectfully,
> Sister Mary Josetta[6]

One morning early in 1962, on very short notice, McMurrin was summoned to an eleven o'clock meeting at the White House. Believing the jacket and slacks he wore inappropriate for greeting the president, he asked me to drive him quickly to his home in Arlington to pick up a suit. On our six-mile return drive he changed clothes in the backseat. Neatly suited, McMurrin was shortly ushered into the Oval Office. He noticed instantly that President Kennedy wore a sport jacket and slacks just like the attire he had so hurriedly jettisoned.

In February of 1962 Commissioner McMurrin agreed to visit the newly created Educational Television Center in Columbia, South Carolina. He invited Keith Engar and me to accompany him. Professor Engar was on leave from the University of Utah for a year of service with the Federal Communications Commission in Washington, D.C.[7] Traveling together, the three of us took an overnight train and arrived at about 8:00 a.m. in Columbia. After watching a demonstration of one of South Carolina's television programs for use in the schools, we were luncheon guests of several state public education officials.

By two o'clock we had completed the purpose of our trip to Columbia and had five hours to wait before boarding the overnight train back to Washington. Recognizing an opportunity for some much-needed rest, Sterling suggested that we rent a hotel room and lie down for the remainder of the afternoon. Keith and I readily agreed. The room we rented had two single beds. Keith and I told Sterling that he should take one of the beds and the two of us would flip for the other bed. He refused, and insisted on being a party to the coin toss. He lost and ended up resting on the floor.

A project to which Commissioner McMurrin devoted a great deal of attention during the early months of 1962 was a U.S. Office of Education's "Conference on the Ideals of American Freedom and the International Dimensions of Education," held March 25–28, in Washington. Two hundred college and university presidents, professors, officers of national educational organizations, and government officials were invited to participate. As the keynote for that conference, Commissioner McMurrin prepared one of his most notable addresses, titled "Education for Freedom in a Free Society." Forcefully and eloquently, he stressed the importance to society as well as to individuals of learning to think critically and objectively. The attendees received his message enthusiastically.

A few weeks later, Abraham Ribicoff confided in McMurrin about his intention to resign as secretary of health, education, and welfare so that he could return to Connecticut and run for the U.S. Senate. Before joining the Kennedy administration, Ribicoff had been Connecticut's governor.

As a cabinet officer he was already growing weary of the requirement that all of his public policy statements be reviewed and approved in advance by the White House. By becoming a senator, he could regain the freedom to say whatever he wanted to say.

McMurrin had enjoyed a close and satisfying working relationship with Ribicoff. In little more than a year, the two had managed to raise dramatically the prestige and enlarge the influence of the U.S. Office of Education. Now, with Ribicoff planning to leave the administration, Sterling told me confidentially that he felt inclined to pull up stakes and move back to Utah.

The final months of Commissioner McMurrin's tenure in the Office of Education were marked by continuing progress for education bills he was supporting before congressional committees. Under consideration were bills to reduce class sizes, increase teachers' salaries, and provide scholarships for college students preparing for teaching careers. Most of these bills later won approval and were signed by the president.

One day in July 1962, McMurrin entered a planning meeting in his office with a small group of staff members working on pending legislation. He sensed an unusual soberness in their demeanor. He asked why everyone seemed so discouraged. He was informed that the United States Supreme Court had just announced its decision that the New York state public-school prayer was unconstitutional. Noticing that one of his colleagues was especially downcast, McMurrin jokingly said, "Peter, I'm surprised. You look like you wrote that prayer yourself." To which Peter Muirhead replied, "I did!"

Before joining the U.S. Office of Education, Muirhead, then a staff member of the New York State Office of Education, had composed the twenty-two-word Regents' Prayer that the highest court in the land now declared to be an infringement of religious freedom. It read, "Almighty God, we acknowledge our dependence upon Thee, and we beg Thy blessing upon us, our parents, our teachers, and our country."[8]

On September 5, 1962, Commissioner McMurrin met with hundreds of employees of the U.S. Office of Education in the auditorium of the Health, Education, and Welfare Building. He told them he was resigning because he wanted to return to teaching and research, and thanked them for their dedication and service to their country. With Secretary Ribicoff's departure, he explained, this seemed an appropriate time to make such a move.

On September 8, President Kennedy signed the following letter:

> Dear Dr. McMurrin:
>
> It is with deep regret that I accept your resignation as Commissioner of Education.
>
> I would like to express to you my personal gratitude for your dedication and loyalty. The field in which you directed your efforts is a vital one to the American people, and your contributions as Commissioner have benefitted the Nation as a whole.
>
> In whatever future course you may follow, you have my very best wishes for success and happiness.
>
> Sincerely,
John Kennedy[9]

And on October 2, by which time Professor McMurrin was back on the University of Utah campus, Senator John Sherman Cooper of Kentucky addressed his colleagues on the Senate floor:

> A few days ago, a great public servant left the scene of public affairs and started back to the college campus, to his classes in philosophy....He was appointed by a Democratic President, but he followed no partisan political pattern; no partisan procedures. He followed the dictates of his conscience and the mandates of great thinkers of all ages.[10]

Sterling McMurrin was welcomed home to the University of Utah with comparable appreciation. There he associated as a faculty member with three academic departments: philosophy, educational administration, and history. He soon succeeded Henry Eyring as dean of the graduate school.

Among the many significant nonuniversity affiliations that were to come, McMurrin became a consultant to the national Committee for Economic Development (CED), an organization of about forty business and university executives interested in studying and making recommendations on the condition of the national economy. He invited me to assist him in preparing three or four CED reports, and I accompanied him to CED meetings in various cities around the country. After a meeting in Boston, we rented a car and drove north to visit Joseph Smith's birthplace in Vermont.

When I decided not to sign up for Brother McMurrin's seminary class as a high school student, I didn't expect to see much of him in the future. As things turned out, he became a very important part of my life. It has been my great privilege to observe, at close hand, McMurrin's incomparable contributions to his country, his university, and his church.

Sterling McMurrin's Mormon heritage was deep and profound. He admitted his heresies while remaining a loyal critic of the church. He always defended it when reporters asked for his comments. He chose to remain a University of Utah professor, declining at least two biddings to serve as its president and many invitations to go elsewhere. After his U.S. commissionership, he served the federal government as an adviser in numerous short-term assignments—always as a staunch advocate of equality and fairness.

Five years after returning to Utah, and in the immediate wake of the assassinations of the Reverend Dr. Martin Luther King, Jr. and presidential candidate Senator Robert Kennedy (who had once participated in an Aspen Institute seminar McMurrin taught), Professor McMurrin addressed the annual banquet of the Salt Lake chapter of the NAACP. On June 21, 1968, he reflected deeply on the state of his country and his church. Noting the presence of fanatical elements within both the black and white populations in America, he said,

> If we [whites] follow ours and you follow yours, together we will bring ruin upon our nation and upon ourselves. We don't want passivity and quiescence; we want militancy, the kind of energetic,

determined, constructive militancy that enabled Dr. Martin Luther
King and other Negro leaders to bring the civil rights movement
into being.[11]

Then, turning to his own religion that continued to deny priesthood privileges and temple rites to those of African descent, he spared no words:

> I firmly believe that the time will come when the Mormon people
> for the most part will have abandoned their crude superstitions
> about Negroes—their children will force them to—and then the
> Church will have a new vision of brotherhood and social justice.
> When that time comes, those who can remember will remember
> with sadness and moral embarrassment the day when their Church
> could have done great things to hasten the achievement of the good
> society, but failed. I am confident that day will come, but I am one
> of the disenchanted, and am now quite sure that when it comes, I
> won't be around.[12]

But that day did dawn just a decade later when the president of the Mormon Church, Spencer W. Kimball, removed the proscription on black
males' access to the priesthood. Sterling McMurrin's clarion voice was
one of the precipitating forces. His Arizona and Washington, D.C., years
had prepared him well for his expanding role as a moral authority. Being
enmeshed in a web of the Latter-day Saint elite seemed to have liberated
his spirit in young adulthood and magnified his influence at the height
of his career. It is not always so. The spark came from within.

NOTES

1. Sterling M. McMurrin Account # MS0032, Special Collections, J. Willard
    Marriott Library, University of Utah, Salt Lake City.
2.   Ibid. Harold B. Lee and Sterling McMurrin were second cousins.
3.   Ibid.

4. Ibid. As a Mormon apostle, David O. McKay had performed the marriage ceremony of Sterling and Natalie McMurrin twenty-three years earlier.

5. McMurrin Papers.

6. Sister Mary Josetta to Sterling McMurrin, December 22, 1961, McMurrin Papers.

7. A faculty member at the University of Utah, Engar was the original program director and then manager of Channel 7, KUED, the University of Utah's television station.

8. McMurrin Papers.

9. Ibid.

10. Ibid.

11. Sterling M. McMurrin, "The Negros among the Mormons" (address to the Salt Lake City Chapter of the NAACP, June 21, 1968), McMurrin Papers.

12. Ibid.

PART III

OBERT C. TANNER

6

THE SPIRITUAL QUEST
OF OBERT C. TANNER

ROBERT ALAN GOLDBERG

The poverty-to-prominence story of Obert C. Tanner is a familiar one, but it bears brief repeating. From a poor family, Obert Tanner developed a work ethic through hard labor on the farm, railroad, and in a series of menial jobs. Working his way through school and college, he gradually pulled himself up by his bootstraps. In the emblematic jewelry business, he found his calling. Beginning as a clerk and errand boy, Tanner eventually organized a major corporation. Business and later philanthropy, however, were not sufficient to occupy his time or mind. He also devoted himself to teaching and studying philosophy. He joined the University of Utah faculty in 1945 and retired after almost thirty years in the classroom.[1]

This is an important history that offers significant insights. But alone, the account misses the rich fabric of Obert Tanner's life and mind. There is too little context and no nuance. Moving this story to the background, the focus here is on another piece of his life. Tanner was a religious man who pursued, what I will call, a "spiritual quest." He described it as a "journey in search of freedom."[2] His was not an escape from something, not a rebellion, but a freedom for something.

Obert Tanner was born into the Church of Jesus Christ of Latter-day Saints and was comfortable in its culture. As he wrote in his autobiography, "I am proud of my church" and "I love my church."[3] He never openly challenged Mormonism, nor would he ever abandon it. But, he chafed in a church whose doctrine and myths constrained him intellectually. As he would put it, uncritical interpretations "pain the thinking man or woman."[4]

This essay seeks to explore how Obert Tanner found his peace, found his freedom. How he maintained his personal integrity and balance without abandoning his community. On his spiritual quest, he was able to transcend Mormonism without rejecting it. Rather, he understood it not as the one true church, but a piece in a mosaic of faith traditions that reach to understand God and humankind. In his framework, Tanner was not given to "final answers," but crafted a practical Christianity of love and progress.[5]

The powerful influence of his mother, Annie Clark Tanner, must be explored at length to understand his journey. He wrote, "All I am and hope to be, I owe to my angel Mother."[6] And, she "was both father and mother to me. I loved her profoundly."[7] In fact, without her spiritual quest as prelude and example, his journey to freedom may not have been possible. Annie wrote a remarkable document detailing her quest. Her book *A Mormon Mother* is a personal and intimate history and sets the context and foundation stones of Obert Tanner's life. As parent and guide, she gave her son the means to accept himself, his religion, and his world.

Annie Clark Tanner's journey was not one of geographic space, but of the mind. She was born in Farmington, Utah, a close-knit and homogeneous Mormon community north of Salt Lake City. Her reading list counted only church publications, and, as she recalled, "we read every word in them."[8] Sunday school and church meetings "were attended faithfully," and the Mormon dietary code, or Word of Wisdom, and tithing were "sacred principles."[9] As a Mormon, she took an oath and with her community "raised our right hand and promised not to trade with outsiders."[10] The community expected submission and dissent was unthinkable. She remembered, "The principle of obedience dominated the teaching of my girlhood, whether it applied to the home, the State, or the Church....Obedience was the basis of our religion."[11] As God's chosen, she declared, "We were the only people on earth to know His great eternal truths."[12]

In building God's kingdom, all played their roles without question. "From the all-seeing eye of God, nothing could be concealed."[13] Silence smothered disagreement, and prayer brought comfort in a culture of one heart and one mind.

Born into polygamy and living within a network of polygamist families, Annie learned early that "celestial marriage" was the "capstone of Mormon religion."[14] She chose to become a plural wife at age nineteen, following not only her culture but also her church's pronouncement of the Principle's divine origin. Annie's commitment to her religion, polygamy, and her husband, Joseph Marion Tanner, was tested in 1888, five years into their marriage. Rather than "jeopardize [her] husband's liberty," Annie went "underground" though she was five months pregnant.[15] This meant, that to escape detection as her husband's second wife, she hid from authorities by shuttling every few days or weeks between safe houses offered by friends, relatives, and sympathetic strangers. Her ordeal took her from community to community in Utah, Idaho, and Wyoming and lasted three years. While her husband maintained a busy public life with his first wife, she could count on little financial or emotional support. Secret conjugal visits with her husband soon produced another baby that she birthed alone. Also in line with church teachings, Annie eventually gave birth to ten children, with Obert her youngest.[16]

But, Annie Tanner would, over time, realize that a prayerful heart and submission would not ease her doubts nor sustain orthodoxy. An unhappy marriage and desperation under the press of poverty and hunger drained her of confidence in her husband's authority and a church that sanctioned his power.

Annie had met her husband Joseph while attending Brigham Young Academy where she studied Mormonism and he was one of her teachers. Annie was immediately attracted to the charismatic Joseph, who was known as an inspiring and deeply religious mentor. "As a teacher," she observed, "he seemed perfect. There seemed to be no limit to his knowledge."[17] After obtaining the permission of his first wife, Joseph asked Annie to marry. Recalling her family experiences and her church's teachings, she readily accepted. Annie was proud to have married Joseph and noted the sanctioned place of women in Mormonism: "To be the wife of a fine leader in Israel was the height of their ambition."[18]

Annie, however, was not prepared for her new role, and her idealized vision of marriage brought immediate disappointment. Citing the needs of his first wife and the press of business affairs and church service, Joseph did not visit Annie for three weeks after their marriage ceremony. Within six months, Joseph had taken a third wife and answered a mission call to spread the gospel in Europe and the Middle East. He was gone for three and a half years, during which Annie supported him with the earnings she made as a teacher. "Already," she wrote, "he manifested a consciousness of his right to 'Rule.' I, too, seemed aware of the fact that he was 'my Lord.' There was no escape from the decree."[19]

Returning from his mission in 1887, Joseph Tanner rapidly climbed the educational hierarchy of the Church of Jesus Christ of Latter-day Saints. Church authorities appointed him acting president of the Brigham Young Academy. He sat on the church's Board of Education, the Board of Examiners that certified teachers for Mormon schools, and the LDS General Sunday School Board that approved published materials for children's education. He also held the position as superintendent of all LDS Church schools. In addition to his church callings, Joseph was appointed as professor at Utah State Agricultural College where he taught history, German, English literature, and logic, among other subjects. He was later named president of the college.[20]

Joseph Tanner's desire to live the Principle of celestial marriage ended his ascent. Despite the Mormon Church's manifesto against plural marriage, Joseph married two more women and so counted five wives. In 1900, he resigned as president of Utah State Agricultural College after the U.S. Congress passed legislation that prohibited funding to state institutions that employed polygamists. In 1904, in the aftermath of the LDS Church's "Second Manifesto" regarding the contracting of plural marriages, Joseph Tanner was released from his ecclesiastical positions. With no income and to avoid prosecution for polygamy, he left the United States and began farming in western Canada. If Joseph was devout about the Principle, his son Obert was more cynical: "I think my father allowed its social rewards to dignify his own desires."[21]

It is curious that a man who dedicated so much of his life to learning as both teacher and administrator would deny his children the benefits of a formal education. Joseph was forthright with wife Annie: "I don't intend to educate all of my children."[22] He bargained with her, agreeing to help satisfy some of her debts if she would send her children to work on his farm. Both their sons and daughters did stints of manual labor not only during summer vacations but also into the school year. Obediently, the children left for the farm. But obedience brought no assurance of parental gratitude, attention, or love. Thus, thirteen-year-old Obert left for Canada on the day he graduated from eighth grade. He stayed for months not seeing his father while doing hard labor without change of clothes, in "wild mountain country." He wrote of his "austere" father: "I never recall his arm on my shoulder or a smile on his face....I never had a father who seemed interested in me."[23] When a farmhand scolded Joseph for his treatment of his son, he laughed and replied, I "wanted to make a man out of him." In turn, Obert "could not feel any affection for him."[24] Obert felt the loss intensely and endured this wound his entire life.

Joseph Tanner's motivations were complex. His parental expectations may have reflected, in part, his own career disappointments. A life of learning, including study at Harvard University, had not spared his dismissal from positions in education or the church. Now, most salient to Joseph's life were the coping skills of perseverance, practicality, and hard work. These beliefs may have also been influenced by research he did for two hagiographic biographies that he wrote of self-educated Mormon pioneers. In them, he attributed the men's success to a life not of books, but of labor. Immigrant and Mormon leader James Jenson "was brought up in a school of hard work."[25] John Riggs Murdock, a member of the Mormon Battalion, church official, polygamist, and legislator experienced "schooling in a new and wonderful life...perhaps after all of greater value and consequence...than the text-book of a schoolroom could ever have been."[26] Thus, echoing his remarks about Obert, he wrote to his son Myron in 1909, "Your education [on the farm] means more than the study of law or medicine. It means character and power to the man who has it. If you stay by me, I will make you a first-class man."[27]

If he rationalized working his children to build their characters, their service also provided him a supply of cheap labor, and he did not hesitate to draw on their resources. Joseph's prioritizing of farmwork also insured that his children's educational achievements would never challenge his own. Apparent as well was Joseph's attempt to leverage the children to assert authority and control over Annie. In reaching for power, he was determined that her dream for their children's future would be subordinated to the present-day needs of his farm.

In this personal crisis, Annie Clark Tanner found the strength to draw the line. She could no longer take comfort in the belief that suffering and struggle were God's will. Tensions with Joseph had been escalating for years. He provided her and her children with little or no financial resources, forcing them to fend for themselves or beg relatives for support. He had repeatedly taken her children from school to do manual labor. Years of living apart from him and raising her children alone, had given Annie a sense of self, a new confidence that she believed other wives in polygamy had also discovered. She declared, "The plural wife, in time, becomes conscious of her own power to make decisions. She learns that it takes more than the authority of the leader in a patriarchal marriage to make a successful home."[28] When Joseph demanded that her youngest child Obert work on the farm rather than return to school, Annie was ready to be tested: "He asked too much—the future of a promising boy. Herewith closed the last possibility of reconciliation."[29]

Annie challenged her insensitive and controlling husband and would no longer submit. But her stand had even greater significance for her life. Buffeted and educated by heartbreak, she began to question the strictures that had long governed her: "At one time, I had been a good follower. Now I began to have opinions of my own. No doubt this change came as a result of experience. I became disillusioned, too, as to the superiority of man's judgment over woman's."[30] She had, observed Obert Tanner, "an analytical mind."[31]

Taking courage, she followed Joseph Smith's suggestion to seek knowledge from "all good books." Thus, she read works other than those prescribed by authorities. Comforted by her belief in "a true and loving God," Annie Tanner wrote, she "surrendered more easily the old ideas of literal interpretations" and the infallibility of man-made institutions.[32] While never abandoning her church, Annie Clark Tanner had left behind the closed world of her childhood and young adulthood.

Annie Tanner was her children's role model. They bore witness to her suffering and understood her values and beliefs. She reared her children to think for themselves and reject simple obedience to authority and institutions. "We were nonconformists," noted Obert.[33] As he also recalled, his mother declared that John Stuart Mill's piece *On Liberty*: "was my Bible."[34] Annie Tanner used books to enlighten herself and her children. Letters between Obert and his mother often end with his request for another book to read. Even when Tanner went on his LDS mission to Germany, she was sure to stock his bookshelf. She remembered,

> I was anxious for Obert to have an understanding of religion in its broadest sense, so I sent him a great many books written by many religious teachers. In religious thought, I reasoned to myself, why not be a citizen of the world and learn what other people are thinking and teaching.[35]

Obert was responsive. He wrote back, "Finer gifts were never made to a young man trying to get his bearings with the world and to find the correct philosophy of life."[36]

His mother's impact was deep, or as he said, "her influence...was as pervasive as the atmosphere itself."[37] Because of her, Obert was steeped in Mormon culture and knowledgeable about its history, doctrines, and institutions. If his father's example offered grounds to reject his faith tradition, his mother's mentoring gave him the latitude to accept it. At the same time, he looked beyond its borders under her watchful eye.

Her influence on Obert occurred not only during his childhood, but also at what was an intellectually and religiously challenging time in his life, his LDS mission during the 1920s. Obert was Annie Tanner's only son to accept the mission call. It was not an easy decision for him. Obert was more a cultural Mormon than a religious one. He enjoyed prayer services and singing hymns, but often left church before the sermon was delivered. Although he had progressed through the different offices of his church, from deacon, teacher, and priest, to elder, he was unsure in his faith and uncertain whether he could teach what he did not believe. He was also enrolled at the University of Utah and did not want to interrupt his education for two years of religious service. In part, he answered the call because of his mother's wish, peer pressure, and community expectations. As important, he convinced himself that the mission field and its intense focus, would provide the opportunity to devote himself completely to answering questions that perplexed him: Is there only a single road to salvation? Why do evil and suffering exist? Can science be reconciled with religion? And, was Mormonism true?[38]

Within the first six months of his mission, Tanner's plan came undone in the daily reality of missionary life and Germany's post-World War I misery. He despaired: "I had not realized the depth of my doubting."[39] He could not find or offer "final answers."[40] He felt a fraud and unable to accomplish his work. Growing despondent, he confessed his lack of faith to his fellow missionaries and asked the mission president for permission to return home.[41]

In the midst of his spiritual crisis and while riding on a streetcar, he experienced an epiphany. It demanded two simultaneous leaps of faith. The first required that he put "on the shelf," as he declared, or compartmentalize cognitions that conflicted.[42] Thus, he boxed off the pursuits of philosophy and science from religion. These disciplines mandated different paths to, and tests of, knowledge. And, they had different ends. He later wrote, "Religion is a way of living while philosophy is a way of thinking. Religion is a search for the good life, philosophy is a search for truth."[43]

At the same time, in a second leap of faith, he reconceived Mormonism's role in the world and his life. It was futile, he resolved, to press the claims of the LDS Church to uniqueness or teach its doctrines as being the one true path to salvation. Yet, he had no intention of rejecting his mother faith. Instead, he transcended his church by finding its common denominator with other faiths. This merging process led him to teach a "pragmatic" or "practical Christianity"—"to love and help people."[44] His was "an undying hope for a better world."[45] The "universal creed of all religions," he wrote, "is the love of God as the purest being, and a love of man."[46] In the life and teachings of Jesus Christ, he found "a searchlight" to reveal the problems that men and women faced and to seek their amelioration.[47] "I preach," he declared, "the gospel of hope and good will."[48]

In essence, on that German streetcar, Obert Tanner had found resolution in a vision first proposed by the interdenominational Social Gospel movement. Rising to prominence in the late nineteenth and early twentieth centuries, ministers of the Social Gospel offered Jesus as a model of compassion and the means to achieve social reform, justice, and harmony. Christian ethics held the answers to economic inequality, war, racial injustice, institutional oppression, and personal selfishness. Later in life, Obert Tanner would be more expansive both in his role models and dreams: "My own definition of religion is based on Plato's trinity; that is, whenever anyone finds ultimate Goodness, Truth, or Beauty...then one participates in religious experience."[49] Thus, his fountains, lecture series, and all manner of philanthropy were the works of a deeply spiritual man. In his words, he was "more a pragmatic Christian than a theological believer."[50]

Obert Tanner's conversion experience was satisfying because it revealed to him the essence of religious belief in a compassionate Christianity. And it enabled him to find comfort within the Mormon community. This was the first step in his spiritual quest, and it became a lifelong pursuit. He had rendered unto Caesar the matter of science and philosophy and rendered unto God the vision of a kingdom governed by loving kindness. Rather than compromise his ideals, he had refreshed his sense of integrity and devotion to the divine.

With the insights gained on his mission, Tanner returned to Utah and began to build up the kingdom as an LDS junior and senior high school seminary schoolteacher. In the classroom, he worked out a formula that would enable students to feel comfortable in Mormonism while exploring the broader meaning of Christianity. Also insuring him the freedom to explore religious commitment was the institutional relationship of seminary classes to the public school system. His students received credit for seminary classes toward graduation from public school only if they focused on ethics and biblical literature, and "avoided all denominational doctrines."[51] Success in the classroom brought Tanner to the attention of Mormon Church authorities, who asked him to write primers to guide other seminary teachers and students.[52]

David O. McKay, the general superintendent of the church's Sunday schools and a longtime member of the Quorum of the Twelve Apostles, was particularly supportive of Tanner's efforts. Like Tanner, he began his mission skeptical of his church's claims. While overcoming his doubts, he rejected "unrighteous dominion" and believed in the "divine right of man to freedom of choice."[53] His biographers Gregory Prince and William Robert Wright noted that: "David O. McKay was an intellectual. He cherished the things of the mind, cultivated his own intellect throughout his life...and vigorously defended the consequences of intellectualism. He did so, not as a matter of personal preference, but because he saw it as one of the key Christ-like virtues."[54] Later as president of the Mormon Church, McKay declared, "Ours is the responsibility...to proclaim the truth that each individual is a child of God and important in his sight; that he is entitled to freedom of thought, freedom of speech, freedom of assembly; that he has the right to worship God according to the dictates of his conscience."[55] In David O. McKay, Obert Tanner found an intellectual mentor and friend, a father figure who represented a church that was open to the mind as well as the heart. It was a church that Obert Tanner could embrace.[56]

Problems of Youth, coauthored with Adam Bennion, was published in 1931 by the CES of the LDS Church and adopted in classes throughout the seminary system. Based on the principle of free agency, Tanner and Bennion proposed a "problem method" that presented hypothetical moral dilemmas that students analyzed and worked to resolve.[57] In tackling such matters as fairness, the Golden Rule, and abstinence from vice, the book presumed "free participation on the part of pupils" and advised teachers "that lecturing is essentially out of place in this course."[58] The authors put forth the theme of the book boldly: "In the field of moral instruction many issues are relative—they call for more *more-or-less-ness* and less 'yes or no-ness."[59] They also cautioned teachers to "respect minority thinking and help your group to appreciate its place in a discussion."[60]

A companion volume, *Looking in on Greatness*, appeared in 1932 and was also immediately adopted into the seminary curriculum. This book moved beyond the problems of young people to develop such ideals as humility, charity, moral courage, sacrifice, and honesty. It also revealed the authors' remarkable intellectual range. Bennion and Tanner used biography to demonstrate these qualities and discussed such role models as Charles Darwin, Elizabeth Barrett Browning, Ralph Waldo Emerson, Anna Shaw, Walt Whitman, Samuel Gompers, and Mahatma Gandhi. Again, the authors advised teachers to "be tolerant of the opinion of a pupil who has difficulty in agreeing with you."[61] Both *Problems of Youth* and *Looking in on Greatness* would be used for decades in seminary instruction.[62]

The success of these primers led church authorities to offer Tanner another assignment, a book about the New Testament and its application to the lives of young people. He quickly accepted: "The universalism of Christ's teachings had always appealed to me."[63] Again, he looked beyond his Mormonism to envision Jesus as unbound by denomination or creed. For Tanner, the savior was the "ideal" example for individuals to follow in their lives and emulate in their dealings with others. As his bibliography demonstrates, academic biblical scholarship was essential in the writing of the book, and Tanner was intent on enabling students to understand differing interpretations of New Testament passages. Mormonism was visible in its absence. Later, when asked to revise the book for a subsequent edition and "color it with Mormonism," he refused to blur Jesus' message with dogma.[64] LDS seminary teachers continued to use his book for almost three decades.[65]

His vision of a universal Christianity did not threaten David O. McKay. In fact, he was so pleased with Obert Tanner's work and interpretations that he offered him a permanent position to "write for the church. Just come down and write whatever may be needed." Despite the rigors of the Great Depression and his great admiration for McKay, Tanner was not prepared to end his search for freedom. Nor could he testify to a faith sufficiently strong to bear the weight of institutional pressures or the vicissitudes of human expectations. He wrote, "I simply did not have enough orthodox conviction for such a lifetime assignment."[66]

Nevertheless, David McKay and Obert Tanner would find another opportunity to collaborate. In fact, their relationship had grown closer even as both men pursued their different lives. A particularly intimate moment had occurred when Obert and Grace Tanner's seven-year-old son Stephen was killed in a tragic accident in 1949. In all, three of their children suffered early deaths. David McKay was there to console them in their grief and spoke at Stephen's funeral. Obert Tanner counted McKay as one of his "closest friends" in the church.[67] When the need arose to write a new manual for college-aged LDS seminary students, McKay, now president of the LDS Church, immediately thought of Tanner. "I was not," recalled Tanner, "about to turn him down on anything that he asked me to do."[68]

He answered President McKay's call, seizing the opportunity to discuss at length the breadth of Christ's story and teachings. He was, however, deeply apprehensive. "I was a liberal," Tanner wrote. "The reading committee would probably be filled with conservatives."[69] Tanner went to McKay with his concerns. McKay reassured him and offered his complete support: "Well, then, we will change the committee."[70] To ensure that Tanner's work would not be censured or the subject of severe editorial critique, McKay appointed Adam Bennion, Tanner's coauthor on the primer series, as committee chair. Disagreements that arose during the book's drafting were handled equitably, and Tanner only balked at issues of "personal integrity."[71] If author and committee reached an impasse, the matter was referred to President McKay. He remembered that "President McKay agreed with all my interpretations."[72]

With an office in the LDS Church headquarters and a large budget to buy reading materials, Obert Tanner went to work on *Christ's Ideals for Living*, which was published in 1955. It was, he wrote, "the most useful book I leave."[73] Like his other church-sponsored books, Mormonism played only a minor and supporting role. Tanner divided each of the book's forty-five chapters into five parts. After introducing the ideal that Jesus exemplified, sections would detail its representation in the New Testament, in Jesus' life, in our lives, and in quotations from LDS leaders. Tanner did not privilege the words of Mormon Church leaders, which remained unexamined, a lifeless listing without comment. He asked teachers of his book to "consider material of the lesson as something like a table prepared and spread with several offerings, from which the teacher and class may select according to their interest."[74]

The true focus of the book was the "our lives" sections. These nuanced and lively chapters took material from the leading works of world literature, "from poets, philosophers, and men and women whose writings add insight and appreciation to the ideals Christ gave to mankind."[75] These sections fueled the book's drive. Here the prose came alive. Here can be seen the hand of Annie Clark Tanner.

Like a university professor teaching an Intellectual Traditions of Western Culture class, Tanner extolled the works of such non-Mormons and free thinkers as Plato, Aristotle, Dante, Voltaire, Kant, Josiah Royce, Oliver Wendell Holmes, Harry Emerson Fosdick, Alfred Tennyson, and Henry David Thoreau. The message was undiluted, direct, and powerful. After finding Christ in their words, he asked students, "What would a man fight for today?"[76] He answered: protection of the rights of minorities; equality of opportunity; and freedom in our economic, political, educational, and religious lives. He found Jesus in support of the United Nations, opposed to war, and against racial discrimination and prejudice. He even enlisted him against the anticommunist hysteria of McCarthyism: "We must not let our fight against totalitarianisms cause us to attack and accuse each other, until we all lose by forcing each other into mental straightjackets."[77] Underlying all of this was his plea for "a free spirit of inquiry [as] the key to progress." He continued: "God has never intended that an honest mind should be humiliated or made unwelcome in the Church by any other member because of honest inquiry. Above all, keep the virtues of integrity, sincerity, and genuineness. Nothing else can be right in a man's life if he is not sincere."[78]

Written in the 1950s, under the protective wing of David O. McKay, Tanner's book was decidedly progressive. It preached a call to action and the creation of a broader outlook and community. "Man," he wrote, "is made in the image of God and should aspire to a God-like character."[79] Tanner was convinced that youthful readers might make the Mormon Church a launch pad for a worldwide movement for change.

Dedicated to President David O. McKay and carrying the church's imprimatur, the book had broad reach within the Mormon educational community. General Superintendent of LDS Sunday Schools George Hill declared it "the finest manual yet produced as a Sunday school text. I predict that it will be regarded as one of the most valuable texts for Sunday schools and general church use, for years to come."[80] As late as 2006, the blog *By Common Consent* placed *Christ's Ideals for Living* first on its list of the "Top 10 Mormon Lesson Manuals." It was as "timeless in its appeal, beautiful to read...an immediate source of comfort and inspiration."[81]

Some would suggest that this moment in church history has passed. Beginning in the 1960s and accelerating in the 1970s and 1980s, social turbulence outside the LDS Church and shifting power dynamics within spurred initiatives that pressed for correlation, standardization, and conformity in thought and behavior. Tolerance of different paths to religious truth and doubts about official doctrine and authorized history harmed a people who faced threats to church and community. As the Mormon world tightened and became more insistent, intellectuals and freethinkers found little room for spiritual understanding and growth. It is not surprising, then, that Obert Tanner distanced himself from the community of his birth. Others, too, made pilgrimage out of Mormonism, voluntarily or not, or remained silent. Nor is it surprising that in 2014, *Christ's Ideals for Living*, while still available for sale from the Deseret Book Company, for a time carried the caveat, "The views expressed herein are the responsibility of the author and do not necessarily represent the position of the Church or of Deseret Book Company." [82]

In his search for freedom, Obert Tanner had succeeded in carving out a space that was within Mormonism and at the same time beyond its reach. His close friends remained influential within the Mormon Church, and he never cut himself off from their company. In the absence of his father, his mother and then later men he respected had encouraged his commitment. He was always at ease with the church's rituals and familiar with its history and doctrine. At the same time, he did not attend Sunday services at the ward house and offered only token tithing. His longtime friend and fellow professor of philosophy Sterling McMurrin explained their sense of identity:

> Our cultural roots were firmly in the LDS Church. Though we held dissident views and were somewhat critical of both the beliefs and practices of the Church, we had very strong ties with it, not only of sentiment and with a sense of participating in its history—to say nothing of bonds of kinship and friendship, but also because we sincerely believed that there were important elements of truth and strength in the Mormon religion and its theology.... To be a Mormon is to belong not simply to a church but to a living community and culture.[83]

In creating his sacred space, Tanner built another community that deflected criticism and pressure to conform. He cast an international shadow and served on the board of governors of the American Association of the United Nations and several times as its delegate to the Geneva Conference of the organization's World Federation. For his work toward international peace and understanding, he received the United Nations Peace Medal. In the business world, he created a multinational corporation with thousands of employees, with offices in nine nations, that counted scores of major companies among its clients. At the University of Utah, he established a strong reputation as teacher and scholar. He endowed the Tanner Lectures in Human Values, an international forum that annually recognizes individuals of uncommon achievement and outstanding ability. His philanthropy touched education, the arts, and medical sciences. This public life of service brought him the National Medal of Arts. Annie Clark Tanner's son had traveled far from his roots in search of freedom. But, he never wandered from his God or lost his bearings on integrity.[84]

His daughter Carolyn Tanner Irish has written, "I do think Obert is as good a critic as religion has (and all religion needs critics!), yet he is unusually kind about it."[85] Never a stranger to Mormonism and proud of his roots, Obert Tanner's faith quest took him to a deeper understanding of God and the human condition. His eyes were on matters of progress, tolerance, justice, and mercy. Self-confident of his path to freedom, he had no desire to critique with voice raised or the flag of rebellion unfurled. Rather, Tanner gently persuaded, by example. He was simply a man too busy with a religious life that touched education, philanthropy, and business. In all of this, he saw the hand of God. If critics chided him for a lack of faith or commitment, or even branded him as an apostate, they never looked into his soul or truly understood Christ's ideals for living.

Obert Tanner at about the time he founded the O. C. Tanner Company in 1927. Courtesy of the Obert C. and Grace A. Tanner Humanities Center.

Grace and Obert circa 1965. Courtesy of the Obert C. and Grace A. Tanner Humanities Center.

Obert and Grace Tanner with four of their six children, 1950s. Back row: Gordon, Joan, and Carolyn. Front: Obert, Steven, and Grace. Courtesy of Carolyn Tanner Irish.

Obert C. Tanner at the height of his career, 1970s. Courtesy of Carolyn Tanner Irish.

Annie Clark Tanner. Courtesy of the Obert C. and Grace A. Tanner
Humanities Center.

NOTES

1. Obert C. Tanner, *One Man's Journey: In Search of Freedom* (Salt Lake City: University of Utah Press, 1994), 48–52.
2. Ibid.
3. Ibid., 61.
4. Ibid., 62.
5. Ibid., 61.
6. Ibid., 15.
7. Obert C. Tanner, introduction to Annie Clark Tanner, *A Mormon Mother: An Autobiography* (Tanner Trust Fund, University of Utah Library, 1969), xxviii.
8. Tanner, *Mormon Mother*, 15.
9. Ibid., 14, 149.
10. Ibid., 28.
11. Ibid., 2, 5.
12. Ibid., 18.
13. Ibid., 16.
14. Ibid., 1.
15. Ibid., 105.
16. Ibid., 102–27.
17. Ibid., 50.
18. Ibid., 23.
19. Ibid., 68, 69 (quote), 73; Margery W. Ward, *A Life Divided: The Biography of Joseph Marion Tanner, 1859–1927* (Salt Lake City: Publishers Press, 1980), 18, 24–25.
20. Ward, *Life Divided*, 24–27, 32.
21. Ibid., 38–51; Tanner, *One Man's Journey*, 13 (quote).
22. Tanner, *Mormon Mother*, 178.
23. Tanner, *One Man's Journey*, 46–47.
24. Ward, *Life Divided*, 51, 54; Tanner, *One Man's Journey*, 43 (quote).
25. Joseph Marion Tanner, *A Biographical Sketch of James Jensen* (Salt Lake City: Deseret News, 1911), 4.
26. Joseph Marion Tanner, *A Biographical Sketch of John Riggs, Murdock* (Salt Lake City: Deseret News, 1909), 5.
27. Tanner, *Mormon Mother*, 197.
28. Ibid., 270.
29. Ibid., 212, 274, 279, 284, 286 (quote).
30. Tanner, Introduction, xxiv; Tanner, *Mormon Mother*, 271 (quote).
31. Tanner, *One Man's Journey*, 15.
32. Tanner, *Mormon Mother*, 218–19.
33. Tanner, *One Man's Journey*, 19.

34. Ibid., 60.

35. Ibid., 309.

36. Ibid., 310; Tanner, introduction, xxix; Tanner, *Mormon Mother*, 253, 92.

37. Tanner, *One Man's Journey*, 20.

38. Tanner, *Mormon Mother*, 301; Tanner, *One Man's Journey*, 57–59, 62, 63, 68.

39. Tanner, *One Man's Journey*, 66.

40. Ibid., 61.

41. Ibid., 63, 66, 68.

42. Ibid., 72.

43. Ibid., 70–71, 134 (quote).

44. Ibid., 72.

45. Ibid., 58.

46. Obert C. Tanner, "Is Religion an Aid to International Understanding?" in *One Man's Search: Addresses by Obert C. Tanner* (Salt Lake City: University of Utah Press, 1989), 163.

47. Tanner, *One Man's Journey*, 73.

48. Ibid., 70–71, 74.

49. Ibid., 57–58.

50. Ibid., 74.

51. Ibid., 107.

52. Ibid., 103, 106, 107–8.

53. Gregory A. Prince, "David O. McKay and the 'Twin Sisters:' Free Agency and Tolerance," *Dialogue: A Journal of Mormon Thought* 33 (Winter, 2000): 2–3.

54. Gregory A. Prince and William Robert Wright, *David O. McKay and the Rise of Modern Mormonism* (Salt Lake City: University of Utah Press, 2005), 40.

55. Prince, "McKay and the Twin Sisters," 26.

56. Prince and Wright, *David O. McKay*, 6–8.

57. Obert C. Tanner and Adam S. Bennion, *Problems of Youth* (Salt Lake City: Church of Jesus Christ of Latter-day Saints, 1931), 3.

58. Ibid., 5.

59. Ibid., 6.

60. Ibid., 7.

61. Adam S. Bennion and Obert C. Tanner, *Looking in on Greatness* (Salt Lake City: Church of Jesus Christ of Latter-day Saints, 1932), 4.

62. Ibid., 3–6; Tanner, *One Man's Journey*, 108.

63. Tanner, *One Man's Journey*, 113.

64. Ibid.

65. Obert C. Tanner, *New Testament Studies* (Salt Lake City: Church of Jesus Christ of Latter-day Saints, 1932), 5, 7, 9, 42–55; Tanner, *One Man's Journey*, 109, 114.

66. Tanner, *One Man's Journey*, 112–13.
67. Ibid., 95.
68. Ibid., 116.
69. Ibid., 117.
70. Ibid., 117; Grace A. Tanner, interview by Gregory A. Prince and William Robert Wright, Salt Lake City, October 10, 1994.
71. Tanner, *One Man's Journey*, 120.
72. Ibid., 115–19, 120 (quote).
73. Ibid., 131.
74. Obert C. Tanner, *Christ's Ideals for Living* (Salt Lake City: Deseret Sunday School Union Board, 1955), 5.
75. Ibid., 4.
76. Ibid., 67.
77. Ibid.
78. Ibid., 92.
79. Ibid., 84.
80. George Hill, quoted in Tanner, *One Man's Journey*, 120.
81. Edward Snow, "The Top 10 Mormon Lesson Manuals…Ever," *By Common Consent*. See http://bycommonconsent.com/2006/02/13/the-top-ten-mormon-lesson-manuals-ever, accessed August 22, 2014.
82. Obert C. Tanner, "Christ's Ideals for Living" *Gospel Link*, see http://gospellink.com/library/contents/713 (accessed August 22, 2014).
83. Dionne Williams, Telephone conversation with the author, Salt Lake City, June 2, 2014; Sterling McMurrin, "In Memoriam: Obert C. Tanner, Symbol of Freedom," *Sunstone* 94 (February 1994): 13–15.
84. Tanner, *One Man's Journey*, 153, 160, 190, 213, 223.
85. Tanner, *One Man's Search*, 144.

7

OBERT TANNER AND THE IDEA OF A UNIVERSITY

MARK MATHESON

"As I mentioned, we had a free American democratic home."
—Annie Clark Tanner

Obert Tanner's regard for universities was profound, and this essay explores his engagement with them during his lifetime.[1] He grew up in the early twentieth century in a small Utah town, and in the world of his youth the Mormon Church was a pervasive institutional presence. It is probably imprecise to see Tanner in these early years simply as a member of a church; he was in fact part of a people, and the formation of his identity in this singular context had a lasting significance. His early experience was informed with an understanding of human life as a deeply cooperative enterprise, even with an element of utopianism, and the ideal of individuals working together for the common good was a permanent part of his cultural inheritance. This communitarian legacy would have a sustained influence on his subsequent thinking about education and politics, and it would shape his ideas about the possibilities inherent in the university as an institution.

But living in this early Mormon society also involved costs to individual liberty, and Tanner felt these constraints. His mother, Annie Clark Tanner, strongly encouraged his inclination toward personal independence. The perpetual surprise in the story of Tanner's life is the role played by Annie and the ethos of individual autonomy and intellectual freedom she established in her home. In the midst of a society based on hierarchy and deference to authority, she built a domestic culture grounded in classic Anglo-American liberalism and the free exchange of ideas. Probably no influence shaped Tanner's life more than growing up in the "free American democratic home" created by his mother. But the principles of individualism and freethinking so deeply imbued in him by this experience, and so cherished by him throughout his life, were in many respects at odds with the theology and practice of the communal and hierarchical church to which his family belonged. Tanner's experience of this cultural divide—between the defining values of his home and those of his church—was integral to his early life, and it influenced his developing aspirations in both education and business.

Tanner particularly valued a small but important liberal movement in the Mormonism of his youth, which attempted to affirm personal and intellectual independence within the collective life of the church. Annie Clark Tanner's home was a remarkable enactment of this lively cultural tendency in the contemporary faith. But the practice and ideas of this movement never prevailed in the institution as a whole, and we will see that as a young adult Tanner declined a promising career in the church because of his concerns about its hierarchical system of governance. Still this liberal stirring within the church was of great spiritual importance to Tanner, and it would resonate throughout his life as an attempt to bring together a communal institution with more liberal traditions of thought and practice.

The most evident aspect of Tanner's life is his rise from poverty to great wealth, which he accomplished with enormous personal effort, but his views never became libertarian. For him a person's responsibility to the community was fundamental, and the freedom of the individual, about which he cared so passionately, was based on social foundations. Later instances of his dedication to a communitarian ideal would come in his active public speaking career following World War II, when he advocated fervently for both the United Nations and public education in America.

Tanner also saw the university as a promising institution for the invest-
ment of his communitarian hopes. A confluence of the liberal tradition in
thought with the cooperative social ethic in Mormonism (as distinct from
its hierarchal relationships) was for Tanner an enduring ideal, and as he
grew into adulthood the university emerged for him as the institution in
which this union was most likely to be realized.

Annie Clark Tanner's autobiography, *A Mormon Mother,* has made the
story of Tanner's parents widely known. Written in longhand in 1941, the
last year of her life, it gives an account of her polygamous marriage to
Joseph Marion Tanner, who was on the faculty of Brigham Young Academy in Provo, Utah, where Annie Clark was a student. After a short courtship, they married in 1883. She was his second wife, and he soon married
again. Throughout his marriage to Annie, he spent little time with her
and provided scant material support. Obert Tanner was born in 1904, the
tenth and last of their children.

In childhood Obert became aware of his father's notable achievements
as a teacher and school administrator, which established him as one of the
foremost educators in early Utah. But Joseph's public career had essentially come to an end before Obert was born, when he resigned from
the presidency of Utah State Agricultural College in 1900. Obert had
little contact with his father, and their relationship was difficult. Under
legal pressure because of his polygamous marriages, Joseph departed for
Canada in 1906. He lived there for the rest of his life and returned only
occasionally to Utah. On one of these visits, Obert confronted his father
about his uncaring attitude toward him personally and his general neglect
of Annie Clark Tanner's family.[2] Obert was fifteen years old, and it was
the last time he and his father ever saw each other.

Much later in life, Tanner sponsored the writing and publication of
a biography of his father, which appeared in 1980. He evidently wanted
to give Joseph his due, particularly for his success as an educator. In his
foreword to the biography, Obert writes that he has "a son's natural pride
in my father's many achievements, especially his great record in improv-
ing the quality of education in his time."[3] This is certainly praise, but the

foreword as a whole is a measured piece of writing. Tanner passes no harsh judgments, but neither is there particular warmth, and he seems to be writing essentially for the record.

His father's example, which included studying law for three years at Harvard and serving as a college president in Utah, probably became important to Tanner as he grew older and pursued his own education. He himself would choose to study law, and in going east to Harvard he was following a path broken in the late pioneer period by his father and a small cohort of outstanding Utah scholars. Two others of this number, John A. Widtsoe and George Thomas, also returned from Harvard to become university presidents in the Utah system. But though he provided an example of a successful career in education, Joseph's influence on Obert's conception of the university was negligible. The values Obert would come to see as defining characteristics of higher learning, including free inquiry and the nurturing of each student's intellectual independence, were in many ways antithetical to his father's educational philosophy.

Annie Clark Tanner's influence on Obert's ideas about the university was of far greater consequence. Though she grew up in a frontier society, Annie had an advanced education. She and her brother were sent by her family to study at Brigham Young Academy, which she refers to in *A Mormon Mother* as "the Church school,"[4] a phrase that suggests its role as a focus for institutional energies. The main subject studied at the school was indeed religion, and as a leading student, Annie earned a certificate in theology, but the curriculum also included astronomy, physics, and history. The head of the academy was Karl Maeser, a devout Mormon who instilled in the school a deeply aspirational culture. Though his first goal was to promote the faith, he seems to have relied on the Mormon doctrine of "free agency" to encourage the students' individuality.

Annie clearly thrived in this environment, and at the end of her life she remembered the inspiring quality of her experience at the academy: "I was delighted by my work there. The world seemed so much bigger and was more beautiful than ever before."[5] Her academic ability was recognized and remarked upon by Maeser, who in speaking to his faculty identified Annie as the most brilliant student in her class. This praise meant a great deal to Obert, who mentions it in his introduction to his mother's book in 1973, as well as in his autobiography. Annie seems never to have forgotten the liberating educational experience she had at the academy, and it clearly helped to create her devotion to higher learning. She also became the epitome of a lifelong learner, in spite of the many practical and emotional hardships she faced, and she imparted her love of education to Obert, from his childhood onward, through both her example and their numerous conversations about books and ideas.

Obert later wrote very thoughtfully about the culture of his childhood home. With her husband almost always absent, Annie was essentially a single mother, and she crafted this culture in accordance with her deepest values. She based her philosophy of child rearing on John Stuart Mill's *On Liberty*, which she read many times, and the evidence is clear that she made her home into a profoundly liberal institution.[6] There was a price to pay for this in how she and her family were regarded by some of their neighbors, and her husband made his own demands for stronger domestic discipline, but she opposed them. He once said to her, "Your children don't know the first letter in the word obedience." She replied, "That's strange, they suit me splendidly."[7] No influence ever moved Annie to change her liberal philosophy and practice as a mother, and Obert always celebrated her for the openness and promise at the heart of the worldview she communicated to her children.

In his own autobiography, *One Man's Journey*, published in 1993 just after his death, Tanner writes about his experience growing up in his mother's home, and he incidentally confirms his father's perception: "Mother held firmly to her philosophy that a child should have the largest possible measure of freedom. I do not remember that she ever asked for obedience."[8] That Annie never asked her children to obey may suggest how spiritually confining she found her marriage and what she called "the old tradition" of the church. Her children, at least her sons, followed her example. Tanner remembers that his five older brothers were "nonconformists" who would energetically set forth their views at family dinners, which became the setting for "the freest of discussions." Annie encouraged this open exchange of ideas because she saw it as integral to her children's education, and according to Tanner, "a good education for her children was the single greatest goal of her life."[9] Tanner's understanding of the university as a place of questioning and debate was shaped significantly by his experience of his mother's dinner table. He wrote later that he and his siblings recognized that their mother was engaged in a lifelong quest for knowledge and truth, and based on the strength of her example, they came to believe with her that "a university was the noblest creation" of humankind.[10]

The extent of Tanner's reflection on his mother's experience is evident in the three introductions he wrote for the printings of Annie Clark Tanner's autobiography. Written respectively in 1941, 1969, and 1973, each is more expansive than the previous one, suggesting the son's growing engagement over time with the significance of his mother's life. In contrast to the somewhat dutiful prose of his foreword to his father's biography, Obert's exploration of Annie's experience in these introductions is intense, searching, and emotional. In the last of the three, which is by far the longest, a note of brooding enters as Obert ponders both the pain of his mother's life and the inner victories she achieved. Many of these victories were over personal disappointments and the difficulties (and potential humiliations) of a life lived in chronic poverty. But arguably even more significant to Tanner, particularly with respect to his developing views on higher education, is what he understood to be the extraordinary progress of his mother's inner life.

Tanner began exploring this subject in the first introductions written in 1941, in which he sets forth Annie's experience as a "journey" of personal development

> From the sunrise to the sunset of this life one sees a person who loved life, enjoyed its work, and particularly one who asked questions and pursued new ideas even into the late evening-time. From those early girlhood years, spent in the intellectual security of revealed truth and clear duty, a long journey has been traveled. Herein lies the genius of this life, if not its greatness.[11]

The later introductions make clear that Tanner did indeed believe that the greatness of his mother's life lay in her achievement of a new freedom of mind and spirit. He writes in the second preface that she overcame the "religious, political, and domestic authoritarianisms" imposed on her, and to such an extent that in her later years "it appeared that nothing people or circumstances might do could shake the foundations of her serenity and personal integrity."[12] Somehow Annie moved from a life formed in deference to hierarchical authority to the realization of her own intellectual and spiritual independence. This was an improbable journey, and for Obert it was always a source of awe. He was no doubt pondering it, as well as his mother's powers of endurance in the face of suffering, in the acknowledgement he makes in the third introduction: "Her life is a mystery to me."[13]

Tanner writes that against her husband's authoritarianism, his mother eventually came to have a "full dissent," and in her search for truth she moved over many years from the religious literalism of her youth to "the authority of scholars and universities."[14] She experienced serious "personal doubts and misgivings" in this process, but she grew through these uncertainties and achieved a genuine independence from traditional "institutional and domestic authority." In speaking of his mother, Tanner would make a fundamental association between education and freedom: "We shared a love of books, lectures, and new ideas. She wanted to pass on a sense of independence to her children, possibly to spare us some of the pain of having to achieve our own intellectual emancipation."[15] We've noted that Annie remarked on the revelatory power of higher education in her own experience, and though her years of formal learning were early and relatively brief, the inspiration they provided seems to have projected her on the extraordinary journey of her inner life. In his introduction to the first edition (1941), Tanner calls Annie's autobiography "the unfolding of a life in its inward workings," a life that "though it ends far away from its native land, never loses a warm feeling towards it, and above all, never fails to understand it."[16] Tanner's use of metaphor here—the "native land" for his mother's inherited Mormon culture and doctrine—is unusual in his writing. It can be read as a gentle understatement of Annie's inner achievement, and this might suggest how politically and culturally sensitive his mother's journey remained at the time her story was first published.

In the final introduction (1973), Tanner writes still more extensively about his relationship with his mother, and near the end he offers a summation. The tone of gratitude and continuing wonder, in prose written more than three decades after her death, indicates her lasting importance to his understanding of both higher education and himself:

> We talked in depth of lectures and books and people and institutions....She gave me my love of books and my pride in the profession of teaching. So indelible was her influence on me, that in my life of both business and teaching, because of her, teaching always came first. She responded to the offer I received to teach at Stanford with the comment: "At last it has come." She looked upon business with approval, but her enthusiasm was reserved for new ideas and lectures and books and opportunities given by universities.[17]

This passage attests to how profoundly the bond between Obert and Annie Clark Tanner was based on their mutual commitment to higher education. The conversations he describes were moments of sustenance and hope in their challenging life circumstances, and in a sense they both came to experience and envision the university as a resource against despair. Tanner knew of it as a worldly institution through reflection on his father's career, but his understanding of it as a place of self-realization was the legacy of Annie Clark Tanner. Having grown up in her home, he would always esteem the university for its interrogative function and its encouragement of lively debate in the search for knowledge and truth. But his mother's achievement of a new inner freedom and wholeness of being was for Tanner the most sublime aspect of her life, and he came to value the university, following her own vision, for its unusual potential to enable the individual's intellectual and spiritual emancipation.

In the fall of his seventeenth year, Obert entered the University of Utah. He took a job at the same time to pay for his schooling and to contribute materially to his mother's support. Hard work was an ideal he adopted early in life, and he experienced it as both a cultural mandate and practical necessity. But while Obert worked his way through the University of Utah, he was also a devoted student whose undergraduate years provided him with a powerful intellectual experience. He took courses in science, philosophy, and literature, and he found they broadened his perspectives. He recalled studying Darwin and finding the theory of evolution compelling, and later during his missionary work in Germany he paid close attention to the Scopes trial unfolding in Tennessee. While an undergraduate he still enjoyed the aesthetic experience of attending church, but his university experience made the content of some of the sermons painful, and he would often slip quietly out of the service after the hymns and before the preaching. Even so, Obert paused in his undergraduate education to serve a two-year mission for the LDS Church, after which he returned to complete his first degree at the University of Utah in 1929.

During his undergraduate years Tanner had his first encounter with the jewelry business. Hired to stoke the furnace at the home of Salt Lake City jeweler William Schubach, he eventually asked for a job in his downtown store. The owner and his young employee had a colorful relationship, in which Tanner was quite assertive about his business abilities. When he announced two years later that he was going to leave the job to spend more time on his studies, Schubach offered him a share of the store's profits if he would stay. It was a large moment: the offer must have been very attractive to a young man who had grown up in poverty and who knew that his mother scrubbed other people's floors for fifteen cents an hour. But Tanner declined, and he did so to continue and complete his university education, which he describes in his account of that time as "the goal of my life."[18] This was an early choice between what would become his two great professional interests, education and business, and his commitment to higher learning came first.

It was also as an undergraduate that Obert had his first experience with teaching. He began to instruct high school students in LDS seminary courses, and he enjoyed this work from the beginning. He was soon recognized for his excellence as a teacher and writer, and a more momentous offer was made to him on the basis of his success. In 1931, Dr. Joseph Merrill, commissioner of education for the LDS Church and former dean of engineering at the University of Utah, invited Tanner to study for his PhD at the University of Chicago and then return to Brigham Young University to chair the Department of Religion. The church would pay for his advanced study at Chicago and reserve his place at BYU, and Dr. Merrill showed Tanner a letter from the president of the church in which all of this was formally promised.

Tanner was deeply honored, and he was already passionate about pursuing graduate work at a great university. But he found himself in a moral dilemma: he was concerned that he was not religiously orthodox enough to commit to this plan, and he believed that accepting might require him to compromise his intellectual integrity. After much thought he declined the offer, a decision that attests to the enduring force of his mother's household culture, with its dedication to individuality and personal conscience. But the cost of preserving his independence in this instance was particularly high, and it was clearly a watershed moment. Tanner never had second thoughts, but he remembered that his decision to decline the church's offer "carried with it a profound sadness."[19]

Tanner started the O. C. Tanner Company, working out of his mother's basement, in 1927. Following the completion of his first degree, he continued to build his business and entered law school at Utah. The great event of his life in this period was his marriage to Grace Adams in 1931. The two of them formed a remarkable partnership that lasted until Obert's death in 1993. Grace had earned a higher degree herself, and she was deeply supportive of her husband's career as a writer and educator. He remembered only a single moment when Grace took exception to his ambitious educational plans. He had finished his law degree and was sworn in to the Utah State Bar in 1936, but on the day of the ceremony he told Grace that he wanted to pack up and pursue a higher degree at "a great university."[20]

Though she was expecting their second child, Grace reconciled herself to Obert's idea, and the young family drove west to the San Francisco Bay area. Tanner wanted to study philosophy at either Berkeley or Stanford, and he apparently left without having made contact with either department. His decision to look west for graduate education is interesting in itself. The typical path for talented students from Utah had been east to Chicago or Ivy League schools, especially Harvard. One of Tanner's mentors and friends in Utah, Adam S. Bennion, had earned his doctorate at Berkeley in the previous decade (though he had first attended Columbia and Chicago), and his example was probably important. Tanner's interest in staying relatively close to his growing business in Salt Lake City was certainly a factor as well. But in some sense the journey west, in all its audacity, was symbolic of a new direction for Tanner. It would be a life-changing decision for him and his family.

Tanner's first stop, while Grace and their son Dean waited in the car, was at Berkeley. The campus was crowded and busy during a class change, but Tanner couldn't find anyone to talk with in the philosophy department. He decided they should drive to Stanford before coming back to Berkeley, and there he was able to meet with Professor Henry Waldgrave Stuart, who was the philosophy department chair. They spoke for an hour in "unhurried conversation," and Obert returned to Grace and told her that they were staying in Palo Alto. They lived there for almost a decade, and Tanner remembered most of it as a time of idyllic happiness.

The intellectual and political ferment of the Great Depression era was galvanizing the Stanford campus, and Tanner participated energetically in the debates that took place in the classroom and on the inner quad. His experience with five contentious older brothers at his mother's table was no doubt helpful; he had grown up in the midst of intense debate, and he writes that he was now arguing with "endless energy."[21] One of his professors, Harold Chapman Brown, was a Marxist, while Henry Waldgrave Stuart had reservations about Marx. Tanner became keenly aware of disagreements between leading scholars on the most fundamental questions. He had come to Stanford, he writes, "in search of better answers," but he was in fact finding ambiguity and a general lack of agreement on just about everything.

Tanner found that one of his professors, Morris Cohen, was particularly gifted at challenging the truth claims of systematic philosophies. He remembered that as a teacher Cohen was a "genius," and ideas "flew back and forth in his class in the best Socratic tradition. I loved it, even when I was wounded in the crossfire."[22] Tanner was not surprised to find intense dialectic at the heart of the university experience, though he had imagined that truth—"Truth, spelled with a capital *T*"—would emerge from the struggle.

In fact his graduate education marks the beginning of Tanner's turn from the search for absolute truth, to which he had been predisposed by his upbringing in a conservative religious culture, to a more pragmatic exploration of values and ideas and the degree to which they might promote freedom for the individual and justice in society. Among the central categories in his thinking, the notion of absolute truth was giving place to the concept of the "ideal"—in the sense of a goal for individual and collective human work—and this would become a very productive idea in Tanner's subsequent writing and philanthropy.

Early in the Palo Alto period, Tanner spent a year studying at Harvard, where philosophy professor Clarence Irving Lewis especially impressed him. He and Grace would become lifelong friends with Lewis and his wife Mabel. As with Professor Cohen at Stanford, Tanner felt a deep gratitude to Professor Lewis and experienced firsthand how an exceptional teacher can advance a student's personal development. These relationships indicate another refinement that emerged during these years in Tanner's conception of a university: he developed a sense of the value of mentors and their unique capacity to welcome students into the community of learning. Tanner was also at the threshold of a university teaching career, and for this the examples of Cohen and Lewis would prove particularly important.

When Tanner returned from Harvard, he received an offer to teach in Stanford's Department of Religious Studies. He had completed an MA in philosophy and was beginning his doctoral work.[23] The courses he taught included Philosophy of Religion, Comparative World Religions, and New Testament Literature. He enjoyed this teaching immensely, and he was very engaged in providing students with dynamic learning experiences, including arranging bus rides for fieldwork at various places of worship in San Francisco. Taught in this way, his Comparative Religions course became steadily more popular, and he was proud that it continued to grow with interested students throughout his Stanford career. Tanner viewed this opportunity to teach as a development from "learning for my own improvement" to a more socially engaged participation in the life and work of the university.

We have seen that Annie Clark Tanner was especially pleased with her son's opportunity to teach at Stanford, and from the beginning she had strongly encouraged his interest in teaching. He established this goal for himself as an adolescent, no doubt in substantial part because of his mother's ideals, but he also recounts an influential experience that took place in his local church. Adam S. Bennion was a mentor and long-time friend to Tanner, who greatly valued his wisdom and thoughtful approach to difficult life questions. When Tanner was seventeen he heard Bennion speak at the Mormon ward house in Farmington, Utah, and he was so inspired he decided that teaching would be his life's work.[24] He wrote a letter about this to his mother, who was in Southern California nursing one of her daughters, and Annie would later write that she was happy to learn, based on the example of Tanner's high-mindedness, that "the ideals of home were [being] carried over in my absence."[25] Tanner wrote that he was deeply impressed by the power of Bennion's oratory, which "kept the audience spellbound." It was a performance that Tanner imagined he might someday emulate, and he wrote to Annie about his dreams for the future and the eminence he hoped to attain.

Bennion was a Mormon of liberal and humanistic inclinations, and he was a powerful role model for Tanner. He would later write that Bennion encouraged him in his own "liberality in religion," and Tanner consulted him when faced with the decision about whether to accept the church's offer to pay for doctoral study at Chicago. Much like Tanner's mother in this respect, Bennion did not dictate or even suggest what Tanner should do, but said simply that they should converse and "walk around the problem" to see it from a variety of perspectives.[26] It seems significant that upon hearing Bennion speak on that memorable occasion in Farmington—a talk delivered in the context of the church as both physical building and religious institution—Tanner's response was to dedicate himself to becoming not a churchman but a teacher. This aspiration suggests how deeply the liberal movement in the church was affiliated with his own idealism about teaching and education.

Tanner seems to have particularly valued his own teaching because of its actively social character, and he was exceptionally careful, no doubt in the spirit of Annie Clark Tanner, not to impose his views on his students. That he taught from 1945 to 1974 in the philosophy department at the University of Utah is an index of his commitment to the profession, since he was also engaged during these years in building the increasingly successful O. C. Tanner Company. His typical day involved teaching on campus in the morning and then driving to work at the company in the afternoon. His friend and colleague Sterling McMurrin wrote that during this period many people, including students and colleagues, did not know that Professor Obert Tanner and business leader O. C. Tanner were the same person.[27]

Tanner respected the seeking in which his students engaged, and he wanted to teach in ways that enabled them to develop their own values and intellectual independence. A number of anecdotes from the period illustrate his convictions about this. He was pleased, for instance, when a curious student approached him after an exam to ask about the professor's views: "I sure would like to know what you personally think about some of the subjects we talked about."[28] The late Chase Peterson, a University of Utah president and close friend of the Tanners, enjoyed telling another story about Obert's teaching. One day after class a student tentatively approached Professor Tanner and said that he didn't know if he agreed with his approach to religious and philosophical questions. Tanner threw his hands up in delight and said, "This is what I've been waiting for!" Obert and Grace's daughter, Carolyn Tanner Irish, retired bishop of the Episcopal Diocese of Utah, has said that during her youth, their neighbors were often confused about what her father's profession was since he seemed involved in a great many things. When Carolyn asked her father how she should respond to such questions, he said, "Just tell them I'm a teacher." Carolyn remembers it as a definitive response that settled the matter, and it confirms Obert's identification with the profession of teaching—his other accomplishments notwithstanding—throughout his successful life in business and public service.

Tanner's experience as a university student and professor expanded his views about the function of higher learning. Particularly during the crucial decade of his graduate work at Stanford and Harvard (1936–1945), his experience of university education and the goals he identified for it became increasingly social. He continued to endorse the quest for personal enlightenment and the Socratic injunction for self-examination, and he always believed that the university was the most promising context for individuals seeking truth and a coherent understanding of the world. Now he developed a new focus on social dimensions of the university experience, including the unique power of mentors and the centrality of teaching. Tanner also became deeply engaged during these years in studying the merits of various social systems, an evolution of his curricular interests that owed much to the exigencies of the Great Depression, and he moved from thinking in terms of absolute truths to a broader and more socially pragmatic concern with values and ideals. In many ways the process of moral and intellectual valuation was becoming central for him, and this developing perspective would strongly influence his later philanthropy.

Though Tanner's business success is not the subject of this essay, it is crucial to his story and to his lifetime relationship with universities. He pursued his business and educational interests simultaneously, and his colleague Sterling McMurrin said that how Tanner succeeded at this was "something of a mystery" even to his closest friends. McMurrin summed up Obert's achievement by noting that not since Thales in the sixth century BCE had a philosopher been so successful in business.[29] Tanner started the O. C. Tanner Company by selling class rings as an itinerant salesman in the 1920s, and before his death it had become the largest manufacturer of recognition jewelry in the United States.

From the beginning, one of Tanner's strongest motives for building his company was the material foundation it would provide for independent thinking, writing, and teaching. There was a moment in his career as a young teacher of LDS seminary courses when church authorities challenged his liberalism, and it caught him off guard. He even describes it as "a turning point in my life," one that led him to devote more energy to business and the independent income it could provide.[30] This important event occurred not long after he had established his company in 1927. In England at this time Virginia Woolf was advancing the same understanding that motivated Tanner—material security as a necessary basis for intellectual freedom—in lectures at Cambridge that would become *A Room of One's Own*.

Almost from the start, Tanner also conceived of his company as an enterprise that would enable him to contribute to the cause of university education. The culmination of his work in this regard is the Tanner Lectures on Human Values, an international lecture series that he and Grace established in the 1970s and that continues to flourish at nine major universities in the United States and England. Obert came to regard the Tanner Lectures as his most important educational legacy, and the context of this study enables us to see that they grew organically from his lasting attachments, formed early in life, to both intellectual freedom and a strong social ethic.

In Sterling McMurrin's book about the early history of the Tanner Lectures on Human Values (1992), he writes that the lectures are the "authentic expression of the personalities and interests of Obert and Grace Tanner."[31] This is the apt judgment of an outstanding scholar and friend. McMurrin in fact suggested to Tanner in 1975 that he begin funding lectures by prominent scholars, and the two worked diligently over a number of years to establish the Tanner Lectures program. These professors of philosophy clearly held the lecture form in high esteem, and this may reflect in part their common experience of the liberal element in Mormon thought and preaching. This seems certainly true of Tanner, who found the learned sermon a powerful form that brought together intellectual rigor, moral insight, and social vision. Adam S. Bennion was working on his doctorate at Berkeley when he gave the talk in church that was so significant to Tanner in 1922. From early in his life Tanner was excited by such moments, in which the critical thinking done in universities came together with a richly communal ethic.

Later in the 1920s, Tanner participated in another event that integrated university scholarship with the life of his communal church. Dr. Joseph Merrill, who would convey to Obert the church's offer of doctoral training and a university career, invited distinguished religious scholars from the University of Chicago to teach summer sessions at BYU. This program flourished for three years and emphasized both biblical scholarship and the teaching of scriptural texts. The sessions were held not on campus but in the pastoral setting of the Wasatch Mountains—an appropriate place for this idealistic project that brought the church together with university learning. Tanner would later give high praise to this moment: "It was a bright period of fine scholarship for BYU, and for all the church."[32] His strong approval for this program is indicative of perhaps his most sustained educational ideal, which was to bring together the university imperatives of intellectual freedom and rigorous scholarship with the cooperative traditions he valued in his Mormon heritage.[33]

Tanner's long engagement with liberal preaching as a literary and educational form was one line of development that led him toward the Tanner Lectures. It was early in his "decade of searching" at Stanford that he spent a year in graduate study at Harvard. Both institutions were distant in many respects from his upbringing in the interior West, but Tanner was beginning to find continuities that were important to him. He saw affinities, for instance, between the talks of Adam S. Bennion and those of other figures he encountered on the national scene. During the year at Harvard, Tanner's interest in this kind of preaching manifested itself in his close attention to the sermons of Harry Emerson Fosdick, the liberal minister of Riverside Church in New York. More than a decade before, he had read some of Fosdick's books during his time as a missionary, and now Tanner listened regularly to Sunday radio broadcasts of Fosdick's sermons.

Fosdick is generally recognized as the leading liberal Protestant theologian of his era, and Dr. Martin Luther King Jr. identified him as the most important American preacher of the twentieth century. His sermons were informed by intellectual rigor, including a full acceptance of science, and by engaged moral questioning and an active social conscience.

Tanner greatly admired the content of these sermons, as he did Fosdick's eloquence and highly influential public career. When Fosdick came to Harvard to speak at Appleton Chapel, Tanner was genuinely enthusiastic and arrived early to get the best possible seat. He would later make a connection between Bennion and Fosdick and identify them as "incomparable preachers."[34] He also saw the similar path that each pursued in his respective faith tradition: Bennion as a representative of the liberal tendency in Mormonism, which was often at odds with more orthodox church traditions, and Fosdick as an exponent of liberalism in the fundamentalist-modernist controversy that was dividing contemporary American Protestantism.

Tanner himself went on to participate in the liberal preaching tradition that Bennion and Fosdick exemplified. During his later years at Stanford he was not only a doctoral student and teacher but also acting chaplain of the university. He gave regular sermons at Memorial Church on the Stanford campus, and he spent much time and energy in their preparation. He had made his first visit to this church a number of years before. The occasion was Obert and Grace's honeymoon in 1931, which included a car tour along the West Coast. They stopped by Stanford and were able to attend an organ recital at Memorial Church. It became a significant moment for Obert:

> As we left, I recall pausing outside to look more carefully at the church. I was standing near enough to touch one of the large stones of which it was built. I recall thinking to myself that the sermons preached here to a university audience must be very intelligent. I would like to hear one of them. This must be a church quite acceptable to everyone. I stood there only a moment, and in my heart I had a wish, barely a flicker, that I might some day return to Stanford.[35]

What we know of Tanner's formative years helps explain why he was especially drawn to this building, a church on a university campus, and the enlightened sermons he believed were preached there. The moment is informed by the tensions in his personal religious and cultural history, and he glimpses a prospect in which the conflicts between the individual's right to intellectual freedom and the coherence of the gathering, the *ecclesia*, might somehow be resolved in a generous institutional union.

Obert Tanner saw the university as a promising setting for the realization of this ideal. For him the institution represented a possible third way, like the liberal movement in the Mormonism of his youth, that would sacrifice neither the individual's freedom nor the creative benefits of a close-knit society. Over the course of his life he pondered the university's power to do two things: to educate the individual student and to constitute an enlightened human community. He believed that at its best, the university can help students toward a fuller development of their intrinsic gifts, a greater freedom of mind and spirit. But his communitarian roots were also of permanent importance in his life and thought, and he seems to have invested the secular university, perhaps not fully realizing it himself, with his attachment to the cooperative element in his church and the constructive social energies it produced.

Tanner's idea of a university was thus idealistic, but it was never naïve. He was a realistic businessman familiar with social injustice, human suffering, and the all-too-human failings of individuals, both within the university and beyond. But he persevered in his hopes for the institution, and he founded the Tanner Lectures on Human Values on the basis of an enduring vision. He established them in a way that guarantees the complete autonomy of each university in choosing its annual lecturer, and the freedom of each speaker from any constraint imposed by the administration of the lectures is absolute. But he also envisioned the Tanner Lectures as annual occasions for gatherings of people of goodwill, as affirmations of human society in themselves and as part of the larger collective work for social justice and human fulfillment. Obert would never have thought in any literal sense of the Tanner Lectures as an opportunity for the gathering of "a church quite acceptable to everyone," but now in their fifth decade, they continue to carry forward his energetic dedication to both individual freedom and a cooperative society.

NOTES

1. Epigraph taken from Annie Clark Tanner, *A Mormon Mother: An Autobiography*, rev. ed. (Salt Lake City: Tanner Trust Fund, University of Utah Library, 1973), 295.
2. Obert C. Tanner, *One Man's Journey: In Search of Freedom* (Salt Lake City: University of Utah Press, 1994), 46–47.
3. Obert C. Tanner, foreword to *A Life Divided: The Biography of Joseph Marion Tanner, 1859–1927*, by Margery W. Ward (Salt Lake City: Publishers Press, 1980), v.
4. Tanner, *Mormon Mother*, 46.
5. Ibid.
6. Tanner, *One Man's Journey*, 60.
7. Tanner, *Mormon Mother*, 252.
8. Tanner, *One Man's Journey*, 18.
9. Tanner, *One Man's Journey*, 19. Annie nurtured her children's independence: "Young people with a tendency to analyze things are not always good followers. My own children were not reared under the old tradition, namely, that obedience is the greatest of all virtues. Rather, they were encouraged to think things out for themselves." See Tanner, *A Mormon Mother*, 227.
10. Obert C. Tanner, introduction to *Mormon Mother*, xx.
11. Ibid., x.
12. Ibid., xii.
13. Ibid., xv.
14. Ibid., xiii.
15. Tanner, *One Man's Journey*, 19.
16. Tanner, *Mormon Mother*, x.
17. Ibid., xxix.
18. Tanner, *One Man's Journey*, 155–57.
19. Ibid., 111.
20. Ibid., 125.
21. Ibid., 129.
22. Ibid., 130.
23. Tanner, *One Man's Journey*, 93–94, 135–38. Tanner did not complete his doctoral work at Stanford, a decision he revisited many times in later life. Dean Tanner, Obert and Grace's oldest son, died suddenly of polio in 1943, and in their grief they felt the pull of home and family in Utah. Tanner was also thinking about the future of his business, and he came to believe that if he was going to make the company great he needed to return to Salt Lake City. Both the Tanner Fountain and the annual Tanner Lecture at Stanford are dedicated to Dean.

24. In *One Man's Journey*, Obert places this event about a decade earlier, when he was roughly eight years old (64). In Annie Clark Tanner's *A Mormon Mother*, she prints Obert's letter to her about it, which is dated early in 1922 (301). This seems more likely to be the correct date of the event, and Obert was then seventeen.
25. Tanner, *Mormon Mother*, 301.
26. Tanner, *One Man's Journey*, 111.
27. Sterling McMurrin, foreword to *One Man's Search: Addresses by Obert C. Tanner* (Salt Lake City: University of Utah Press, 1989), xiii.
28. Tanner, *One Man's Journey*, 139.
29. McMurrin, foreword to *One Man's Search*, xiii.
30. Tanner, *One Man's Journey*, 159–60.
31. Sterling M. McMurrin, *The Tanner Lectures on Human Values: A History of the Early Years* (Salt Lake City: Trustees of the Tanner Lectures on Human Values, 1992), 57.
32. Tanner, *One Man's Journey*, 110.
33. Ibid. This summer-school experiment was discontinued due to the influence of more orthodox elements in the Mormon Church.
34. Tanner, *One Man's Journey*, 64.
35. Ibid., 128.

8

OBERT C. TANNER'S MORMONISM

The O. C. Tanner Company as a Window into His Soul

KENT MURDOCK

Obert Clark Tanner died in October 1993 at the age of eighty-nine. Newspapers and television stations reported his death and chronicled the remarkable story of his life. His memorial service was held in Abravanel Hall in Salt Lake City. Thousands attended, with music provided by the Utah Symphony and the Mormon Tabernacle Choir. Prominent religious and community leaders eulogized him. His family and more than two thousand employees mourned his passing. What sort of life had he lived to garner such attention?

Obert Tanner was an accomplished man. Beginning life in poverty, he was a student, Mormon missionary, family man, university professor, jeweler, author, philanthropist, and founder of a company that is the preeminent business of its kind in the world. He had a circle of friends who loved and respected him, a family that revered him, and thousands of employees who held him in the highest possible esteem. Of what was such a man made?

My essay breaks this question down by asking, How did Obert Tanner's Mormonism play out in his life and affect his accomplishments? How did his Mormonism frame his business, the O.C. Tanner Company?

There are no easy answers because Obert Tanner was hardly one-dimensional. Although Mormon precepts and traditions definitely appear in his life, they are woven into a tapestry of nature and nurture, religion and philosophy, education and experience. Thus, there is fertile ground for speculation about the relative influence that poverty had on Tanner as well as his relationship with his mother, distant father, family life, religious odyssey, and academic and business careers. Moreover, in my interactions with him, I found evidence of Plato's rationalism, Kant's *Critique of Pure Reason*, Edmund Burke's conservatism, biblical axioms, William James' pragmatism, Newtonian physics, Alfred Sloan's concept of the enterprise, Hegel's dialectic, Jesus' kindness, and Lao Tsu's common sense.[1] Yet Obert Tanner's Mormon core was essential to his understanding of the world. His Mormonism was a significant piece of the larger mosaic that is the full portrait of the man.[2]

I begin with a story that frames this essay. When I retired from the O. C. Tanner Company in 2009, a newly employed Sudanese refugee addressed me at a company meeting: "I do not know you, but God will bless you for what you have done here. I never knew such a place existed on this earth."[3] If she had known Obert Tanner, she would have realized that her comments were for him. What was "such a place" and why did it seem a heaven on earth? The answer, of course, is found in the tangible manifestations of the values, character, heart, and hard work of Obert C. Tanner.

A Religious Man

Obert Tanner had a profound faith in God: "Religion is a trust," he wrote, "a hope that the noblest in human life will finally be sustained."[4] At his foundation was a religious upbringing at the knee of his revered mother and in the Mormon Church. Of his early life Tanner said, "Overall, my environment gave me a love for my church."[5] He served an LDS mission in Germany, during which he went through the spiritual crisis described in Robert Goldberg's essay in this volume. Interestingly, Tanner rejected a strictly materialist viewpoint during his quest: "I did not want to believe that the whole creation is just billions of atoms going at it blindly."[6] Reflecting on his philosophical inclinations, he observed that he did not want to relinquish the unique value of a religious view of mankind: "I did not want to reduce religion to ethics; the mystery of life was too great for that."[7] Coming from his early crisis of faith, he retained a distinctly religious and Christian orientation: "The basis for my religious faith now became the life and teachings of Jesus Christ."[8]

Notwithstanding his passion for and study of philosophy, Tanner always reserved a place in his life for God. In a speech given at the University of Utah, he declared, "No university can change human nature or answer our questions about ultimate meaning, purpose, or destiny of human life."[9] Clearly, his love of philosophy, intellect, and reason blended with his faith. Said Tanner: "My own definition of religion is based on Plato's trinity; that is, whenever anyone finds some ultimate Goodness, Truth, or Beauty, to which one becomes committed, then one participates in religious experience. This means that the work of science, art, public life—all may be the expression of genuine religious life."[10]

These ideals were borne out in my observations of Obert Tanner's demeanor, character, and certainly his works. He believed that a life should be lived according to universal principles. He respected others and attached importance to their moral behavior. He was not arrogant, but reverent, forever trying to do the "right" thing. He was more interested in creation than profit. He felt the need to serve the community and to be liberal with his means. Although many would contend that none of these are the exclusive province of religious feeling or Mormonism, Tanner would say that he learned these principles from his mother and in Sunday school and they became authentically his own as he defined religion for himself: "I came to believe that, generally, religion offered the best, the finest way to live. It was not in politics, not in school, not in business, but in religion that I found the best expression of noble ideals."[11]

One aspect of Tanner's Mormonism was acceptance of a central tenet of Christian and Mormon theology, that there is an essential spiritual reality in the nature of man. He said,

> It may be, then, that if God is left out of some new religion in a new age, this would be true: that man the sinner would lose his strongest help; that man the sufferer would lose his securest refuge; that man

the thinker would lose his greatest thought; that man the worker would lose his greatest motive; that man the lover would lose his fairest vision; and that man the mortal would lose his only hope.[12]

In regard to Mormonism, Tanner was always an individual. He was not a member of the LDS Church as minion or interchangeable unit. He was, in the sense referred to by the Apostle Paul and C. S. Lewis, a member who was like an organ in a body: unlike others in the body, but essential and complementary to the whole. Thus he believed that religion must be authentic and was key to finding meaning in life. While he did not participate in all the meetings, rituals, and observances of his church, Tanner loved its leaders and never departed from his people, or his love of the Mormon religion.

Applied Values, Philosophy, and Religion

Obert Tanner was a man of action, someone who not only thought about the great questions, but who lived life fully and passionately. He wrote and spoke of important things in an effort to leave the world a better place. He was a teacher who saw his students' successes as his most significant accomplishments. He was a philanthropist who eschewed a large personal fortune to contribute to and create beauty in the community. He was a capitalist who conceived ideas, took risks, competed vigorously, overcame challenges, and built something economically viable and valuable. And his life was touched by tragedy. He was the father of six children but lost three of his sons while they were boys, two to terrible accidents and one to polio. Few could fully comprehend his and his wife Grace's grief.

I knew him as a man engaged with life on its terms, carving out his path thoughtfully, and from time to time, repentantly. Making amends, changing his mind or approach, reconciling himself with others—these were his standard practices. As he wrote in his autobiography, the Mormon doctrine of "eternal progression" was particularly appealing because it meant that individuals continue "to grow and learn throughout eternity."[13] Although his opinions were strongly held and urged with great force, Tanner, unlike some who attain great prosperity and power, was contemplative, reflective, and introspective. He marched to the tune of authentically held principles and virtues. He sought propriety and right conduct. Tanner spoke and wrote with integrity, seeking to express his honest thoughts and feelings, not to impress his audience.

That same integrity pervades the atmosphere of the O. C. Tanner Company. The chief financial officer of the company enjoyed telling of Obert Tanner's instructions when he was hired. Tanner insisted that all books of account, records, ledgers, and financial statements be accurate and truthful. Tanner informed him that the company should pay its full share of taxes. There were to be no dishonest dealings or crafty accounting or any shading of the truth.[14] The same admonition was the essence of his's instructions to every department and employee. The mandate was clear: do the right thing, tell the truth, and keep promises.

He practiced what he preached. Tanner was once confronted with a forgotten document that he had signed several decades earlier. It contained a statement that ran counter to what he had said in times more recent. He looked with obvious surprise at the document, acknowledged his signature, and immediately had me prepare a corrective letter acknowledging the earlier statement and offering an apology.

Similarly, when we discovered that the company's employee discount policy was unlawful because it allowed executives a 50 percent discount and other employees only 25 percent, he authorized a flat 40 percent discount for all. At the same time, he specifically retained his practice of giving a 50 percent discount to Mormon general authorities, other clergy, and university presidents.

Obert Tanner respected integrity in others and in the processes of civil society. When a proposal was made to name Symphony Hall in Salt Lake City for Maurice Abravanel, the first conductor of the Utah Symphony, Tanner wrote to county officials in opposition, opining that public buildings should not be named after individuals. When the county council nevertheless voted to name the building Abravanel Hall, Tanner respected the decision and instructed us to call county officials and tell them that he would pay for the brass nameplate at the building's entrance.

Obert Tanner supported higher education with fervor and was unabashed in his admiration of the academic world and those who excelled in it. This respect obviously came from his mother's love of poetry, philosophy, and literature, and also from the Mormon doctrine of lifetime learning, expressed scripturally in the Lord's injunction to "seek ye out of the best books words of wisdom; seek learning, even by study and by faith."[15] In 1991, four current and former university presidents sat on the board of directors of the O. C. Tanner Company. He gave O. C. Tanner Company stock to a trust for Utah universities, which included the University of Utah, Utah State University, and Southern Utah University. He organized and endowed the Tanner Lectures on Human Values. He donated fountains and faculty and philosophy reading rooms to Stanford, Harvard, Utah State University, and the University of Utah. And of course, he taught philosophy for thirty years at the University of Utah.

A favorite verse in the Mormon canon of scripture recounts Jesus Christ telling the prophet Joseph Smith: "Verily I say, men should be anxiously engaged in a good cause, and do many things of their own free will, and bring to pass much righteousness; for the power is in them, wherein they are agents unto themselves."[16] Obert Tanner lived these words. He consistently devoted himself to good works. He "tithed" his company in his own way, annually donating 10 percent of its gross profit to the Tanner Charitable Trust. From the trust, tens of millions of dollars went to worthy causes, including those for the advancement of Utah's universities, arts, and charities. Because of his leadership and resources, Utah possesses the Utah Shakespeare Festival in Cedar City, the Tanner Amphitheatre in Zion National Park, Abravanel Hall, the Capitol Theatre, the Grace Adams Tanner Alumni House at the University of Utah, numerous public fountains, the Utah Symphony, the Tanner Gift of Music, Tanner Park, and countless other objects of his generosity. Tanner's perennial question to his chief financial officer was, "What is my give-ability?"[17] Meaning, how much can I give away and stay within 10 percent of the predicted gross profits? Since his death in 1993, his daughter Carolyn has continued her father's tradition, and under her leadership, the company continues to pay its 10 percent in support of the community.

Faith in Practice: The O. C. Tanner Company

The company began in 1927 when Obert Tanner sold pins to gradu-ating high school seniors in Spanish Fork, Utah, to acknowledge their achievement. Now the company sells and administers employee rec-ognition programs and products for corporations all over the world. It employs about two thousand people in the United States, Canada, and Great Britain. Nearly 70 percent of the employees are women, and the company employs people from forty-eight countries. In 2015, *Fortune* magazine honored in Tanners' creation as one of "The 100 Best Companies to Work For" in America.[18]

The O. C. Tanner Company proved to be Obert Tanner's lever to repair the world. Of his business experience and its intersection with the religious and philosophical worlds, he said, "Business provided, for me, a whole different perspective on the world than what I had gained through my religious and philosophical vocations. The latter in turn helped to make my company much more than just another enterprise. All together, they have given me a life of daily excitement and extraor-dinary satisfaction."[19]

The O. C. Tanner Company's success stems from his ability to find leaders and employees capable of appreciating and demonstrating his fundamental values. To them, he modeled the values and practices of the small Mormon community in which he was raised. There, he had wit-nessed mutual affection, service, kindness, and charity amid the normal give and take of social and economic interactions. Tanner learned that people working together are able to accomplish more than the aggregate of self-interested individuals. He had been taught that Mormons exalt the principle of self-reliance, with each assigned to carry a portion of the load according to ability; all could serve and contribute. Thus, he never tried to do for his employees what they could do for themselves. Nor did he lessen his expectations of their capabilities and the results he sought from them. Men and women, he was convinced, required room to grow and develop through their responsibilities.

He characterized his business this way: "I sometimes reflect that O. C. Tanner Company's work, expressed in symbolic terms, is that of putting a drop of oil on the bearings of the free enterprise system."[20] His ideas were not just window dressing. Since the beginning of the business, they have guided business strategy, innovation, marketing, and the intellectual property shared with clients. The business is founded and run on an intractable philosophy of the nature of man, an ethic or religious principle originating, so far as the company is concerned, in the heart and mind of Obert Tanner.

He refused to scrimp on salaries, wages, or investments. He pressed experimentation and innovation. Employee suggestions and input into the production process are encouraged. The team atmosphere is palpable. Because employees are engaged and feel valued as participants in the enterprise, they put their hearts and souls into their work, making the business even more profitable. Tanner nurtured all of this, and his legacy continues. His values run through the company like oxygen in the atmosphere. According to Don Ostler, the second CEO of the company: "The O. C. Tanner Company was created in the image of its founder. Its values and business philosophies come from Tanner, who was the architect, builder, and leader of the business for sixty-six years."[21]

Obert Tanner's employees appreciated him for his good works. One observed at the time of his death, "The fountains and the flowers are only the outer beauty of the company. The real beauty was the kindness and love Mr. Tanner showed to each of us." Another agreed: "Mr. Tanner's legacy to me is that he treated all his employees as equals and was continuously concerned about our welfare." A third echoed these thoughts: "Mr. Tanner gave so much to others. I admire him for retaining his integrity, honesty, and respect for humankind. I am honored to have rubbed shoulders with Mr. Tanner."[22]

Tanner was not an armchair idealist about freedom. He was practical in his wisdom. He understood the conditions and limitations of life and business and operating within the limitations of human nature, prevailing trends, popular opinion, and the myriad controls of government. He accepted the rules and regulations that impacted the company, even if he thought interference was excessive. He believed that it was a privilege to do business in America, and never balked at paying his fair share of taxes—a pragmatic adjustment to reality and another stake of integrity driven into the ground for his employees to witness.

A remarkable aspect of Obert Tanner's quest for freedom was subordination of his will and desires to the greater mandate of his cherished principles. I came to appreciate him as a slave to principle. In one discussion concerning a business adversary who angered him greatly, he reasoned his way to and fastened upon the principle of magnanimity as the "correct" method to resolving the issue. His actions de-escalated the conflict and engendered a reciprocation that eventually resolved the conflict. Tanner simply felt it was the right thing to do for the benefit of the company and all concerned.

One day I ran head first into his kindness. I reported with pride that gains in efficiency had enabled us to reduce our employee count to less than two thousand for the first time in some months. Tanner thought for a moment and said, "I am kind of proud of employing two thousand people; that has a nice ring to it." He went on to say, as he did on other occasions, "the creation of jobs is like a religion to me." Indeed, he noted in his autobiography that employing men and women "may be the major accomplishment of my eighty-nine years."[23] In a speech to his employees in 1985, he informed them that he had secured the company's future by locking it in a trust to prevent it being sold or merged. "When I leave," he said, "I want a smooth transition, things to go on as if I were here. This will mean job security for the people I esteem so highly."[24]

Obert Tanner harmonized his philosophical, religious, and business approaches. He observed, "I have come to realize, as many will agree, that there is one sure and successful way to deal with people in our free enterprise system, and that way is the application of the Golden Rule."[25] To Tanner, this was not merely the principle of reciprocity embodied in most ethical systems; this was the principle of selflessness and service evinced in the life and teachings of Jesus Christ. He not only preached it; he practiced it. Thus, initially trying the legal approach of making contracts with his sales people (he was after all a lawyer), and failing in court to enforce certain protective provisions, Tanner reasoned his way to an unwritten understanding that the relationship should be governed by the Golden Rule. No more written contract, clauses, paragraphs, or legalese.[26] One day, I asked him why, as a philosopher, he did not use Kant's categorical imperative as his statement of the salesman's contract rather than the Golden Rule. An hour of spirited lecture later, I had my answer. Kant's enunciation of the principle, no matter how apt, lacked the life and spirit of Christ's declaration!

Never Far from Home

Near the end of his life, Obert Tanner was clearly a world citizen who appreciated diverse peoples, philosophies, and religions. But he retained his love and pride in his Mormon heritage. Thus, he returned to his small-town roots and chose to be buried by family members under a modest headstone in the Farmington, Utah, cemetery.

His favorite fountain of the dozens he built is in the center of the LDS Church's original plaza east of Main Street in Salt Lake City. President Nathan Eldon Tanner, a relative and a member of the First Presidency of the Church, had asked him to consider designing and building a fountain there. Recalling the project near the end of his life, Tanner wrote, "If possible, I wanted a design that would express, in a symbolic way, the distinctive spiritual values of the Mormon religion.... Some architects were attracted to still pools of water that would reflect the temple spires. They cited persuasively the transcendent beauty of the reflection pools in front of the great Taj Mahal." To Obert Tanner, the comparison was "flawed"; the idea was Islamic, not Mormon. He noted, "The Taj Mahal pools express the eternal and unchanging, the serene and final will of Allah in all things. Such a philosophy gives peace of mind to those who believe that 'God will have it so,' but that is not the dynamic of the Mormon religion." For Mormons, Tanner maintained, "human beings and God are partners. Whatever impedes human joy and happiness should be overcome. Water moves and thereby can express change and progress." Thus, he "designed a fountain where the jets would run a cycle from small jets to larger ones, so that as it played, the fountain would become more complete, more whole, more perfect, and more beautiful, thus portraying the Mormon ideals of growth, participation, and progress and, evoking that favorite doctrinal point of mine, the law of eternal progression." Written at the very end of his life, this sentiment revealed his great affection for, as he called them, "the distinctive spiritual values of the Mormon religion."[27]

At the O. C. Tanner Company, the same affinity repeatedly manifested itself in his relentless efforts to make progress. He called it "a search for a future better beyond our present best," and he spoke often of "reaching for the fringes of perfection, and sometimes coming near," certainly a similar thought, and one also directly related to the Platonic ideal of perfection that he loved.

One day near the end of his life while we were talking in my office, Tanner expressed his pride in the company and remarked, "I suppose I could say it is a Mormon company, and I'm happy about that." There was much about the company that was Mormon. His longtime friend and CEO Don Ostler had served as a Mormon bishop and stake president, and the overwhelming majority of executives in the company and a significant fraction of the employees were of the LDS faith. His handpicked board of directors at that time consisted largely of Mormons, including prominent men in the church who served as outside directors: Dallin Oaks, Rex Lee, Stephen Nadauld, and Chase Peterson. Carolyn, Tanner's daughter and chair-elect of the board, affectionately referred to pictures of the directors as a "wall of Mormon men," which was quite true. I had also been selected by Obert—and Carolyn and Don—as the president and intended future CEO with knowledge that I was an active Mormon, having served at one time as his bishop. I never heard him say anything directly about his personal relationship to the church or his beliefs as to the truth claims of Mormonism. He seemed unconcerned with such matters or who believed what.[28] Nonetheless, he always spoke with great affection of leaders of the church, and he responded with all resources when called upon by any one of them for assistance.

Obert Tanner was quite comfortable in Mormon culture and at ease with fellow Mormons. He trusted Mormons (not blindly, but they did receive the benefit of the doubt from him). This is apparent in the trust instruments that govern the O. C. Tanner Company and declare what kind of person may be considered for a position as an outside director on the board: "only those individuals will be selected who have...personal experience with and appreciation...of the social and cultural conditions in [Salt Lake City]." If that was not sufficient, the provision continues that no one may be deemed to have that personal experience and appreciation "who does not in his or her personal life and affairs embrace the standards, including industry, honesty and loyalty, of those who pioneered the colonization of Great Salt Lake Valley, Utah."[29] It is no surprise, then, that when Tanner chose those he felt most comfortable working with, an apostle of the Mormon Church, a Mormon Church general authority, the president of church-run Brigham Young University, and a practicing Mormon with a pioneer heritage received the nod. As can be discerned from the carefully wrought language of this trust provision, he clearly felt that Mormon values were at the foundation of his prosperous company and were necessary to preserve its success.

Another of his great gestures of beauty, the "Gift of Music" concerts that are free to the public because of the O. C. Tanner endowment, were designed with his longtime neighbor and friend, Gordon B. Hinckley, who later became president of the LDS Church. The concerts drew the Mormon Tabernacle Choir and the Utah Symphony together in an evening of entertainment for the people of the Salt Lake Valley. The free concerts now run for two nights every other year in the LDS Conference Center and are attended by 40,000 people.

At Tanner's memorial service in Abravanel Hall, President Gordon B. Hinckley paid homage to his respected friend: "Those of us who have been the beneficiaries of Obert's generosity, and I think that includes all of us, know that in the getting of wealth, through his giving, he emphasized the ideal of Jesus whom he loved so much."[30] President Hinckley's tribute would have pleased Obert very much.

Obert C. Tanner lived a long life rich in learning, giving, building, and loving. He left a legacy as a seeker of truth, love, and beauty: husband, father, philosopher, teacher, entrepreneur, and philanthropist. He charted an independent course but never forgot his Mormon roots. Like the diamonds he loved to sell, he was a man of many facets. His life touched mine in profound ways and I am grateful to have walked along with him a part of the way. What a joy to have worked in the space he created and have it said, "I never knew such a place existed on this earth."

NOTES

1. For more on this, see his autobiography, Obert C. Tanner, *One Man's Journey: In Search of Freedom* (Salt Lake City: University of Utah Press, 1994).
2. The author began doing outside legal work for Obert Tanner and the company in January 1991 and was hired to be the president of O. C. Tanner Company in October 1991. He became CEO in March 1997 and continued in that capacity until his retirement in June 2009. He worked with Obert C. Tanner virtually on a daily basis during the last thirty-three months of Obert's life.
3. Statement by Akon Majok, May 28, 2009, O. C. Tanner Company night shift meeting.
4. Tanner, *One Man's Journey*, 58.
5. Ibid., 60.
6. Ibid., 71.
7. Ibid., 74.
8. Ibid., 72.
9. Obert C. Tanner, "A New Religion for a New Age," in *One Man's Search* (Salt Lake City: University of Utah Press, 1989) 152.
10. Tanner, *One Man's Journey*, 57–58.
11. Ibid., 63.
12. Tanner, "A New Religion for a New Age," 152.
13. Tanner, *One Man's Journey*, 72.
14. Statement of Robert K. Anger, longtime controller and then chief financial officer of the O. C. Tanner Company. Anger observed that in his experience as an auditor for a major firm, Obert's approach was refreshing and different than that of many companies. He called it "liberating."
15. Doctrine and Covenants 88:118. Mormonism combines spiritual and practical considerations for living according to gospel principles. Mormon scripture also contains the Lord's commandment to "teach one another the doctrine of the kingdom.... Of things both in heaven and in the earth, and under the earth; things which have been, things which are, things which must shortly come to pass; things which are at home, things which are abroad; the wars and the perplexities of the nations;

and the judgments which are on the land; and a knowledge also of countries and kingdoms." Doctrine and Covenants 88:77–78.

16. Ibid., 58:27–28.

17. Statement of Robert K. Anger, overheard on occasion by the author and other executives.

18. *Fortune*, 171, March 15, 2015, 147. O.C. Tanner is ranked fortieth.

19. Tanner, *One Man's Journey*, 184.

20. Obert C. Tanner, *"Commitment to Beauty,"* (New York: Newcomen Society in North America, 1982), 8.

21. *Obert C. Tanner, An Uncommon Man* (Salt Lake City: O. C. Tanner Company, 1993), brochure without numbered pages.

22. Ibid.

23. Tanner, *One Man's Journey*, 180.

24. Obert C. Tanner, "The Nature and Future of the O.C. Tanner Company" (Salt Lake City: O.C. Tanner Company, 1985), 8.

25. Tanner, *Commitment to Beauty* also 19.

26. Only a few key employees who were privy to sensitive competitive information and strategy were required to sign a confidentiality agreement.

27. Tanner, *One Man's Journey*, 204–5.

28. See Tanner, *One Man's Journey*, 74. Perhaps a clue is given in his statement: "Well, I became a converted Christian. I was totally committed as a follower of Jesus Christ, though I suppose I was more a pragmatic Christian than a theological believer."

29. Nineteenth Amendment to the O. C. Tanner Trust of Voting Shares, 23–24.

30. Tanner, "Uncommon Man".

PART IV

LOWELL BENNION

9

LOWELL BENNION AND THE THINGS THAT MATTER MOST

MARY LYTHGOE BRADFORD

Lowell Bennion was a legend in his time—a fact that embarrassed him. A list of his awards and accolades takes up two pages in his biography, ranging from "One of the Most Caring People in America" to "A Concurrent Resolution of the Legislature and the Governor Honoring Lowell L. Bennion for His Life of Devotion to the Values of Service, Love and Self-Worth and the Powerful Influence [of] His Life and Example."[1]

I was with him at the Utah Capitol for this honor at the invitation of my legislator sister-in-law. Lowell might have invited his biographer, but he did not even invite his wife Merle to the ceremony. The "whereases" rolled on from State Senator Scott Howell, detailing his many contributions and honoring a life "that teaches the difference one person's service can make in the lives of all of us and illustrates the joy his life exemplifies as he has given of himself to others." Lowell Bennion then spoke briefly: "Most of what I did, I did with others."[2]

He would have enjoyed this, his latest honor, being celebrated with Sterling McMurrin and Obert Tanner in a symposium at the University of Utah. McMurrin and Tanner influenced him in many ways. One of his mottos, "Religion is the faith that the things that matter most are not ultimately at the mercy of things that matter least" came to him through McMurrin from his Professor W. E. Montague. Obert Tanner's definition of beauty and truth and his fine lesson manuals were also inspirational.

The three men grew from the same soil, and were products of the LDS Church Educational System (CES). They were so close that after Lowell Bennion founded the LDS Institute at the University of Arizona, McMurrin replaced him as director.

Bennion would not have advertised himself as an intellectual—indeed, he would not have advertised himself at all. It is apt, however. He was a thinker, and his way of thinking has kept many members in the Mormon Church while helping his students to think for themselves. (It is difficult to know when we are thinking for ourselves, but the struggle is worth the effort). Eugene England, a student at the University of Utah's LDS Institute of Religion in 1950, recalled one of Bennion's classes on the nature of God. When a student asked, "If God is no respecter of persons, why is there a difference between blacks and others?" England immediately spoke up: "Well, God is also a God of justice, and since blacks were not valiant in the preexistence, they are cursed." England reported that Bennion "simply asked me how I knew [this]...[and] when I had no answer but tradition, he gently suggested that God...would surely let blacks know what they had done wrong and how they could repent...and since God had done no such thing, it seemed better to believe that blacks...were no different... from the rest of us."[3]

From this encounter, England realized "with shame that many of my beliefs...were based on very flimsy and unexamined foundations and were inconsistent with some great central principles that I claimed to believe."[4] Noting his mentor's role, England wrote, "It was educed. Led out of me from inside, in the central act of education that was Lowell Bennion's great gift and the heart of his legacy."[5] Thereafter, he determined that "any religious principle must be consistent within its whole context...and that its reliability is greatly strengthened by verification through a variety of ways of knowing, reason and experience as well as authority."[6]

After his Swiss-German LDS mission, Lowell Bennion remained in Europe for graduate school. His educator father Milton Bennion arranged for his doctoral study at the University of Erlangen in Germany though he soon transferred to the University of Vienna in Austria. There he began to examine the voluminous work of recently deceased social theorist

Max Weber under the tutelage of professors who had been profoundly influenced by his far-reaching ideas about bureaucracy, capitalism, rationalization, and alienation. Hit with a barrage of new insights about the nature and uses of authority in complex organizations, Bennion began to see his own culture with new eyes. He read everything Weber wrote in the original German, and set out to write his doctoral dissertation on this great thinker's methods.[7]

To continue his work, Bennion and his bride Merle Colton moved to Paris and then to the University of Strasbourg. Although preparing to defend his thesis in French, he had written it in English at the behest of Maurice Halbwach, his major professor. The reason? Weber's theories were hardly known in the United States, so Bennion's work might help introduce the scholar to American academicians.[8]

Max Weber's Methodology was published in Paris in 1933 with a print run of one hundred copies—as was the practice with European doctoral dissertations at that time. With the first systematic English language treatment of Weber's work under his belt, Bennion was poised to parlay this achievement into an academic career in the United States. But he and Merle, having lost their first child as an infant, were anxious to return home to Utah. In the depths of the Great Depression, his best job opportunity there was to teach in the LDS CES. Given Bennion's deep religious convictions and intellectual fascination with the LDS Church as an organization, this was a natural fit.

As Laurie DiPadova-Stocks, a former student of Bennion, expressed many times: "Lowell Bennion had Max Weber in his bones."[9] During his long career as teacher and humanitarian, he found a remarkable "synergy" in Weber's ideas.[10] It was Weber who first described the "inherently contradictory systems in religious organizations," teaching that value judgments must be separated from facts; scientists must pursue truth without personal or political benefit. Bennion taught his students Weber's worldview, that we "live in two worlds: the empirical factual reality and the world of values."[11] Religious values cannot be proven in the same way as scientific facts. In his book, *The Things That Matter Most*, Bennion clarified this seminal view. To understand him as an intellectual is to understand his debt to Weber. Weber provided Lowell Bennion with a framework for his own faith in the Gospel of Jesus Christ.

At the University of Utah in the 1950s, I entered his classes, a dewy-eyed literature major hoping to write books someday. Lowell Bennion encouraged me, asking if I would proofread his manuscript *Religion and the Pursuit of Truth* in which he applied Weberian philosophy to the Gospel of Jesus Christ. This book recognizes the difficulty of harmonizing religious faith with education: "We have inherited two traditions: the faith and morality of the Hebrews and early Christians, and the life of reason initiated by the Greek philosophers." [12] Bennion admitted that the two will never see "eye to eye," but a marriage can be consummated if individual differences can be respected and a working relationship achieved. Bennion counseled with students who learned disturbing truths in their university courses. He advised them to test the authorities by analyzing the evidence behind their claims—but with humility. "Integrity," he insisted, "is the first law of life." [13] By analyzing, then synthesizing, students could keep their faith while progressing in secular knowledge.

Bennion spoke of various ways of knowing the truth—intuition, mysticism, and revelation. He insisted that students develop a multifaceted philosophy composed of self, everyday experiences, their studies in the humanities and sciences, and religion. "To leave any one [approach] entirely untapped," he declared, is to go through life with limited vision." [14] Bennion concluded that the "best" religion "keeps open the gates to heaven and the doors to human experience in other fields." [15]

When I began researching Bennion, I found that he had already focused his intellect on the important facts of his life. During oral history interviews conducted for the LDS Church, Maureen Beecher noticed a classical, organizational patterning. Bennion divided his career into three parts: the Sanctuary, the Halls of Ivy, and the Real World. Translation: The LDS Institute of Religion, the University of Utah, and the Community Services Council of Salt Lake City. I organized my research around these, setting up interviews with family, colleagues, and friends. It was a labor of love for nearly a decade. Bennion and his cast of characters were unusually patient and helpful. With characteristic humor, he chided me for "talking to everyone who has ever breathed in the same room with me."

Of course, the three segments were not equal in importance, and they needed to be fleshed out, but it was obvious that his twenty-seven years in the "Sanctuary" were most prominent. It was there that he could practice the "things that mattered most": teaching young people how to think, organizing them into wholesome social activities and service projects, and giving them a place to go with their doubts and problems. He eschewed the growing emphasis on perfection. Making a list and checking it twice led to a preoccupation with self. Better was to emphasize, like the Buddhists, the concept of balance. In seeking balance, we can look outward instead of inward. His Christian advice was to forget self in serving others. This was not an easy thing for students just learning to grow into themselves, so a combination of courses at the LDS Institute and membership in Bennion's coed LDS fraternity offered an inviting path to education and maturity.[16]

When the Bennions returned from Europe, John A. Widstoe, who knew Lowell in the mission field, asked him to found the Institute of Religion at the University of Utah that was to be housed in the University Ward. When Bennion asked, "What should I teach?" Widstoe responded, "What can you teach?"[17] Together they planned to survey Mormon professionals who could help locate students for the institute. John Ballif, dean of students at the university and Sunday school president in the University Ward, shared lists that enabled Bennion to visit four hundred out-of-town students. The institute could become a home away from home for them. By organizing a well-balanced religious and socially attractive meeting place to mix and mingle, he set the stage for open discussion. His goal at the institute was to be a "magnet not a net."[18] His advisors suggested that he not seek university credit for his courses lest it provoke "Mormon versus non-Mormon fights in the Board of Regents and faculty."[19] Bennion embraced this concept, since he wanted students to study religion as a personal choice.

David O. McKay, then second counselor to LDS Church President Heber J. Grant, phoned his friend Milton, Bennion's father, and arranged a meeting. Lowell Bennion remembered this as a sort of "intellectual swearing-in." After sounding him out on various subjects, McKay said, "I don't care what you do and what you draw upon, but be true to yourself and loyal to the cause."[20] This added to the comfort he felt with church leaders who had often gathered around his family's dinner table. His brother, M. Lynn Bennion, had just been appointed supervisor of the church seminary system, and his friend Franklin L. West, a PhD from Chicago, was made commissioner of the CES.

On January 2, 1935, Lowell Bennion left his rented home to walk to the University Ward chapel, where students enrolled for institute classes. On that first day, he recorded sixty-five students and the next day 140 more students. By week's end he had registered "thirty mature students" in the course based on Max Weber, with the daunting title, "Religion and the Rise of our Modern Economic System." Both students and their friends seemed anxious to learn, and Bennion responded by designing more courses and opening up his home to discussion groups. He maintained an open-door policy, a standing invitation for students to drop by at almost anytime. As a student, I remember being puzzled by this. How could such a busy man be always available?[21]

One day I asked him a question: "I have two proposals of marriage. Which should I take?" He looked at me searchingly and replied, "What makes you think you have to choose? You can choose not to choose."[22] His finely-honed Socratic method cut through the false dilemma. Later I realized that this canny response came from his habit of listening to and learning from his students. He knew me well enough to understand that when the right man appeared, I would not be asking advice but informing him of my choice.

Most of his inventions and innovations were responses to student needs. When a student complained, "I am tired of just passing sacrament and ushering. Why don't we do something worthwhile?" Bennion answered, "Meet me Saturday in your work clothes." This was the first of the many service projects performed for the elderly that would become his hallmark. At Christmas time, students serenaded widows and homebound ward members, branched out to hospitals, and subbed for Santa.[23]

Lowell Bennion was troubled when students told him that their professors were casting doubt on the Book of Mormon's historicity. "I didn't have enough background to deal with student questions," he said. So, at his father's suggestion, he took his wife and baby for a summer semester at the University of Washington. He enrolled in anthropology, sociology, and religion classes. After a vigorous semester, he concluded that the Book of Mormon was not a scientific work. "It is not a history nor a geographical treatise.... Rather, it is a profoundly religious record relating religion to life."[24] He abandoned any attempt to "prove" the book through external evidence. From then on he would teach it as a document for the purpose of persuading readers to come to God. He now felt he could present it as an honest, true-to-life experience "concerning our relationship to Jesus Christ."[25]

When a group of returned-missionary students expressed the need for activities to make us "brothers," he invited them to his home to discuss a constitution for a new fraternity. Twenty-six students met in a simple ceremony where they extended the right hand of fellowship, calling themselves Alpha chapter but with no other authority except that of Lowell Bennion. Too many had been stung by Greek fraternities, so they wished to promote LDS intellectuality, fraternity, leadership, and culture.[26] Young women students asked, "Why can't we have a sorority?" and Bennion answered, "You can," so they formed the Omega chapter at his home. Thus, Lambda Delta Sigma, the LDS fraternity, was born. Bennion's friend Obert Tanner manufactured the pin symbolizing membership.[27]

Lowell and Merle Bennion were proud of these laboratories of brotherhood and sisterhood. Bennion observed, "It was a marvelous thing to have these men and women...together in the same organization."[28] And it was marvelous to be part of an increasingly well-educated body of instructors. Bennion's brother Lynn, with a doctorate from the University of California, Berkeley, wrote in his memoirs: "I remember [educators] Daryl Chase, Russell Swenson, Wesley Lloyd, Sidney Sperry, and Antone Cannon were among those who went to the University of Chicago's Divinity School with" the blessing of Apostle Joseph Merrill." He noted that the "idea was...to lead...the finest religious education in America." [29]

But the forces of anti-intellectualism were gathering in the LDS Church. Joseph Fielding Smith, apostle and church historian, censured papers written by two Utah State Agricultural College institute teachers—W. W. Henderson and Heber Snell. Their papers summarized modern criticism's questioning of the literalness of biblical narratives, their authorship, and their traditional dating. Smith charged that reading Old Testament narratives as anything but literal "would weaken students' faith" and "force people to reject all that has come through Joseph Smith."[30] Smith declared that "if the views expressed in the papers by these men...are the views being taught in our Church School system, then I am in favor of closing our schools and seminaries...and for the good of the youth of Zion, the sooner it is done the better."[31] This was one of the first volleys in the conflict between intellectual and literal approaches to teaching Mormon students. Bennion took no position on this but focused on the religious life of the students, avoiding the temptation to become a specialist in a limited area. He shunned the tendency to elaborate on the unknown or "dwell on things which God has only touched on lightly."[32] Instead of having their faith shaken, scholar Laurie DiPadova-Stocks claimed that his students were more insulated from faith upheavals than other faithful Latter-day Saints.[33]

Lynn Bennion and Frank West problem-solved and field-tested lessons for the institutes and seminaries to challenge students to think. They claimed to be "in harmony with a sound philosophy of education which puts the child at the center...and takes into account his interests and needs and guides him toward lofty religious goals."[34] They participated in a two-month CES convention that was meant to showcase the scholarship of its best teachers. The two were shocked when J. Reuben Clark, first counselor to President Heber J. Grant, took the podium and denounced church educators for teaching the philosophies of the world, announcing that institutes and seminaries were "of doubtful procedure" and could be discontinued at any time.[35] Lowell Bennion missed this speech because he was organizing an institute at the University of Arizona, a two-year assignment that he and Merle took on as an adventure.

Back in Utah during the war years, 1941–1943, Bennion found prime teaching opportunities. His intellectual curiosity made him a generalist with a broad background. When he created a class on world religions, he began with Max Weber's theories and then "I got the best books and dug out for myself."[36] After scrutinizing dating habits, he created a curriculum for courtship and marriage classes. In his courses, Bennion was progressive on the subject of birth control. His view that "a woman is not just a machine for turning out children" meshed with President David O. McKay's 1947 declaration that "when the health of the mother demands it, the proper spacing of children may be determined by seeking medical counsel, by compliance with the processes of nature, or by continence."[37] Bennion emphasized family goals based on the sacred and eternal nature of the human personality with the home as its primary institution. He guided his classes through the relative advantages of temple and civil marriages, advantages and disadvantages of large families, and the mutual obligations of parents to children. In making room for religion in the home, he invented a prototype of family home evening.[38]

In 1945 Lowell Bennion sent a carefully worded letter to David O. McKay, then president of the Quorum of the Twelve Apostles, confessing that he was troubled by defending the policy of denying priesthood to worthy black members. He found it difficult telling them that they had been unfaithful in the pre-existence, if there was even a suspicion of a black ancestor. McKay acknowledged the problem and affirmed his hope that African-American men would someday be given the priesthood. Though this was not entirely satisfactory to Bennion, it did offer hope for dialogue. When students raised the issue, Bennion usually responded with "I don't know—I just can't answer that."[39]

The 1950s were a decade that students later called the "heyday" of the institute at the University of Utah. Enrollment increased and the faculty expanded. The organization's goals were clear: "To interact personally with all the students, build safe bridges from the university to the church, and…help students formulate a lasting philosophy of life."[40] Although some of his courses still carried the same titles as in 1940, Bennion updated them to meet contemporary needs. He told students,

> The purpose of life is self-realization and fulfillment for all peo-
> ple ...to achieve quality living, to enlarge our souls, to meet our
> potential.... the purpose of life is within life, not outside it.... The
> Mormon belief in a celestial kingdom is not a "reward."...We should
> not have to sacrifice this life for the next....If there were no life after
> this one, this life would still be worth living. Living the gospel and
> loving others are intrinsically worthwhile, not just stepping-stones
> to a future life.[41]

Bennion believed that intelligence was coeternal with God. God, he
taught, is good, impartial, and not responsible for evil. "God may have to
struggle with and work with nature, as a contractor has to use imperfect
materials....God...has to work with me and He needs my cooperation."[42]

The crowning recognition of his efforts came in 1958 when President
McKay came to the institute and invited him to speak to the priesthood
session of the coming LDS General Conference. The subject, he said,
was "going steady...too much, too soon. They won't listen to old fuddy-
duddies, so I want you to tell them how to date." When Bennion offered
to submit his speech ahead of time, President McKay said, "No. You know
more about it than I do."[43]

In addition to interactions with students, Bennion's influence came
through his many publications. In 1953, he published his most influential church manual, *An Introduction to the Gospel,* used in the Sunday
schools during the decade. His goal was to write so that both the casual
inquirer and educated member could understand. Bennion taught that
"Jesus spoke profound thoughts in simple language."[44] His upbeat manual
for youth, *Goals for Living,* was first published in 1952 and reprinted in
1962. It posed such questions as, "How long has it been since you arose
with a thrill to greet the dawn?" and "When did I last kneel in prayer
overwhelmed with gratitude for the gift of life?"[45] In 1959 CES published
his *Introduction to the Book of Mormon and Its Teachings* and *Religion
and the Pursuit of Truth.*

He wrote scores of articles for church magazines, and CES also published his ideas for missionary work. Bennion struggled against the

tendency, in Eugene England's words, to "pulverize the gospel, to analyze and defend and explain it in small chunks that may...in fact, contradict each other." England continued, Bennion's writings demonstrate the "coherent moral and spiritual force available in Mormon thought."[46]

Bennion's books and articles grew naturally out of his class work and speaking engagements that were grounded in a strong sense of audience. He was much in demand at community and church meetings. He spoke at graduations, BYU gatherings, PTA convocations, and on television. He gave countless funeral sermons where his unsentimental yet comforting theology eased the pain of loss while giving hope for the living.

In his excitement at the ascendency of President McKay, Lowell Bennion failed to give heed to the appointment in 1951 of Ernest L. Wilkinson to the helm of Brigham Young University. Ezra Taft Benson, later secretary of agriculture during the Eisenhower administration, had recommended Wilkinson, a Washington, D.C., attorney without educational experience. Wilkinson immediately made plans to replace LDS institutes with junior colleges and it was not long before the entire CES was brought under his "unification" program.[47]

Wilkinson's agenda for the University of Utah was soon clear: divide and conquer. To facilitate the replacement of institutes with junior colleges that would serve as feeders to Brigham Young University, he advised Bennion to begin sending his students to the church school. He also advised Bennion to obtain permission to offer university credit for institute classes, keep attendance records, and give grades. Wilkinson stressed the need for loyal instructors, and keeping a file on liberal faculty members. He planted student spies in the classes of suspect professors. Wilkinson lost some support, however, when church leaders noticed the price tags on some of his schemes.[48]

When two hundred CES instructors and directors converged at their convention in June 1954, the *Church News* billed it as "graduate courses in religion."[49] Harold B. Lee was in charge of "Advanced Theology" with lectures by J. Reuben Clark, Joseph Fielding Smith, Adam S. Bennion, Marion G. Romney, and Henry D. Moyle—the executive committee of the Mormon Church's board of education. Bennion attended the final session. He heard Apostle Mark E. Petersen defend the priesthood exclusion of blacks: "Is it not a reasonable belief that the Lord would select the choice spirits for the better grades of nations?" Asserting that he knew of "no scripture having to do with the removal of the curse from the Negro," he advised the instructors not to speculate about it.⁵⁰ Lowell Bennion spoke from the floor, thanking Petersen for raising questions and then told of President McKay's interventions that allowed temple marriages with those of suspected mixed ancestry. He asked "If Negroes sinned, what sin could they have committed that a merciful God wouldn't be willing to forgive?"⁵¹

The next morning Lowell Bennion responded to Joseph Fielding Smith's lecture on the age of the Earth. Smith insisted on a figure of six thousand years and concluded with a threat: "If you don't [agree,] you have no business in the church school system."⁵² Bennion spoke from the floor:

> I defend the faith against [principles that contradict basic gospel truths such as] there is no God...or that Christ was not the son of God, or that man is not immortal...but when it comes down to details like the [age of] the earth...[and other questions to which] we don't have the final answer...I try not to agitate the student against science, or to get him to feel he must choose between science and the gospel...I do everything...to help [him] believe in the gospel and respect the scientific method.⁵³

Bennion argued for diversity of thought and knew that Mormon scientists like Henry Eyring and Fred J. Pack disagreed with Smith's view. Apostle Smith replied that he was willing to "leave the age of the Earth alone," but that teachers have an "absolute duty" to teach their students that Adam "was not descended from a monkey."⁵⁴ Although Bennion felt the clouds gathering above his sanctuary, he resolutely concentrated on "the things that mattered most"—walking with students along the paths of learning and faith.

Across the street from the institute, University of Utah President A. Ray Olpin saw opportunity in the growing conflict and met with Lowell

Bennion in the spring of 1961. With the encouragement of President McKay, he told Bennion that he was seeking a new dean, who would offer an open door to students needing mentoring. Bennion was flattered, but responded that he was a "poor administrator" who was hoping for time for "writing and creative activities." Olpin insisted that Bennion "would not be burdened with administrative details" and pressed him to accept. Bennion still hesitated, unwilling to leave his position at the institute.[55]

In 1962, however, Bennion was told that he would be replaced. When informed, Olpin again offered the dean of students position to him with a salary higher than he had received at the institute. But Olpin could not persuade Bennion, who needed time to meet with his family, pray, and meditate. Eventually, Olpin appointed Neal Maxwell with the suggestion that he hire Bennion as assistant dean. Bennion hoped to secure an audience with McKay to discuss the situation. Finally, he received a telephone call from LDS leader Hugh B. Brown, who, in speaking for President McKay, told Bennion that he would be of greater service to the university. In June, Bennion accepted the University of Utah's offer, rather than a number of other church education opportunities that Wilkinson had suggested. Lowell Bennion would come to feel that by refusing to intervene, President McKay had acted to protect his free agency.[56] For the remainder of his life, Bennion expressed only feelings of love, respect, and appreciation for President McKay.[57]

Ernest Wilkinson saw the university's offer to Bennion as a way out of the dilemma. He could now claim that Bennion had accepted a better position. When the word of his removal from the institute surfaced, letters and telephone calls expressing anger and disappointment inundated church leaders. Still, if he was happy about his appointment, Bennion was upset with Wilkinson's press release announcing his departure: "The Institute directorship was left blank when Dr. Bennion resigned to accept a position as assistant dean of students at the University of Utah." Bennion was even more exasperated when Wilkinson requested that he "stop all the rumors" about his removal.[58] Bennion wrote Wilkinson a long letter explaining that he would have preferred to remain at the institute where "I felt I could serve God and man best." He asked Wilkinson to "tell me why I was released and by whom in order to pass on the truth to those who inquire."[59] Apparently, Wilkinson never replied.

Lowell Bennion's friend and neighbor, Obert Tanner, saw the dismissal as an ethical breach:

> The church had a very great man and a very good man, and the church should have been more careful. If you were to ask why Christianity lived, it's because mankind took a good man and nailed him to the cross, put a spear wound in his side, and a crown of thorns on his head—and mankind can't forget it....I'm not criticizing the church. They did what they thought was right. I just think they did wrong.[60]

The stress of that summer of 1962 was relieved one night when Bennion had a powerful dream: "I looked to the foot of the bed—and there was Jesus Christ looking at me and smiling. He held out his arms in blessing, and I felt peace and comfort."[61]

Bennion's continuing faith and activity in the church was puzzling to some, inspiring to others. He said,

> Next to my family [the church] has done the most to shape my life and give me life's values...but I distinguish between gospel and church. The church is the...vehicle to inculcate the gospel into [our] lives.... It is both divine and human. I love my country but not everything it does. I love my...family but I don't agree with all their choices.... The Church can be the church of God and still be imperfect because it consists of men—good men—but of men, including leaders, who are human as well as inspired.[62]

The issue of civil rights remained one of the most agonizing issues facing liberal and believing Mormons. In 1963, Bennion accepted an invitation to debate Chauncey Riddle, a highly regarded BYU professor. The topic was billed as "liberalism vs. conservatism," but the "negro question" became the crux of the discussion. Most people, not understanding

Wilkinson's role in Bennion's departure from the institute, believed that his attitude toward the priesthood ban on black men was the cause of his dismissal. Students and members of the community jammed the Joseph Smith Building auditorium, standing along the sides, filling doorways, and spilling into the hall. Lowell Bennion spoke first: "A society without a good conservative element is not a well-balanced society. The color-giving, life-giving element in our society is the liberal element. The Mormon religion contains both elements. The standard works are conservative, as is the authoritative, bureaucratic structure of our church." The liberal mind, he continued, is unafraid to focus on anything, including religion. "Religion may transcend reason," he suggested. "The liberal person would question anything that contradicted his own experience…and the logic of his experience." [63] Bennion maintained that revelation and intuition should be checked by reason and experience, while reason and experience should be checked by revelation and intuition.

Riddle abruptly asked, "Is it moral to deny the Negro the priesthood?" Bennion responded with another question: "What would you do if you were taught facts contrary to the gospel of Jesus Christ and your inspiration after thoughtful…prayer?" Riddle replied, "If we challenge a revelation on the basis of whether it is moral or not we are on shaky ground."[64]

Bennion's gentle reply: "I am willing to walk by faith in darkness, but when I am called upon to do something that is against…what I think is the heart and soul of the Gospel.…I just can't be happy with the present practice of the church to deny the Negro the priesthood." The audience burst into applause. Riddle then made the familiar argument that "there is a reason for it, we just don't know what it is," and "since only a small segment of the earth's population can have the priesthood, Negroes should be happy with membership only."[65]

Bennion then declared, "I am not fighting the church on this. I love President McKay and I have told him how I feel and he has had me teach for two decades." He concluded, "If it were your child being turned away because of his skin color, how would you feel?" He looked to the large audience: "I have a feeling that God's revelations…depend upon our minds…our eagerness…It may be that the Lord can't get through to us.... Therefore we ought to be searching and praying even over this Negro problem."[66]

Although the audience was divided on the outcome, Bennion was satisfied that he had been able to speak on the priesthood ban in public. He firmly believed that a change was in the offing. In April 1962, he received a call from Hugh B. Brown, second counselor in the LDS Church's First Presidency, assuring him of that. Almost immediately, though, church-owned KSL radio reported that Brown claimed he had been misquoted and Joseph Fielding Smith maintained "Church doctrine does not provide admission...of Negroes to the priesthood in mortality."[67] The ban would remain in place for almost two more decades.

Lowell Bennion would now go on to fulfill the other two segments of his life's work: the Halls of Ivy and the Real World. His longtime friend Boyer Jarvis, executive assistant to President Olpin, was pleased that Bennion's appointment gave him "access to the entire student body in ways he never had before."[68] He met with all students appearing before the Student Behavior Committee, and Olpin handed counseling chores concerning misbehaving student athletes to him. Regarding these duties, Bennion said, "I wasn't there to defend the students regardless of circumstance but to see that justice seasoned with mercy was executed."[69] Dean of Women Virginia Frobes reported that "[Bennion] never gave up on a student...he never saw failure."[70] During the turbulent 1960s when student activism swept a generation, University of Utah President James Fletcher recalled that Bennion was especially helpful in talking to the LDS contingent. In reviewing a document on campus security, Bennion noted, "We need a paragraph reminding officers that college students are not youngsters to be disciplined, but adults. All members of the campus community...should be treated as...self-directing agents."[71] Without requesting the promotion, Lowell Bennion was made full professor in spring 1969. Dean Frobes listed his achievements as "revising and formalizing a new student disciplinary system for the university, bringing together religious leaders, and providing the student with meaningful religious experience."[72] Three years later he was tenured.

Lowell Bennion expressed satisfaction that during the late 1960s and early 1970s, the University of Utah avoided the ugly distrust that shut down universities across the country. He avoided affiliation with groups or movements, listening instead to anyone who wished to talk. In 1972, he headed a committee that drafted a thirty-five-page student code. When it was adopted, it included a student bill of rights modeled after the U.S. Constitution's Bill of Rights. It was not just a list of prohibitions, but emphasized the right of students to appeal. "It was a pioneering effort," said his colleague Ramona Adams, "and schools all over the country asked for copies."[73]

Later in the summer of 1972, Professor of Political Science and the Director of the Hinckley Institute of Politics J. D. Williams asked Bennion to run on the Democratic ticket for the state legislature. Bennion was familiar with the work of the legislature because he had lobbied committees for laws to benefit the delinquent, homeless, and elderly. With Williams's help, he ran a campaign consisting of low-key meetings and a single flyer. The *Deseret News* recorded his promise to "scrutinize every proposal including my own to see whom it will benefit, who it will injure, and is it worth the cost."[74] His chief interests were education and social services, the two most costly functions of state government. When a local leader asked Bennion what he was willing to do for his vote, he replied, "I don't need your vote." He lost, but the 54 to 46 percent margin was the closest a Democrat had ever come to winning that seat. Williams concluded that Bennion could have won if he had had the "necessary fire in the belly."[75]

In 1972, at the age of sixty-four years, Bennion moved from the university to the Community Services Council (CSC) in downtown Salt Lake. This was the final leg of his life journey. As a professor, scholar, and administrator, he had earned the right to retire to his books and garden. But driving him were words from the Bhagavad Gita: "to action alone thou hast a right, not to its fruits."[76] His declining years became his harvesting time, drawing on his skills as humanitarian, mentor, and networker.

The CSC was an umbrella agency that facilitated 140 government and private agencies providing social, health, and recreational assistance.

Bennion's focus was on direct services. He noticed that people in dire straits had "plenty of advocates in the community, but we need people who can deliver a service."[77] His goal was simple: "I went in there with the idea that we could figure out what the problems were and do something about them."[78] He excelled at small group networking, building a diverse team on the council, including attorneys, business leaders, coordinators from the Catholic Church, a member of the Mormon presiding bishopric, and a community-relations coordinator for the Salt Lake School District. He developed or revised the Utah Food Bank, Salt Lake Information and Referral Center, Volunteer Center, Community Helping Community, Ouelessebougou-Utah Alliance, Utah Independent Living Center, and elderly and handicapped services. Bennion also formed Functional Fashions to design clothing with Velcro fastenings and zippers instead of buttons for the physically challenged. Clients experienced the boost in self-esteem that comes from dressing and attending to their hygienic needs themselves. He also focused many programs on the elderly "because they need services and they appreciate them and are not begging for them."[79]

Meanwhile, in 1980 the seventy-two-year-old Lowell Bennion was called as bishop of his East Millcreek Ward in Salt Lake City. In his three years as bishop, he visited everyone in the ward. His counselor reported that "he would just quietly appear on the doorstep with a loaf of bread, sometimes of his own making."[80]

Lowell Bennion retired formally from CSC in the fall of 1988 when he was eighty years old. He retained the title of executive director emeritus, with office space whenever he wished. He was given the Richard D. Bass achievement award, an unrestricted $5,000 grant to recognize his accomplishments. He immediately gave the money to "undisclosed recipients."[81]

Still much in demand, he was asked to serve on the LDS Church's committee on aging, where he promptly suggested programs such as chore service, telephone reassurance, and "befriending." He also proposed that the church select a ward where there are one hundred widows and assign an affluent ward to take care of them. He recommended that LDS meetinghouses provide day care and preschool services. The establishment of the Bennion Community Service Center at the University of Utah now helps new generations of students learn his values by providing an option to engage in service learning activities. Bennion also founded the Teton Valley Boys Ranch, "building self-esteem and forging character in physical achievement."[82]

A few days after their sixty-sixth wedding anniversary in September 1994, Bennion's wife Merle died quietly in her sleep. Lowell Bennion lived two more years in his daughter's basement apartment where he could talk with visitors and occasionally visit "the sick and afflicted." Parkinson's disease took him on February 22, 1996. The main speaker at his large funeral was his neighbor and friend, LDS Church President Gordon B. Hinckley.[83]

Lowell Bennion was an intellectual, but not of the ivory tower. His thoughts were deep, coherent, and unified. His creative mind was focused on service to others, always pointed outward. Mormon students found that the methods of inquiry learned in his classes helped insulate them against the winds of doubt. When a newspaper columnist asked him to choose an epitaph for his tombstone, he replied with one of his favorite scriptures: "What doth the Lord require of thee, but to do justly, and to love mercy, and to walk humbly with thy God."[84]

Lowell Bennion left thirty books and study manuals, more than one hundred essays on topics in sociology, philosophy, ethics, scripture, history, education, and politics. Mormon studies scholar Philip Barlow analyzed his impact: "it is doubtful that more than a handful of modern figures have wielded greater enduring influence on major sectors of Mormondom."[85]

Poet Emma Lou Thayne summed up Bennion's legacy as "the connectedness of a universe [where a] God is as real as [Lowell's] ... garden or his intuitive concern for the well-being of a friend."[86] It may well be that when a complete history of Mormonism is written, the quiet voice of "Brother B." will be heard above the rest.

Lowell Bennion at age twenty, just before his marriage to Merle and his departure for a mission to Germany. Courtesy of Ellen Bennion Stone.

Lowell and Merle in Paris, 1931, after having been separated by his mission for thirty-two months. Courtesy of Ellen Bennion Stone.

Family celebration of Lowell's eightieth birthday and Merle and Lowell's sixtieth wedding anniversary. Children, left to right: Ellen Bennion Stone, Lowell C. (Ben) Bennion, Douglas C. Bennion, Steven D. Bennion, and Howard W. Bennion. Seated: Merle and Lowell Bennion. Courtesy of Ellen Bennion Stone.

Lowell Bennion as professor of sociology and associate dean of students at the University of Utah, circa 1970. Courtesy of Ellen Bennion Stone.

Lowell Bennion at his Teton Boy's Ranch, circa 1968. Courtesy of Ellen Bennion Stone.

NOTES

1. Resolution of the Senate, Utah State Legislature, Febreary 10, 1992.
2. Ibid.
3. Eugene L. England, ed., *The Best of Lowell L. Bennion: Selected Writings, 1928–1988* (Salt Lake City: Deseret Book, 1988), xiv.
4. Eugene L. England, "The Legacy of Lowell L. Bennion," *Sunstone* 103 (September, 1996): 27
5. Ibid.
6. Eugene L. England, "The Achievement of Lowell Bennion," *Sunstone* 11 (July, 1988): 25
7. Mary Lythgoe Bradford, *Lowell L. Bennion: Teacher, Counselor, Humanitarian* (Salt Lake City: Dialogue Foundation, 1995), 52.
8. Ibid., 52–53.
9. Laurie Newman DiPadova-Stocks, "Lesson for Today from Lowell Bennion's Journey with Max Weber," *Sunstone* 159 (June, 2010): 57.
10. Laurie Newman DiPadova and Ralph S. Brower, "A Piece of Lost History: Max Weber and Lowell L. Bennion," *The American Sociologist* 23 (Spetember 1992), 49.
11. Ibid.
12. Lowell L. Bennion, *Religion and the Pursuit of Truth* (Salt Lake City: Deseret Book, 1959), iii.
13. Lowell Bennion, "Memories," 43. Copy in the author's possession.
14. Glenn Schwendiman, class notes for "The Place of Religion in One's Philosophy of Life," taught by Lowell Bennion, March 25, 1935, LDS Institute of Religion, University of Utah. Copy in the author's possession.
15. Lowell Bennion, "How Shall We Judge One Religion as 'Better' Than Another?" address to Humanities-Social Sciences seminar, University of Utah, February 7, 1956. 8. Copy in the author's possession.
16. Bradford, *Lowell L. Bennion*, 108–9.
17. Peggy Fletcher Stack, "A Saint for All Seasons: An Interview with Lowell L. Bennion," *Sunstone* 46 (Feb., 1985), 7.
18. Douglas D. Alder, "Lowell L. Bennion: The Things That Matter Most," in *Teachers Who Touch Lives: Methods of the Masters*, ed. Philip Barlow (Bountiful, UT: Horizon Publishers, 1988), 27.
19. Milton Bennion to Lowell L. Bennion, September 14, 1937. Copy in the author's possession.
20. Lowell Bennion, "Memories," 43, quoted in Bradford, *Lowell L. Bennion*, 65.
21. Bradford, *Lowell L. Bennion*, 66.

22. Ibid., 117.

23. Ibid., 110–11.

24. Lowell L. Bennion, "I Gained New Light on Christ's Relationship to Our Sins," in *Converted to Christ through the Book of Mormon*, ed. Eugene L. England (Salt Lake City: Deseret Book, 1989), 158.

25. Ibid.

26. "Institute Record," October 11, 1936, 66.

27. Lambda Delta Sigma Notes, December 1936–May 1941, Lambda Delta Sigma Minutes, LDS Institute of Religion, Salt Lake City. Copy in the author's possession. Bradford, *Lowell L. Bennion*, 73.

28. Lowell L. Bennion, "Oral History," 89, quoted in Bradford, *Lowell L. Bennion*, 73.

29. Glenn Schwendiman to Mary Bradford, May 18, 1988.

30. Joseph Fielding Smith to Franklin L. West, March 11, 1937, Sterling M. McMurrin Papers, Special Collections, J. Willard, Marriott Library, University of Utah, Salt Lake City.

31. Ibid.

32. Bennion, "Memories," 44.

33. DiPadova-Stocks, "Lessons for Today," 57.

34. Milton Lynn Bennion, *Recollections of a School Man: The Autobiography of M. Lynn Bennion* (Salt Lake City: Western Epics, 1987), 101.

35. Gary Bergera and Ronald Priddis, *Brigham Young University: A House of Faith* (Salt Lake City: Signature Books, 1987), 61.

36. Bennion, "Oral History," 93, quoted in Bradford, *Lowell L. Bennion*, 90.

37. Class notes of Mary L. Bradford, "Courtship and Marriage," February 13, 1952; Lester Bush, "Birth Control among the Mormons: Introduction to a Persistent Question," *Dialogue: A Journal of Mormon Thought* 10 (Autumn, 1976): 25.

38. Bradford, *Lowell L. Bennion*, 112–15

39. Quoted in Bradford, *Lowell L. Bennion*, 93–94.

40. Bennion, "Oral History," 105, quoted in Bradford, *Lowell L. Bennion*, 107.

41. Quoted in Bradford, *Lowell L. Bennion*, 113.

42. Lowell Bennion class, notes kept by Louis and Mavonne Moench. Copy in author's possession.

43. Bennion, "Oral History," 126, Quoted in Bradford, *Lowell L. Bennion*, 117–18.

44. Bennion, "Oral History," 141, Quoted in Bradford, *Lowell L. Bennion*, 118.

45. Lowell L. Bennion, *Goals for Living* (Salt Lake City: 1953), 14–15.

46. England, *Best of Lowell L. Bennion*, xxiii.

47. Bradford, *Lowell L. Bennion*, 130.

48. Ibid., 130–31.

49. "Elder Lee Conducts Course for Teachers," *Church News*, June 24,1954.

50. Mark Petersen, "Race Problems—As they Affect the Church," in "Compilation on the Negro in Mormonism," comp. Lester Bush, bound typescript, 1970. Copy in the author's possession.

51. Quoted in Bradford, *Lowell L. Bennion*, 132.

52. Joseph Fielding Smith, "The Origin of Man," August 28, 1954, copy in the author's possession. See also, *Church News,* July 31 and August 21, 1954.

53. Quoted in Bradford, *Lowell L. Bennion*, 133.

54. Ibid., 134.

55. A. Ray Olpin, "Diary," June 30, 1961, Olpin Collection, Presidential Papers, University of Utah Archives; Bradford, *Lowell L. Bennion*, 140–42.

56. Bradford, *Lowell L. Bennion*, 163.

57. Ibid., 143–45.

58. "Dr. J. J. Christensen Gets Institute Post," *Deseret News*, August 5, 1962; "New Director Named for U. of U. Institute of Religion," *Church News*, August 11, 1962.

59. Lowell L. Bennion to Ernest Wilkinson, August 20, 1962. Copy in the author's possession.

60. Obert C. Tanner, interviewed by Mary Bradford, May 10, 1988.

61. Lowell L. Bennion, conversation with Mary Bradford, September 19, 1988.

62. Bennion, "Memories," 64.

63. "The Liberal and Conservative View in Mormonism, Dr. Lowell L. Bennion and Dr. Chauncy Riddle," March 28, 1963, typescript. Copy in the author's possession; Bradford, *Lowell L. Bennion*, 245–50.

64. Ibid.

65. Ibid.

66. Ibid.

67. Lester Bush, "Negro in Mormonism," 176, typescript. Copy in the author's possession.

68. Boyer and Pat Jarvis, interviewed by Mary L. Bradford, July 15, 1987.

69. Bennion, "Oral History," 157–58; Bradford, *Lowell L. Bennion*, 224–25.

70. Bennion, "Oral History," 159.

71. Lowell L. Bennion to campus security, January 20, 1965. Copy in the author's possession.

72. William F. Prokasy to Thomas C. King, February 5, 1969, University of Utah Archives; Bradford, *Lowell L. Bennion*, 231.

73. Ramona B. Adams, interviewed by Mary L. Bradford, February 12, 1988.

74. "House District 17, Lowell L. Bennion, Democrat," *Deseret News*, October 24, 1972.
75. J. D. Williams, interview by Mary L. Bradford, February 18, 1988.
76. Quoted in Bradford, *Lowell L. Bennion*, 265.
77. Bennion, "Oral History," 4.
78. Ibid., 8.
79. Ibid., 2.
80. Kent Murdock, interviewed by Mary L. Bradford, May 9, 1988.
81. Bradford, *Lowell L. Bennion*, 279.
82. Ibid., 212.
83. Ibid., 355.
84. Dennis L. Lythgoe, "Epitaphs," *Deseret News*, January 1, 1993.
85. Quoted in Bradford, *Lowell L. Bennion*, 332.
86. Emma Lou Thayne, Foreword to Bradford, *Lowell L. Bennion*, viii.

10

LOWELL BENNION, RACE, AND JUSTICE

GREGORY A. PRINCE

No subject caused the Mormon Church more internal division and external derision during the twentieth century than its policy of excluding
men of black African lineage from ordination to its lay priesthood. Initiated by Brigham Young in the context of racist pre–Civil War American
society,[1] the ban became increasingly problematic as church proselytizing activities encountered mixed-race populations, particularly in South
Africa and Brazil, and as the civil rights movement within the United
States became increasingly vocal in condemning the policy and staging
protests against the church and Brigham Young University.

Shortly after David O. McKay became president of the LDS Church in
1951, he traveled to South Africa to see, firsthand, the detrimental effect
that the exclusionary policy was having on the church in that country. The
experience was consciousness altering for him. He made an important
and unplanned procedural change while addressing the missionaries, and
shortly after returning home began to challenge the policy itself.

Lowell Bennion met McKay upon embarking on a career as a teacher
in the church's Institute of Religion program in the mid-1930s. The
exclusionary policy was the basis of other intersections of the two men,
first a decade and then two decades later. Both men hoped for change.
Bennion assumed that it would change in the immediate future, while
McKay privately believed that one missing piece separated him from

changing it, a piece that he never found. Although the policy was not abolished until nearly a decade after McKay's death, Bennion was the means through which McKay made an important symbolic gesture that nibbled at its periphery.

Two Men of Like Minds

Bennion served an LDS proselytizing mission to Germany and then stayed in Europe and earned a PhD in sociology from the University of Strasbourg in 1933.

Returning to Salt Lake City, he became the founding director of the LDS Institute of Religion at the University of Utah in 1935, a decade after the first such institute was established at the University of Idaho. McKay, who the year prior had entered the LDS First Presidency as second counselor to President Heber J. Grant, was an educator by profession and earlier had served as church commissioner of education. He invited Bennion to his office for an informal chat about the new institute position, and signaled him to express his opinions, rather than merely parrot the institutional church.

Bennion, with McKay's encouragement, became an outspoken proponent of personal and institutional morality, even when his views clashed with professional and ecclesiastical superiors. McKay implicitly endorsed Bennion's worldview, even when it differed from his, by occasionally consulting with him—consultations that were noted by others. In an oral history, Bennion reminisced that, "Over a period of about thirty years while engaged in teaching religion to LDS college youth, I was privileged either at his invitation or my request to have a half-dozen conversations with him about questions critical to me at the time." Bennion well remembered McKay's advice: "Be true to yourself and loyal to the Gospel of Jesus Christ and whatever else you do will be all right." Bennion broached thorny questions about evolution and family planning. "What shall I teach," I asked, "in these areas?" McKay replied, "What is your belief?" McKay then "gave me the feeling that we were thinking together, that he was incorporating my reflections into his own."[2] One of Bennion's institute colleagues, who moved from the professional to the ecclesiastical ranks, observed, "Lowell was as close, in the fifties, to David O. McKay as any outsider ever was."[3]

Apostolic Racism

Although the exclusionary policy was a century old by the early 1950s, many church members and most outsiders were not aware of its existence, for it blended seamlessly with a culture that viewed racism as an acceptable status quo. The year 1954 was transformational, bringing both national and church-specific challenges to that status quo.

On May 17, the United States Supreme Court ruled unanimously in favor of named plaintiff Oliver L. Brown, who three years earlier had filed a lawsuit against the board of education of Topeka, Kansas, challenging its policy of school segregation. *Brown v. Board of Education* was a milestone in the struggle for civil rights in the United States—and a threat to the established order within the LDS Church.

Earlier that year, McKay had traveled to South Africa, becoming the first general officer of the church to visit that country. Having seen, from a distance, the disruptive effect of a church policy that required a man to trace his ancestral lines to Europe prior to qualifying for priesthood ordination, he made the trip "to observe conditions as they are." Speaking to a conference of missionaries, he addressed the issue of the priesthood ban head-on, apparently for the first time in a public setting. He told the missionaries that he had first encountered the issue in Hawaii in 1921. A black man had married a Polynesian woman who was a member of the church. All of their children were "active and worthy." He continued, "My sympathies were so aroused that I wrote home to President Grant asking if he would please make an exception so we could ordain that man to the Priesthood." President Grant answered, "David, I am as sympathetic as you are, but until the Lord gives us a revelation regarding that matter, we shall have to maintain the policy of the Church."[4]

While acknowledging that the force of revelation was required to eliminate the ban, McKay softened its boundary by reversing the policy requiring the tracing of ancestral lines: "Unless there is evidence of Negro blood you need not compel a man to prove that he has none in his veins."[5]

Upon returning to Utah, McKay charged a committee within the Quorum of the Twelve Apostles to examine, in detail, the history of the priesthood ban. On May 17, the same day the verdict in *Brown v. Board of Education* was announced, a colleague wrote to Apostle Adam Bennion, a member of the committee, "You indicated that the Church leadership is even now undertaking a careful reevaluation of our doctrine in this respect."[6] The reevaluation prompted McKay to do what none of his predecessors is known to have done: challenge the policy by taking it to the source. Future Church Historian Leonard Arrington noted in his autobiography, "I knew something about the apostolic study because I heard Adam S. Bennion, who was a member of the committee, refer to the work in an informal talk he made to the Mormon Seminar in Salt Lake City on May 13, 1954. McKay, Bennion said, had pled with the Lord without result and finally concluded the time was not yet ripe."[7]

McKay's colleagues in the hierarchy were not uniformly of the same progressive bent. Apostle Mark E. Petersen soon gave a lecture to Mormon educators, Lowell Bennion being among them, that sought to shore up traditional—and racist—arguments on which the exclusionary policy rested. The lecture should be viewed not only in the context of earlier events in South Africa, Salt Lake City, and the United States Supreme Court, but also in light of the fact that among the listeners was Joseph Fielding Smith, who succeeded McKay as church president in 1970 and whose own speeches and writings unapologetically defended the policy. Speaking to some two hundred CES instructors and directors, Petersen held forth for over two hours on the spiritual inferiority that he insisted was inherent in black Africans and their descendants.

He first made an assumption that was supported neither by scripture nor by any natural evidence: "Is there any reason to think that the same principle of rewards and punishments did not apply to us and our deeds in the pre-existent world as will apply hereafter?" He then denigrated "the children of God in darkest Africa" both by assuming that they were cursed to have been born there, and that since God "is not a respecter of persons," they got what they deserved.

Moving to the subject of priesthood, he invoked the common, though scripturally unjustified (and subsequently debunked by modern LDS Church leaders) "curse of Cain," which not only explained the policy of excluding them from the priesthood, but also justified ancient and modern racial segregation. After all, he said, "[God] segregated them."

Denying that LDS policy revealed any prejudice, he added insult to injury by allowing that if a black person accepted Mormonism—not a likely event at the time— and lived a righteous life, he might enter the Celestial Kingdom—the highest of three, in LDS theology—but "he will go there as a servant." There was no ambiguity in Petersen's theology; indeed, his word was final: "I know of no scripture having to do with the removal of the curse from the Negro."

He concluded with yet another insult and then a reinforcement of the righteousness of racial segregation. Beginning with a racial slur—"I would be willing to let every Negro drive a Cadillac if they could afford it"—he invoked God's will to justify continuing racial segregation, in words on a par with those of southern segregationists: "I think the Lord segregated the Negro and who is man to change that segregation? It reminds me of the scripture on marriage, 'what God hath joined together, let not man put asunder.' Only here we have the reverse of the thing—what God hath separated, let not man bring together again."[8]

Lowell Bennion's sensitivity about the policy had been raised a short time earlier by an incident that occurred at the Institute of Religion:

> A boy came to me after Sunday School at the Institute with tears in his eyes. A freshman. He said, "They asked me to pass the sacrament today and I couldn't." I said, "Why not? Are you a member of the Church?" He said, "Yes." "Do you hold the Priesthood?" "No." I said, "Why not?" He said, "Well it's believed in our town that my grandmother in South Carolina had black blood, Negro blood, so my brothers and I have been denied the Priesthood. My older

brother has quit the Church and gone away angry. I was President of the Seminary class last year and I didn't miss MIA or Sacrament Meeting." I said, "Why have you stayed in the Church?" He said, "My mother asked me to and I love her."[9]

So it was against the backdrop of that incident that, at the conclusion of Petersen's remarks, Bennion raised his hand and challenged his assertions. He cited several conversations that he had had in the course of his work at the Institute of Religion, among them with the same student who had said, "'If the Negroes sinned, what sin could they commit for which a merciful God'—as you speak of, Brother Petersen—'would not be willing to forgive, if they repented…with a contrite heart and a broken spirit?'"[10] The following day his colleague at the institute, T. Edgar Lyon, wrote Bennion a note of gratitude for his courage in confronting openly a senior ecclesiastical leader: "Your words fell like manna from heaven on a starving people…." He continued, "You said everything that I had thought, but said it ten time[s] more pointedly and in a nicer spirit than I could have….Others there felt the same way, but none had courage to speak out as you did."[11]

The day after Petersen's lecture, Joseph Fielding Smith gave a two-hour lecture that focused on his newly published book, *Man, His Origin and Destiny*, which was a scathing and unscientific attack on biological evolution. He also endorsed Petersen's statements on race. Once again, Bennion voiced his opposition to an apostle's views.

A short time later, Smith and Petersen invited Bennion and Lyon to meet. "[Smith] called us in to…try to convince us that his position was right. He didn't succeed."[12] Not satisfied with the meeting, Bennion and Lyon, along with fellow institute instructor George Boyd, made an appointment to see Church President David O. McKay. McKay reassured the men that although Smith sat in a high church position as president of the Quorum of the Twelve Apostles—and thus McKay's successor—his teachings and writings on the subject of evolution "did not represent the position of the Church."[13]

McKay elected not to discuss the issue of race and priesthood at the meeting. Had he done so, it is likely that subsequent misunderstandings

and conflicts that directly affected Bennion would have been circumvented. That McKay's views on the issue differed from those of
Smith and Petersen is clear in retrospect, for several months earlier,
and shortly after returning from South Africa, McKay had visited privately with Sterling McMurrin, whose church membership was in peril
because of his unorthodox views on evolution and race. McKay reassured McMurrin that he had every right to hold those views without
placing his membership at risk, and then surprised him by saying that
he accepted biological evolution, and that he viewed the priesthood ban
as a policy, not a fixed doctrine, and one that would eventually change.
McMurrin considered the meeting confidential, however, and did not
discuss McKay's views on the ban for another fourteen years, either
publicly or privately.[14]

Pushing the Envelope

Three years after Bennion's encounter with the college freshman who was
not allowed to pass the sacrament, the same student returned to his office
with a related dilemma. "He said his younger sister, whom I had met,
wanted to be married in the temple in June, and he was going to see what
he could do to bring it to pass," remembered Bennion. He had appealed to
the Quorum of the Twelve, but hardliners in that body refused, invoking
the policy that a "single drop" of Negro blood disqualified a male from the
priesthood, and both a male and a female from marriage in the temple.

In desperation, only three days prior to the scheduled wedding, the
student called Bennion, who responded, "Let me see what I can do." He
immediately went to work, leveraging his close relationship to Hugh B.
Brown, first counselor in the First Presidency, to obtain an appointment
early the following morning with McKay. He explained the situation to
McKay and remarked: "In my experience the gospel builds life. Here I see
it tearing it apart, tearing it down." McKay was sympathetic and replied,
"When problems like this come to me I say to myself, 'Sometime I shall
meet my Father-in-Heaven and what will he say?'" Bennion answered,
"He'll forgive you if you err on the side of mercy." McKay wondered if it

was too late to act. When Bennion mentioned that there was still time, McKay was determined: "Leave it to me."[15]

Thus began a flurry of activity on the part of McKay, just one day prior to the appointed day of the wedding. In a single day the president of the church made phone calls to Marion Romney of the Quorum of the Twelve Apostles; Arthur Brown, the couple's former stake president; Lowell Bennion; Paul Anderson, the groom-to-be; and A. Ray Olpin, the couple's stake president. McKay's diary distilled the content of those phone conversations. "[Dr. Bennion] came in the interest of Paul Anderson and Joyce Marshall, a young couple who wish to be married in the Temple, but the young lady has been unable to obtain a recommend as it is rumored that she has negro blood in her veins." Upon checking with local ecclesiastical leaders, however, he concluded that there was no evidence to substantiate the rumor. Although the rumor had been sufficient rationale for members of the Quorum of the Twelve Apostles to refuse authorization of the temple marriage—"guilty until proven innocent"—McKay concluded the opposite. In a final phone call to the stake president he said, "All that you have and that the others have is hearsay. So if they are otherwise worthy, you may inform the Bishop to issue a recommend to this young couple."[16]

The marriage proceeded on schedule, and two weeks later Bennion wrote to McKay, "Last Sunday, Eldon Marshall from Fillmore called to see us and we received a full account of the marriage of his sister, Joyce, and Paul Anderson, in the temple. His mother, who has weathered the strain of ostracism alone these many years, was privileged to accompany them."[17]

The Marshall case was the first of several instances where the policy regarding blacks and ordination was temporarily set aside while individuals were given the benefit of the doubt. Sterling McMurrin recalled, "There were two instances very similar, of cases that Lowell took to President McKay, and President McKay saw to it, personally, that these people were admitted to the temple, in connection with the marriages."[18] And John Vandenberg, a general authority who frequently sat in on meetings where such matters were discussed, recalled, "President McKay would always say, 'Well, if we don't know, give him the benefit of the doubt and go ahead and ordain him.'"[19]

Challenging the Policy Directly

Bennion's aversion to the policy was founded in two considerations, one theoretical and one practical. On the theoretical side, he questioned and then rejected the predominant rationale that supported the policy, which essentially was that since God is just, and since black Africans and their descendants occupied an inferior status on earth, the only way to justify that status was to infer that their actions in a premortal existence were to blame.

While it is not clear when Bennion first questioned the theological basis of the policy, by the late 1940s his thinking on the subject was advanced enough that he wrote an article, entitled "Race," that included this statement: "Having read the first five books of the Bible.... I can find absolutely nothing that pertains to race directly.... Most people fall for this because it sounds good and appeals to their imagination. But, as an argument, it has no foundation and should not be used."[20] Indeed, the argument lacked foundation because it followed, rather than preceded the policy. In other words, Brigham Young initiated the policy in the late 1840s in the midst of a racist, pre–Civil War environment that did not call for a theological explanation.[21] Only upon subsequent reflection did church leaders, including Young, construct a scaffolding to support it. By cherry-picking the biblical and Latter-day Saint canon, the leaders pieced together a porous argument that was sufficient to satisfy uncritical church members, but that failed under critical examination.

Although Bennion never published his article on race, he occasionally made his viewpoints clear in public settings. One such setting was in Logan, Utah, in the 1950s, and it involved a debate between Bennion and Jerome Stoffel, a Roman Catholic priest who was the director of the Newman Center at Utah State University. One of Bennion's institute colleagues recalled the debate:

> Stoffel said that he couldn't call Mormons prejudiced based on their doctrine, because they believed priesthood denial was based on

something that blacks did in the pre-earth life. Lowell really got after him for saying that, and said that we didn't know, or didn't have a doctrine that it was because of something that they did in a pre-earth life. I was a little surprised to hear that. I thought that maybe Lowell would be pleased that Stoffel would have, in a sense, kind of supported it. I always remembered that, and thought that if Bennion, as smart as he was, wasn't sure, then we had better be a little careful on some of those things. [22]

Bennion also realized that there were limits to what he, as a church employee, could say publicly to challenge the policy. One of his students in the 1950s recalled that rather than making the policy a matter of public confrontation, he "dealt with the dilemma mainly by loving black people and keeping up a dialogue with black leaders."[23] Nonetheless, Bennion was vocal enough to provoke Ernest L. Wilkinson, who was not only the president of Brigham Young University, but also chancellor of the CES, and thus Bennion's boss. In a 1962 letter to David O. McKay, Wilkinson voiced his frustration with what he viewed as Bennion's intransigence. He complained that Bennion had declared being unable "to give a satisfactory explanation for the failure of the Church to allow the negro to receive the priesthood…[and] he has taught that the time would soon come when the Church would give the priesthood to the negro and that the policy of denying them the priesthood was unfair and not in accordance with the justice of god." Wilkinson mentioned that he counseled Bennion: "I told him that he ought to be able to justify the failure to give the priesthood to the negro by taking into account the conduct of the negroes in the pre-existence, but it was apparent to me that he does not quite accept this explanation."[24]

Paired with Bennion's rejection of the theological support for the policy was an abiding concern with the policy's practical consequences. One colleague noted, "Lowell Bennion was right when he said, 'I really believe more in helping the people over here than the dead,'"[25] and he saw the policy hurting, rather than helping people.

In the 1950s the primary detrimental effect of the policy was internal, with the Marshall family being a case in point. But as the civil rights movement developed in the early 1960s, the damage became institutional as well. A dramatic example was the collapse of the Nigerian Mission.

Given the racial demographic of the country—well over 95 percent black—Nigeria would have been one of the least likely places in the world for the Mormon Church to establish itself in the pre-1978 era. However, in the late 1950s a request made to the church by Nigerian citizen Honesty John Ekong for literature led to the "self-conversion" of thousands of Nigerians.[26] Repeated requests to church headquarters for formal inclusion of these people led to several fact-finding visits to Nigeria, to discussions within the First Presidency and Quorum of the Twelve Apostles, and ultimately to a decision to open a proselytizing mission in the country, in spite of the obvious logistical challenges of operating an all-lay church without a local lay priesthood. Late in 1962, LaMar Williams was formally called as president of the Nigerian Mission, and in January 1963 the church issued a press release announcing the opening of the mission.

Only two months later, and before Williams and several missionaries received permission from the Nigerian government to begin proselytizing activities, a Nigerian student, Ambrose Chukwuo, who was enrolled at California State Polytechnic College in San Luis Obispo, wrote a scathing denunciation of the church's priesthood ban that was published in the *Nigerian Outlook*, a newspaper in Enugo, Nigeria. In spite of a flurry of activity at church headquarters to control the damage, fallout in Nigeria was sufficiently severe that plans for the mission were shelved for another fifteen years. Bennion conveyed his reaction to the news in a letter to fellow institute instructor George Boyd: "[I] blush in shame and anger to read it. We have sown the wind and are reaping the whirlwind."[27]

Coincident with the Nigerian problem was one at home, in the form of a threat by the NAACP to picket the church's October General Conference unless it issued an official statement supportive of civil rights. Despite reticence by Church President David O. McKay, Hugh

B. Brown, a counselor to McKay, called upon Sterling McMurrin, a lapsed and yet sympathetic church member with strong ties to the local NAACP chapter, to draft a statement. While McKay would not consent to it being represented as an official First Presidency statement, Brown's presentation said differently. McMurrin recalled, "He read it at the beginning of his sermon very much as if he were reading a separate official statement from the First Presidency. Then he set it aside and proceeded with his own address. It was most effective."[28] While the statement headed off threatened picketing, Bennion saw it as largely cosmetic. To George Boyd he addressed his concern: "Our discrimination in regard to the priesthood cuts too deeply into self-respect to be accepted by the Negroes here or nationally."[29]

Two years later, in October 1965, Bennion published an article that was implicitly critical of the priesthood policy and that was all the more remarkable for having been published in one of the church's magazines, *The Instructor*. While not addressing the policy directly, he lashed out at practices of any origin whose effect was to posit racial superiority. He observed that the "biggest problem" in the world is "the need of men of all races, cultures, and societies to feel their own worth and dignity as human beings. Man has a long and shameful history of subjugating and humiliating his fellowman for economic, political, religious, racial, or other reasons." This must end, he declared: "We are all children of the same earth and of the same Creator. God loves one as He does another. Can we do less?"[30]

Three years later, in a written critique of a book chapter, Bennion made his strongest statement in condemning the policy, and apparently for the first time advocated openly for it to end. Calling this "the most critical social issue facing the Mormon Church today," he blamed it for increasing racial prejudice among church members, called it a practice, and not a doctrine, and asserted that "no new revelation is needed to change doctrine; there need only be a change of practice."[31]

There is no evidence that Bennion ever pleaded his case directly to McKay. However, McKay's counselor, Hugh B. Brown, was clearly a thought partner of Bennion regarding the policy. In April 1962, shortly before the church's annual General Conference, Brown telephoned Bennion and assured him that a change in the policy was imminent, but no change occurred.[32] The following year, Brown went public in an interview with Wallace Turner that was the basis of a *New York Times* article: "We are in the middle of a survey looking toward the possibility of admitting Negroes.... The whole problem...is being considered by the leaders of the church in the light of racial relationships everywhere."[33] Other church leaders quickly walked back Brown's assertions, but Brown did not give up. In the late 1960s, after first learning of McKay's 1954 conversation with Sterling McMurrin, in which McKay said that the policy was not doctrinal and would eventually change, Brown tried to change it by an end run while McKay was incapacitated, and while Harold B. Lee, a senior apostle and perhaps the staunchest defender of the priesthood ban, was out of town. Brown later told his grandson that his actions were the cause for his being released from the First Presidency upon the death of McKay—the first time a sitting counselor had been released since the death of Brigham Young in 1877.[34] His champion on the subject thwarted, Bennion retreated publicly on the issue.

Paying the Price

Bennion's views on the priesthood ban were not the only source of friction with Ernest Wilkinson, but they were significant. His open challenge of Apostle Mark Petersen's racist remarks in 1954 was a breach of the normal deference paid to church leaders, and the presence of senior apostle and future Church President Joseph Fielding Smith, combined with the fact that the meeting occurred on Wilkinson's BYU campus, left a bad taste in Wilkinson's mouth. Bennion's subsequent meetings with Apostles Smith and Petersen, and then with David O. McKay, were also problematic with Wilkinson, for they circumvented normal chain-of-command protocol. Shortly after the McKay meeting, Wilkinson dispatched a lieutenant to meet with Bennion, George Boyd, and T. Edgar Lyon, "apparently to scold us for going directly to President McKay instead of going through channels—himself and the executive committee."[35]

Bennion's continuing, indirect challenges to the policy were also a source of irritation to Wilkinson. The aforementioned case of Joyce Marshall was not the only instance in which Bennion went to the church president and succeeded in nibbling at the periphery of the policy.[36] Indeed, Wilkinson's previously cited, 1962 letter to McKay complained in detail about Bennion's continuing resistance to the policy. The letter was one of the final moves in Wilkinson's long-term effort to remove Bennion from his position as founding director of the LDS Institute of Religion at the University of Utah. At one point Wilkinson worked behind the scenes to engineer a transition from the institute to a faculty position at the university. Sterling McMurrin was involved in the matter and recalled the details: "I used to be Dean of Letters and Science at the University. I offered him a position as Professor of Sociology. He didn't want to go to the University, he wanted to stay where he was. He liked working with the Church, and he liked personal counseling with the students."[37]

Wilkinson persisted in his efforts to remove Bennion from the institute. On June 12, 1962, one month prior to his letter complaining about Bennion's intransigence concerning the priesthood ban, he met with McKay and suggested two options regarding Bennion's future. These Wilkinson outlined as a potential position in the Dean of Students office at the University of Utah, or an assignment the next year writing textbooks for church schools. McKay asked Wilkinson to submit in writing a detailed outline of the latter task.[38]

Bennion, who had perhaps as much access to McKay as anyone at his church level, once again appealed to him in an attempt to retain his position at the institute. This time, however, his appeal failed. Sterling McMurrin recounted the sad episode. University officials offered Bennion a position with the Dean of Students office, "But he didn't want to leave the Institute. Wilkinson told him he had a choice of getting out or coming to BYU and teaching. He didn't want to go down there." Bennion then conferred with President [Hugh B.] Brown. Brown was "sympathetic" and went to McKay, who invited Bennion to visit him. President McKay, supporting Wilkinson and attempting to ease the hurt, counseled Bennion, "If you've had a good offer of that position at the University, my advice to you is that you should take it." This greatly disappointed Lowell Bennion. "He had supposed that President McKay would come out and say, 'Look, if you want to be in that Institute, you're going to be there,' and he'd tell Wilkinson to lay off. But he didn't. Well, it was a gain for the University," McMurrin said. [39]

Indeed, it was a gain for the university. But Bennion's heart never left the LDS Institute of Religion. George Boyd, who had served with Bennion at the institute and who was also removed from his position by Wilkinson, recalled Bennion's state of mind: "He wanted to stay with the Institute. Finally, he went to the university, but he was never happy over there." Regarding McKay, he remarked, he "was getting old and weary, and didn't want to continue the battle."[40]

The Revelation

Bennion's activism on racial issues in the church bore some fruits. To his students and some colleagues he imbued a philosophy of toler-ance, acceptance, and love. On one notable occasion his intervention with Church President David O. McKay salvaged a marriage and likely kept an extended family within the church. The incident, in turn, showcased a notable aspect of McKay's persona when he stated that he was willing to defend before the Lord an action that went contrary to the opinions of his colleagues.

But as much as Bennion wished to have the discriminatory policy on ordination reversed, and as much as he acted to effect such a rever-sal, the policy stood unchanged for nearly a decade after McKay's death. Neither Bennion nor McKay's closest associates in the church hierar-chy understood why McKay did not move on the policy. Perhaps, it was because he never articulated fully to them his bedrock belief that only a revelation could change it. And even though on multiple occasions he sought such a revelation, a fact that not even his counselors knew, he never received it.

Sixteen years after Bennion's forced departure from the Institute of Religion, he received a phone call from his neighbor, Stuart Poelman, informing him that the First Presidency and Quorum of the Twelve Apostles had just announced the lifting of the ban on priesthood ordination of black males. Bennion's son recalled, "He was thrilled about the black revelation. Dad was not an emotional man, but that was [one] time there was emotion in his voice."⁴¹ When approached by Mary Bradford, the editor of *Dialogue: A Journal of Mormon Thought* and his subsequent biographer, with a request that he record for publication his feelings about the revelation, he gently declined. "Let's just be happy and go on."⁴²

NOTES

1. In December 2013, the church broke new ground by acknowledging on its website both the post–Joseph Smith origin of the policy and the racism that underlay it. Church of Jesus Christ of Latter-day Saints, "Race and the Priesthood," https://www.lds.org/topics/race-and-the-priesthood?lang=eng (accessed December 9, 2014).

2. Lowell L. Bennion, "My Memories of President David O. McKay," *Dialogue: A Journal of Mormon Thought* 4 (Winter, 1969:, 47–48.

3. Paul H. Dunn, interviewed by Gregory A. Prince, June 5,1995.

4. "Minutes of a Special Meeting by President David O. McKay, 17th January, 1954," in David O. McKay, "Diaries," January, 1954. David O. McKay Papers, accession 668, Special Collections, J. Willard Marriott Library, University of Utah, Salt Lake City.

5. Ibid. McKay's engagement with the exclusionary policy, and with civil rights in general, is treated in detail in Gregory A. Prince and William. Robert Wright, *David O. McKay and the Rise of Modern Mormonism* (Salt Lake City: University of Utah Press, 2005), chapter 4.

6. Wallace R. Bennett to Adam S. Bennion, May 17, 1954. Cited in Lester E. Bush Jr., "Compilation on Blacks and Priesthood," undated, unpublished manuscript, p. 259. Lester E. Bush Papers, Ms. 685, Manuscripts Division, J. Williard Marriott Library, University of Utah, Salt Lake City.

7. Leonard J. Arrington, *Adventures of a Church Historian* (Urbana: University of Illinois Press, 1998),183.

8. Mark E. Petersen, "Race Problems—as They Affect the Church" lecture given at Brigham Young University on August 27,1954. As shocking as such statements are to many contemporary readers, similar views are still held by many Latter-day Saints—including Dr. Randy Bott, now retired from his former position as professor of religion at BYU, who in 2012 made similar claims to reporter Jason Horowitz. See "The genesis

of a church's stand on race," *Washington Post*, February 28, 2012. The story resulted in a swift and unprecedented statement by the church that called out Bott by name and disavowed the statements that "absolutely do not represent the teaching and doctrines of The Church of Jesus Christ of Latter-day Saints.... We condemn racism, including any and all past racism by individuals both inside and outside the Church." See Church of Jesus Christ of Latter-day Saints, "Church Statement Regarding '*Washington Post*' Article on Race and the Church," mormonnewsroom.org, (accessed February 29, 2012).

9.   Lowell Bennion, interview by Maureen Ursenbach Beecher, March 9, 1985. LDS Archives, Ms. 200 730, Salt Lake City.

10. Mary Lythgoe Bradford, *Lowell L. Bennion: Teacher, Counselor, Humanitarian* (Salt Lake City: Dialogue Foundation, 1995), *Bennion*, 132.

11. T. Edgar Lyon to Lowell L. Bennion, August 28, 1954. In: T. Edgar Lyon, Jr., *T. Edgar Lyon: A Teacher in Zion* (Provo, UT: BYU Studies, 2002), 242.

12. Quoted in Bradford, *Bennion*, 135.

13. Lyon, *T. Edgar Lyon*, 243.

14. This episode is discussed in detail in Prince, *David O. McKay*, Chapter 4.

15. Lowell Bennion, interviewed by Maureen Ursenbach Beecher, 9 March 1985. LDS Archives Mss. 200 730.

16. David O. McKay Diary, June 13, 1957.

17. Lowell L. Bennion to David O. McKay, June 27, 1957, in David O. McKay, Diaries, entry dated June 13, 1957. The McKay diaries were kept by his secretary, Clare Middlemiss, and consisted of typescript in loose-leaf binders. On occasion, such as this entry, Middlemiss would insert a later document that shed light on the diary entry. Hence, the apparent anachronism.

18. Sterling M. McMurrin, interview by Gregory A. Prince, January 14, 1996.

19. John H. Vandenberg, interview by Gordon Irving, November 15, 1984, LDS Archives, Ms. 200 727, Salt Lake City.

20. Lowell L. Bennion, "Race," unpublished essay, quoted in Bradford, *Bennion*, 94.

21. The first scholar to document such a beginning of the policy was Lester E. Bush, Jr., "Mormonism's Negro Doctrine: An Historical Overview," *Dialogue: A Journal of Mormon Thought* 8 (1973), 11–68. Subsequent scholarship, while adding details, has confirmed Bush's basic narrative. The most recent book on the subject is Russell W. Stevenson, *For the Cause of Righteousness: A Global History of Blacks and Mormonism, 1830–2013* (Salt Lake City: Greg Kofford Books, 2014).

22. Kenneth Godfrey, interview by Gregory A. Prince, August 4, 1999.

23. Douglas D. Alder, "Lowell L. Bennion: The Things That Matter Most," in *Teachers Who Touch Lives: Methods of the Masters*, comp. Philip L. Barlow (Bountiful, UT: Horizon Publishers, 1988), 26.

24. Ernest L. Wilkinson to David O. McKay, July 13, 1962, quoted in: Bradford, *Bennion*, 166.

25. Irene Bates, interview by Gregory A. Prince, October 3, 2000.

26. For a detailed account of the Nigerian Mission, see Prince, *David O. McKay*, chapter 4.

27. Lowell L. Bennion to George Boyd, October 21, 1963, quoted in Bradford, *Bennion*, 246.

28. Sterling M. McMurrin, "A Note on the 1963 Civil Rights Statement," *Dialogue: A Journal of Mormon Thought* 12 (Summer 1978), 60–63.

29. Lowell L. Bennion to George Boyd, undated letter, quoted in Bradford, *Bennion*, 250.

30. Lowell L. Bennion, "Religion and Social Responsibility," *The Instructor* (October, 1965): 391.

31. Lowell L. Bennion, "Commentary [on David L. Brewer]," quoted in: Bradford, *Bennion*, 252–53. Donald R. Cutler, ed., "The Mormons," in *The Religious Situation: 1968* (Boston: Beacon Press, 1968), 549.

32. Lowell L. Bennion, interviewed by Mary L. Bradford, 12 September 1990, quoted in Bradford, *Bennion*, 250.

33. Wallace Turner, "Mormons Weigh Stand on Negro," *New York Times*, June 7, 1963.

34. Edwin B. Firmage, interviewed by Gregory A. Prince, June 6, 1995.

35. Quoted in Bradford, *Bennion*, 137.

36. McMurrin interview by Prince.

37. Ibid.

38. Ernest L. Wilkinson, "Memorandum of Conference with President David O. McKay on Tuesday, June 12, 1962," in David O. McKay, "Diaries," June 12, 1962..

39. McMurrin, interview by Prince.

40. George Boyd, interview by Gregory A. Prince, January 15, 1996.

41. Douglas C. Bennion, interview by Mary L. Bradford, May 19, 1987, quoted in Bradford, *Bennion*, 258.

42. Bradford, *Bennion*, 258.

11

LOWELL, A TEACHER BY HEART

EMMA LOU WARNER THAYNE

It was fall 1941, a few months before Pearl Harbor, December 7. I was a sixteen-year-old, very green freshman at the University of Utah. I'd been told to go to the LDS Institute of Religion and be sure to get a class from Dr. Bennion. "The Institute" was part of the old University Ward built in 1925, just west of the campus. Above its front doors, under a portrait of Christ, a single sentence declared, "He went up into the mountains and taught them." I liked it.

On the second floor among a throng of students, I signed up for a class titled "The Religion of the Latter-day Saints." Little did I know what to expect. Dr. Lowell Bennion became to my college days what he was to thousands—an electric current in my believing. He was able to plug a student in to brave new things to think about, while at the same time repairing frays in the cord that attached to credible essentials—all with a companionable incisiveness that endeared as it chastened.

His appearance probably started the process. Even then, in his early thirties, he was wonderfully bald, gnomelike, with a thick fringe of curly hair below that mirror we all came to revere. Entering a classroom at the Institute of Religion, makeshift at best, Dr. Bennion came headfirst, twinkling like a boy with adventure on his mind. Even serious, he was smiling. As he came, his face, handsome, ruddy with expectation, was always turned toward us, ahead of the stride that never seemed to keep up with the impulses that persuaded it. His shoulders were those of an athlete, and his arms stretched long to the hands that could have held a baby in one palm. Natty, he walked like a youngster pulling a sleigh. (Nearly forty years later, leading a tour to Israel, he strode the Mount of Beatitudes with an eagerness to see that lent an angling to his gait and radiance to his looking.)

Maybe, though, it was only physically that he came headfirst. Thinker that he was, scholar, intellectual, it was his heart and spirit that made a journey with him indelible. Keenly in touch with both the human and the divine, he could extract from any scripture or journey what mattered most. From what could be worn-out materials—faith, life, death, philosophical gleanings, historical and sociological artifacts—he constructed new trails with new scenery on every side, all of it pertinent and current. With Lowell Bennion, everything was immediate, warm, and personally specific.

He and T. Edgar Lyon were the leaders of the institute and best of friends. A joke told about them was of a naïve student, a girl, asking Dr. Bennion, "How do I learn about the three degrees of immorality?" (She meant *immortality*.) Bennion said in a flash, "Oh, that's my partner's area of expertise." His laugh was hearty and contagious even as he taught the pleasure of thinking, as a stimulating activity for its own sake. He contended that human beings are rational creatures, that Latter-day Saints should have no difficulty believing that "the glory of God is intelligence." All of us seemed to go right along with him. I wonder how many of those students were like me. It was my first experience with this kind of teaching in a classroom. Dr. Bennion insisted that religion, like music, philosophy, or science, has no meaning until it is individualized. Religious life expands beyond intellectual experiences with the gospel. Religion's unique function is to help us face the unknown and embrace our own urgency to find meaning in our total existence.

Bennion taught that religion must be deeply concerned with human relationships and values, such ultimate values as freedom, integrity, love, and hope. While much may be taught from a religious point of view, much must also be learned intuitively and experientially. He talked of conversations with President David O. McKay and learning about handling such critical issues as birth control, evolution, and the denial of the priesthood to black members of the church. He epitomized learning to be open-minded, undogmatic, willing to listen, alert to difficulties, firm in his own convictions but tolerant of those with whom he disagreed. Early in his leadership of the institute, President McKay called Bennion into his office to share some advice he would always hold dear: "Be true to yourself and loyal to the cause," McKay counseled, "and if you are, feel free to draw upon your best thinking and experience from any source."

In recent years, when some leaders of the faith roundly criticized intellectuals, Bennion responded that one cannot be too intellectual, too thoughtful, or too eager to think in matters religious. Only when intellectuals are arrogant, lacking in humility, disrespectful of faith, or intolerant of any knowledge source but reason are they following a dangerous path. Lowell Bennion liked to think of himself as being liberal. To him, this meant broad-minded and not bound by authoritarianism, orthodoxy, dogma, tradition, or unexamined convention. Like Jesus and the prophets, he believed it his duty to promote justice, relieve suffering, and change society even at the risk of personal rejection.

Partly because of this, he was disarming and effective in his multiple settings. In front of a class, at his boys' ranch, at the pulpit, or at a gathering, he was at home and made others feel that way too—comfortable with possibilities for their own growth. His was a conviviality born of constructive curiosity and a feeling of closeness to God and his world.

Lowell Bennion made the betterment of humanity his profession. He was "Dr." Bennion to those thousands at the university; "Brother" Bennion to his Institute of Religion students and colleagues; "Dean" to his university students; "director" of two LDS institutes and of the Community Services Council; "founder" of Lambda Delta Sigma; "husband," "father," "grandfather" to his family; and "Bishop" to his neighborhood flock. But his most fitting title remains "friend." Love was his trademark, humanity his trade. And to it he brought a ceaseless effort reminiscent of Tennyson's ideal: "to strive, to seek, to find, and not to yield."

Bennion was a man for whom position could readily be sacrificed on the unshakeable altar of honor. In the cause of justice to his fellow beings

of every race, creed, color, and persuasion, he was a constant if often har-
ried champion of right over prejudice as a prevailing practice. In dark
times for liberals in the church, times that discouraged if not embittered
lesser men, you could sense his sadness. But to those of us who sought
him out to gain perspective or gather new strength, he remained perpetu-
ally wise and hopeful. Bracingly patient, he returned time and again to his
appraisal of what matters most. With sanity and grace, with head, heart,
and giant spirit, he inspired me over the decades. No one could have had
a more gracious influence on those of us fortunate enough to become
close to Lowell Bennion.

Bennion owed much to the distinctly open-minded characteristics of
his father Milton Bennion. He earned a secondary teaching certificate by
practice teaching at the Stewart Normal School where his father had once
been principal. His teaching style echoed the willingness of his father to
listen and to recognize the value of many lines of learning. This carried,
too, into the manuals Bennion wrote for the LDS Church.

I remember the thrill of finding that Lowell Bennion had written a
manual for the class of fourteen- and fifteen-year-old girls I was teaching.
In it was the illustration I remembered from one of my classes with him
at the institute. It pictured a barn with many small windows and several
hatches opening to the sky. Each opening, he said, afforded a valid view,
from the sides, the top, or the front, but limited by the range of view from
that opening. He labeled these windows: philosophy, religion, history, art,
poetry/literature, athletics, and science. All perspectives were necessary to
gain a full understanding of who we are and how the world works. This
analogy has stayed in my mind as an illustration of a balanced education.
He taught that "to leave any one of these disciplines unacknowledged
meant a limited vision. To tap each source—to know its flow of knowledge and inspiration—is to live most fully."

I learned from Lowell Bennion the important difference between a
prophet and a priest. Prophets break the existing order, are not bound by
the past. Prophets speak for God afresh in the interest of mankind. They
create new forms for timeless concepts that meet the problems of the day
and are quickly responsive to need.

The other type of religious leader, priests, are men and women whose primary concern is to conserve the religion as it came from the founder. Priests build and maintain the church, welding the believers into a meaningful fellowship. Prophets and priests both play meaningful roles, one to create, the other to preserve. As Bennion's student, I saw him play either role with sincerity. His first concern was always "the worth of souls," now as well as in eternity. He saw more potential for good than evil in human nature.

From him as a teacher I learned to think beyond the square, to appreciate differing views of truth. But I learned most to respect his willingness and ability to examine others' ideas. That was in the 1940s. I graduated in 1945, having, with my classmates, witnessed the entirety of the "good war" to defeat Nazism. We supported every phase and welcomed the atom bomb for bringing it to an end. But to Bennion there was no such thing as a good war. I had much to learn from him.

In the 1960s and 1970s he was professor of sociology and associate dean of students at the University of Utah where I was teaching freshman English. I went to him to calm my concerns about issues my Mormon students brought up like the denial of priesthood for black men and of equal opportunities for women in the LDS Church. At about this time, Florence Jacobsen, president of the Young Women's organization of the church, asked me to chair a committee to write six lesson manuals that would conform to an astounding outline. It was a miracle of good sense and inspiration. Lowell Bennion, and equally brilliant Edith Shepherd, had prepared the writing guide to challenge and enlighten young people from their early years to adulthood. Every lesson culminated in a practical application of existence in real life, bringing alive themes like, "Who is my neighbor?" and "Did Christ ever encounter a nonperson?"

From the 1970s on, my husband Mel and I gained new access to his beliefs and imagination in what became known as the Bennion Study Group. It was mostly university people whose ideas and backgrounds differed like stones in a stream but who relished each other's offerings. Thanks to the spirit that was Lowell Bennion. Meeting in each other's homes one evening each month, we felt safe in expressing ourselves about any topic. I never learned so much about variations on believing as I did from the members of this group. We all looked to him as our guide. We all knew of his unconcealed support of priesthood for blacks. One of our occasional visitors was Ruffin Bridgeforth, head of the black Mormon organization Genesis. His experiences moved us all. Then, when the revelation granting priesthood privileges to black men came in June 1978, I asked Bennion, "Do you feel exonerated for your long-denied hopes?" He answered typically, "No. I have lots else to think about."

In 1990 Lowell Bennion and his wife Merle led a group to Israel as part of a tour. Mel and I took our three teenage daughters to let them in on his mystic influence as a teacher. On a Sunday in Jerusalem he spoke about grace, a topic seldom brought to life in a Mormon meeting. He taught us about appreciating the glories afforded us with no deserving or expressed asking on our part. But the highlight our girls remembered best was being on the Mount of Beatitudes. I later wrote of this moment:

> Clumps of olive and eucalyptus become the still hour. Palm branches sigh the liturgy of the patience I never could muster. An Israeli hoses a barnyard. Two youngsters climb a new tractor stalled on the edge of a field. The past opens and closes. A cock crows. A cow moos. Monastery bells ring like the survival of innocence. Suspension. This is a place that is a place. A place that has become The Word. Today the word is Lowell, his rustic simplicity bringing life to the Beatitudes.[1]

That day, he was the light filling us with light.

In later years I visited him and brightly beautiful, white-haired Merle at their home. Gradually his Parkinson's took over. His health, "tolerably good" according to him but drastically limited by any usual definition, brought falls and increasingly difficult recoveries. He had to give up driving—his shoulders, which had lifted tons of food and medicine to thousands in need—refused to work for him. He finally needed help to get a fork to his mouth, his vigorous body had so shriveled and weakened. But his mind and his soul never were. Nor his resolve to stay real.

For more than fifty years he had, as he had for countless others, offered consistent counsel to my constant asking: Should I go to graduate school when I have five teenager daughters, a husband, and a household to run? How might I write or speak for peace in a time of world turmoil? How can I champion the cause of free expression in the church we both love, and still retain a Lowell Bennion faith in questing? His answers are the essence of what he taught:

> Consider the overall benefit. Overcome evil with good.
> Tell the devil to go to hell.
> Be responsible for finding the full measure of your creation. Act out of love, not fear or grievance.
> Whatever you do, do with joy and with faith.
> Keep your own voice and write with your own pen.
> Stay in the church. It's lots more rewarding there than on the outside.

In his eighty-fifth year, after a long visit with him and Merle about what seemed unsolvable problems, I asked him to give me a blessing. I'd never asked before—only for advice. He gave me a blessing like no other I'd known. Since he couldn't raise his arms or stand steadily, I had to sit between his knees, facing out toward Merle, for him to reach to put his huge hands on my head. I felt the loving weight of them, like being engulfed by a magnet. Without a sign of the hesitation I'd come to expect in his speech, he gave me a blessing so private, so knowing, that I felt intimately connected to the Lord who has been with him forever. I will be alive to it as long as I live.

Lowell Bennion lives in the hearts and memories of those who knew him—in person, in print, or by his words—like the light that was his intimate companion, I say what countless others have said or would like to say: Thank you, my friend. For letting me know. And for leaving words and inspiration from a life lived to its fullest and from going up to the mountain to teach us.

NOTES

1. Emma Lou Thayne, *Once in Israel* (Provo, UT: BYU Press, 1980), xx.

PART V

REFLECTION

12

PUBLIC MEN AND THE CHALLENGE OF THEIR PRIVATE WORLDS

A Conversation

LINDA KING NEWELL WITH CAROLYN TANNER IRISH, WILLIAM MCMURRIN, ELLEN BENNION STONE

Sterling McMurrin, Obert Tanner, and Lowell Bennion were storied men. They told stories and they lived lives that made stories. No one is more aware of this than members of their families. Sterling's nephew William McMurrin, Obert's daughter Carolyn Tanner Irish, and Lowell's daughter Ellen Bennion Stone have shared some of their memories of our three subjects. These recollections are personal glimpses into their everyday lives that give us a deeper sense of who they were.

In framing questions for this conversation, I had only to draw on my association with each of these men and their wives. In July 1974, my husband Jack and I unloaded our worldly possessions and settled our children in Salt Lake City where Jack would begin his career at the University of Utah. Within just a few weeks of our arrival, we were invited to participate in a study group that Lowell Bennion headed. This association led to a long friendship with Lowell and Merle that lasted until her death in 1994 and his in 1996. Emma Lou Thayne—whose essay appears earlier in this volume—and her husband Mel were part of that group, as were others who became wonderful friends.

Several years later we were invited to be part of another group called the Monday Nighters. Sterling and Natalie McMurrin, Obert and Grace Tanner, Lynn (Lowell's brother) and Catherine Bennion, and a handful of others,[1] ranging in age from their late seventies to early nineties, had met on the first Monday of each month since the late 1940s. None of them, however, wanted to be the sole survivor of the group, or as they said, "the last one standing." They decided, therefore, to invite a few younger people into their circle. Fortunately for us, Jack and I were the first of those "youngsters." We never knew why they chose us. We didn't know any of them well, and some not at all.

At that time, they took turns telling their life stories. During these meetings, in the company of some of their closest friends, they spoke from the heart, uncensored and without self-consciousness. Their stories provided insights into their varied lives and made Jack and me feel that we *really* knew them.[2]

Carolyn Tanner Irish grew up in Salt Lake City in the same Mormon LDS ward as the Lowell and Merle Bennion family. Years later she joined the Episcopal Church and received her master of divinity degree from the Virginia Theological Seminary. Carolyn was ordained to the priesthood of the Episcopal Diocese of Washington, D.C. In December 1995, she was elected bishop of the Episcopal Diocese of Utah, becoming the first woman bishop in Utah (an irony not lost on Mormon feminists).

Carolyn: Since you mentioned that I was the first woman bishop in Utah, I'll start with a story. The Episcopal congregation in Logan had bumper stickers made to hand out at our convention. They said, "Honk if your bishop is a woman." They also had one made for my husband Fred that said, "Honk if your woman is a bishop." I had a wonderful nearly fifteen years in that role in Utah.

I have only positive feelings about growing up in the LDS Church. Mine was a wonderful childhood. I was always busy at the neighborhood ward. Even after I stopped being quite literal about religious life, I went to church every Sunday and to mutual.[3] I regard the LDS Church with affection. My friend Gordon B. Hinckley, whom I knew as a neighbor in my childhood, later became LDS Church president (1995–2008) and personally welcomed me back as bishop.

Obert did not live to see me become bishop of the Episcopal Diocese of Utah, but when I graduated from seminary, he was there. He came to my ordination as a priest, and as a deacon. People often ask me, "Did it upset your father when you became an Episcopalian and were ordained in that church?" He was so proud of me.

I remember when I was in junior high school, Dad said, "This Sunday we're going to visit a Catholic church," Back then, you didn't quite want to say the word "Catholic" out loud, but I went along. I thought the Mass was pretty much like what the Episcopal Church calls the Eucharist. Two or three Sundays later, we went to a Baptist church. They were pretty noisy, but otherwise, they talked about Jesus loving people. I think the Lutheran church was the third one. Dad wanted to go there because he thought it was closest to the Anglican Church, and his ancestors came from England. Then came the Unitarians. At the Unitarian church, you could talk about anything—probably not God so much—but anything else.

After these visits, Obert said to me, "Carolyn, do you think it makes a difference to God which door you go in?" I thought about his question for days. What would it mean to say, "Yes, it makes a big difference to God," or "No, it doesn't make any difference to God?" This was the beginning of my sense that there is not one true church, and I abide with that today. Our dinner conversations were, "What did you learn today? Well, do you believe that?" It was a philosophy course, and, ultimately, he was a philosopher.

I studied philosophy in college, and moved away from a literal interpretation of the Bible. I became deeply familiar with spiritual teachings of different faiths. Spiritual life has a different language. You can't be literal about the life of the spirit. The interface between the human spirit and the Holy Spirit requires some depth, some silence, some willingness to let its reality develop. And that's where religion took me in my later years, away from just doctrine, and a great deal of it came from Obert and his willingness to openly question.

Linda: William McMurrin grew up in Los Angeles, and now lives in St. George, Utah. His relationship with his Uncle Sterling was very close.

Bill: What were Lowell Bennion, Obert Tanner, and Sterling McMurrin like beyond their professional roles—beyond academia? There probably isn't a more interesting way to view their personal lives than through the stories they told and the ones we tell about them. Sterling's stories offer a window into who he was, and how he viewed the world. Certainly, his tales could entertain, but often they left us with more to think about. Maybe that's why they are memorable. My generation of McMurrins would agree that Sterling never took himself too seriously, that he was always the person we most wanted to be around, talk to, and listen to.

He had an unusual interest in us. Despite observing that some of us were "the center of confusion," he genuinely wanted to know what we were doing, what we were studying, what professional fields we might pursue. Because of his attentiveness, we felt that we, too, might do something important—eventually.

Sterling had an intense loyalty to family. This was true for his immediate family: Natalie and their five children, Trudy, Jim, Joe, Laurie, and Melanie. It also included his extended family—his brothers Blain, Keith, and Hal, who lived in California. Whenever any of the California McMurrins visited Salt Lake City, even without notice, Natalie and Sterling welcomed us with a bed and meals. These visits always held stimulating conversation on a wide range of subjects, gracious generosity, and evenings filled with stories.

Sterling and his three brothers were close. Their relationship also bonded my generation. I was in my last year of college when Sterling, Keith, and Hal's families built cabins near each other on the Kolob Plateau above Zion National Park. Sterling referred to himself as a carpenter's helper. His real contribution, however, was entertainment. Our work may have gone a little faster if we hadn't stopped so often to hear his stories— faster, but not as engaging.

Sterling loved horses—particularly Tennessee walking horses, which he and I raised together. I think they connected him to his youth on the ranch—that was the beginning. They are mild tempered, have a very smooth gait, and a lot of stamina; they can go all day.

Often after spending most of our day riding in the back country, we would settle the horses down with feed and water, and Sterling would say, "Come up to our place and we'll see if Natalie has a cold drink for us." Then he would say with a wink, "We can sit around and criticize the church for a while." In a plaintive voice he would ask Natalie, "Have you got a cold drink for a couple of hardworking men?" She would produce a cold drink, and Sterling would ask, "Have you got something for the other hand?" And out came the cookies.

On one occasion Sterling and I went out for our evening entertainment—watching the horses graze in the meadow—and he commented, "You know what the best thing about these horses is?" I was expecting him to comment on their gait, stamina, or mild temperament. He said, "They're all Mormons." I still laugh at that. He then observed, "You know when Joseph Smith was asked if there are animals in heaven, he replied, 'Oh yes, and I intend to have my horse Jupiter in heaven.' If Joseph Smith gets his horse Jupiter in heaven, I'm going to have Sonny."

A number of times I have been asked if Sterling *really* rode horses. For many people, picturing him astride a horse was simply out of character with the academic persona they knew. After Sterling's death, historian Everett Cooley said to me, "Sterling recently asked me what he should do with all his books." Cooley asked him how many books he was talking about. Sterling replied, "Well, I did a rough count the other day, and there are about seven thousand books in our house." Cooley said, "Does anyone need seven thousand books?" Sterling replied, "A man can never have too many books or too many horses." At the time of his death, I counted thirty-two horses that we had owned through the years.

Linda: In 1940 Lowell and Merle purchased four acres in the East Millcreek area of Salt Lake City to raise their family in the country. Ellen grew up there with her four brothers and still lives on part of that property. In fact, she has never lived anywhere else. By 1986, age had caught up with Lowell and Merle, so Ellen and her husband Neil invited them to move into the apartment on the lower floor of their home. Neil died in 1989. Merle and Lowell continued to live in Ellen's home until they passed away.

Ellen: Talking about the personal family life of my father, Lowell Bennion, is easy because he was what you saw: a man who lived what he believed, what he valued. If he taught a principle, he lived that principle. This extended through all aspects of his life. His love of the Savior, his belief in his teachings and what he exemplified became an integral part of everyday living. My father's intellectual understanding of life and what values really do matter, drove him. Service was the foundation of what he did. It became so intense in his later years that it superseded most other activities.

Our parents had four sons and two daughters: Laurel, Lowell (Ben), Douglas, Steven, Howard, and then me. None of us remember many family vacations—maybe a handful—and these were tied to his speaking engagements. We remember service projects: carrying food to people in need, painting widows' houses, cleaning up their yards. We also remember planting the garden, milking the cow, and working at the Idaho boys ranch that Father founded. Whatever Father did, he did with enthusiasm, vigor, and often not great practicality. He once determined that he needed a project for his four sons. Already, he had hitched them (and me when I was old enough) to the plow to work the garden—a plow I still have in my yard. So they planted a field full of pines to grow Christmas trees. Unfortunately, he forgot to protect the trees from hungry animals. That project soon ended.

He worked hard at the university, then came home and worked hard physically. I believe it was because he had to keep his feelings—his emotion—in check, and his outlet became physical work. He was a master at counseling literally thousands of students. My brothers and I were puzzled as to why it was so difficult for him to talk with us about our personal problems. We decided it was because he just loved us so much. If his chastisements were strong, it was because he wanted us to be better than we were.

When people found out we were Lowell Bennion's children, they would have expectations, like assuming that we loved to do service projects. Once after a talk he had given, a woman approached him. Within my hearing, she asked him what he had sacrificed for all the service that he did. He said, "I haven't sacrificed anything." I know he believed that. Perhaps because I was a teenager, I responded that his family had made the sacrifices. He believed we were so blessed and the needs of others were so great that we had to give, that it wasn't a sacrifice but simply a part of what he valued.

In addition, we were taught to give without expecting anything in return. On one occasion, Father and my brother Howard delivered carpet to a woman in dire need. On the way home, Howard said, "She didn't even thank us for the carpet or bringing it to her home." Father replied with one of his favorite sayings, found in the Bhagavad Gita: "To action alone hast thou a right, not to its fruits." He believed that and lived it. He would say, "I try to act with conviction, with good motives, and get satisfaction out of action rather than the fruit of my action, which is often beyond my control." I believe this is why, when he was let go as director of the LDS Institute of Religion, he didn't dwell on it. He never talked about it at home. He moved on to the next part in his life. It was, at least outwardly, much harder on my mother than on him.

My husband Neil and I lived in the same LDS ward as my parents, and I remember attending a ward council meeting that Father conducted. As the discussion wore on, I recall thinking that this is taking too long. *I know you could solve the problem, Father; why don't you just tell them what to do?* I tackled him after the meeting with that question. He responded, "How will they learn if I solve the problem for them?" He taught people by helping them work things out for themselves.

One event that reveals much about Father occurred when Victor Cline, a prominent marriage and family psychologist, presented a seminar on marriage to members of our Mormon ward. At one point he asked each of us to find a quiet place in the building and think about where we wanted to be in ten years and what we wanted to be doing. I happened to walk back into the chapel with Father and asked him his thoughts. He said his greatest fear was that he wouldn't live long enough to accomplish all that needed to be done.

Early on he saw the realities of the world. He sought out the less fortunate and determined ways to help them, often taking others to serve as well. My mother loved to travel, and for a while he went with her, but he finally reached a point where he said, "I don't have time to go. I have too much to do here." Mother traveled without him after that.

Father tended to do things to the extreme—be it working too hard, getting up in the aisle to dance when he watched *The Sound of Music* (to the embarrassment of his children), his laugh, speaking three or four times in one week. He often missed important family occasions. Always it was for someone else. He thought about loving your neighbor and how best to do that. The examples of his parents and the teachers he admired helped frame the way he lived his life. He lived what he taught and he was true to himself.

Linda: Carolyn, we know that Obert came from a polygamous family, and his father, Joseph Marion Tanner, abandoned his mother, Annie Clark Tanner, and her children when he moved to Canada to escape prosecution for polygamy. How did that affect him?

Carolyn: His mother had to support her family. They were very poor. Her father provided a home for them in Farmington, but she taught school, cleaned people's houses, and delivered their babies. As a small boy, Obert earned a nickel a week working for his uncle on the farm. He also walked along the railroad tracks gathering coal that had fallen off the train. It was used to heat their house. Annie was wonderful to Obert, but he was not close to his five brothers. They were bullies. He was a little fellow, skinny, buckteeth, kind of a funny-looking kid, and they were bigger and made fun of him. I will say this, though: they all graduated from college, which in that day, was not the norm.

Obert saw very little of his father growing up. When he did come to town, he was very cold to Obert. On one of his rare visits to Farmington, Obert waited for him at the train station. As soon as he saw his father, he ran after him, calling, "Father, Father, it's me. It's Obert. Don't you know me, Father?" He didn't even stop to acknowledge his son.

As an adult, Obert was very good to his father's other plural wives. On certain Sundays during my growing-up years, he would say, "I'll go and take Aunt Lora for a ride." Lora was one of his father's plural wives who had outlived him. Obert looked after them all. He made sure they had a roof over their heads and their mortgages paid. He was good to women.

Linda: Ellen, what about Lowell's relationship with his father?

Ellen: Father's experience was the antithesis of what Obert experienced. He had great admiration for his father, Milton Bennion—his integrity and intellect. When Father was in his eighties, I took him to the doctor because he was having trouble raising his arms above his lap. The doctor examined his shoulders and asked if they were painful. "No," he replied, leaving the doctor incredulous because there was no cartilage left in either shoulder. He had watched his own father suffer with diabetes before insulin, including three amputations, with absolute stoicism. He admired this, and, I believe, he was determined to live that example.

He had a good relationship with both his parents. They weren't necessarily warm, demonstrative people, but there was much respect within the family. Father loved his siblings. His father was from a polygamist family with lots of brothers. As a child I also remember going on Sundays to visit some of my great aunts and uncles who were very old. That's how you showed the respect and love that were so much a part of the Bennion family.

Linda: Bill, how do you think the early mix of ranch work and scholarship influenced Sterling?

Bill: Sterling and his three brothers grew up as city kids for half of the year and ranch hands for the other half. They worked alongside of tough-as-could-be ranch hands and lived in one of several bunkhouses with them. Sterling said of this time, "We worked with horses all day long, and at the end of the day, our entertainment was to go out and lean on the fence, watch the horses eat, and tell stories." These experiences provided the underpinnings of Sterling's ability to move freely from conversation about Greek philosophers to one about grazing sheep and cattle.

Linda: Obert had a particular talent of imitating others' voices when he told stories. I can recall his telling about his experience as a young man working in the jewelry store owned by German immigrant William Schubach. Perhaps it was Obert's shyness that rankled his employer, who was not pleased with the young man's progress. As Obert told it (and he did so with a heavy accent), Mr. Schubach said, "Tannah, you will nevah, nevah be a salesman!"

Carolyn: And Obert said back to him, "Yes, I will, but I can't do it with you standing around watching me all the time." He pushed back. And he was a good salesman whether he was preaching the gospel or selling jewelry. He had been cleaning and stoking furnaces for some of the people who lived up on the avenues to get money for school. He would start at four each morning to get their furnaces going so the houses would be warm when the occupants started their day. One of his customers was Mr. Schubach. Obert applied for a job in this man's jewelry store. He thought he could make a little more money, and maybe get some new skills.

Linda: Lowell, Sterling, and Obert married strong, intelligent women. Bill, we know that Sterling met Natalie when they were students at the University of Utah. What can you tell us about their marriage?

Bill: I think they had an exceptional marriage—Sterling believed they did. He liked to say, "Natalie and I have never had an argument. The reason we have been married so long, is because we have an agreement. I make all the important decisions in the family, and Natalie makes all the minor decisions. It works well. We bought a new car last year, and Natalie picked it out, picked the color, picked the model. When we bought our house, Natalie chose the house, and figured out how much money we could spend on it." By now everyone is wondering what the important decisions were. He would continue. "I decide things like whether or not the United States should stay in the United Nations."

Linda: Carolyn, your mother was from Parowan. Tell us a little about how she and Obert met.

Carolyn: They knew each other at the University of Utah when they were students, but it didn't take immediately. Later Obert served a mission with my mother's brother, Ray Adams, who told him more about Grace. He liked what he heard. When he got back he went straight to Parowan to find her. They courted, and it was a lifelong love affair through many joyous and sorrowful times.

I want to share something about Obert's faith crisis when he was on his mission. He served in the 1920s in eastern Germany after World War I. He noticed that women worked the fields rather than men. Most of the men had died in the war. He had a hard time knocking on their doors and talking about God in the face of their suffering. Suffering is an amazing teacher. It can teach us and strengthen us in ways we don't know—ways we would never seek. Obert did not try to convert people to something else. He felt that the whole idea was not to make Episcopalians into Mormons or the other way around. It was to make Mormons and Episcopalians better Christians.

Linda: Ellen, what about Lowell and Merle? How did they meet?

Ellen: Mother was orphaned by the time she was eight and was moved around within the larger family. As a teenager she attended East High School and began dating a boy who was not Mormon. This concerned her grandparents, so they sent her to LDS High School. This handsome young man sat behind her in one of her classes, and that's where they met. Father finished there at sixteen and then went to the University of Utah, but they continued their courtship. Father graduated at age twenty. He and my mother married the following September.

Father immediately left to serve in the LDS Swiss-German Mission. Mother stayed here, found an apartment, and worked. Toward the end, she lived with the Bennions. My parents did not see each other for two and a half years, until she finally joined him in Paris at the end of his mission. One treasure we have is a box of beautiful, tender love letters that Father wrote to Mother while he was on his mission. Unfortunately, he didn't save hers.

During their five years in Europe, while Father worked on his doctorate and dissertation, they learned to love opera, shared in the joy of being together, and experienced the loss of their first child, a daughter named Laurel, at the age of six months. The apartment was cool, and mother pinned the blanket down across the baby so she wouldn't kick it off. Somehow, Laurel swallowed a safety pin. The doctors removed it, but the wound became infected. This was before the wide use of penicillin, and she died. That haunted my mother for her entire life.

Linda: Carolyn, Obert and Grace also had some very tragic experiences regarding your brothers that affected you deeply as well.

Carolyn: My parents had a family of five children, three boys and two girls. We were about two years apart. When we were two, four, six, eight, and ten, all of us contracted polio. We were living in Palo Alto, where my dad taught at Stanford. Three were not expected to live; only my oldest brother, Dean Obert, died. The rest of us recovered. My mother did not want to stay in California after that, so we moved back to Utah.

About four years later my younger brother Stephen was run over by a car up in Brighton in the parking lot. He was six and I was eight. That was the worst because it happened in front of my parents. Five years after that my brother Gordon, who was two years older than I, was killed the day he was to graduate from high school. He had been up Mill Creek Canyon to a party and rode back with someone who had been drinking. The truck hit a tree and my brother went through the roof. So there were five; these tragedies left two—my sister and me. My mother later had a baby boy, David, when she was in her forties.

I remember a comment that a visitor made the evening of Stevie's death. He said something about how we didn't know why God had to take Stevie home, but someday they would learn the reason. It was such an awful death. When it was time for him to leave, my father escorted him to the door and in a very kindly way said, "I cannot see the hand of God in what happened to our Stevie today. I think God is weeping with us."

That phrase stayed with me, and frankly, it helped open me to a religious life later on. Twenty years after Stevie's death, the image of a weeping God was understandable. I learned a lot about grief during that time.

Linda: Once I asked Sterling how your parents coped with these losses. He told me Obert insisted that they were not going to be objects of pity. He said, "We will continue with our lives with our heads up." They did that with dignity and courage.

Carolyn: I don't think they would have survived without the McMurrins and the Bennions and other friends, particularly in the ward. After that I couldn't get away fast enough. Just two years later I went to Stanford, and the first thing I did when I landed in California was light up a cigarette.

My father's way through this was work. He worked all the time. He taught philosophy at the university every morning, then went to the business every afternoon, not because he was drawn to business, but because he did not want to raise his family on a teacher's salary. It surprised him when it became so successful. He didn't set out to become wealthy, and he didn't have a rich lifestyle. He said once, "I don't know anybody who lost so much but still has so much." Obert liked helping people—liked providing good jobs and a supportive, esthetic workplace. He enjoyed making good things happen in the community. He loved beauty.

Linda: Sterling and Obert shared an office at the university. Sterling liked to tell about how Obert's desk would get piled so high with mail and papers that he couldn't use it. So he would hold the wastebasket against the end of the desk and sweep his arm across the whole length, pushing everything into it. Sterling would protest, "Obert, stop! You have pay checks in there." And he'd say, "Ah, what the hell," and kept on shoving.

Carolyn: Those two had a special friendship, partly because they were philosophers. They could talk forever.

Linda: All three of these couples were married in the Salt Lake Mormon Temple. I understand that neither Obert and Grace nor Sterling and Natalie ever went back again. Bill, what was Sterling's view of the temple?

Bill: Sterling's opinion of temple rites was mixed. He respected the spiritual nature of religious ritual and the commitment of individual Mormons to temple work. He was respectful of the symbolism. He felt, however, that the time and energy doing temple work could be better spent elsewhere. With the exception of genealogy, which is clearly linked to the temple, he found the Mormon emphasis on the dead strange, and quite unsophisticated. But, like many things, he could laugh about it. He would say, "Oh I think temple work is a wonderful thing. I'm all in favor of it—it keeps the old people off the streets."

Carolyn: When I was a teenager, Obert took my sister and me on a journey through Mormon history sites. We started in Vermont, then followed the Mormon trail back to Salt Lake, stopping at all the great places. But in New York it was over a hundred degrees. We were near Palmyra when he pulled the car over, opened the trunk, got out a sweater, and put it on. And we were thinking, what is this? We figured it out later. He didn't want the people there to know he wasn't wearing temple garments.

Linda: Bill, tell us more about how Sterling interacted with you and your cousins?

Bill: As we got older, Sterling typically assumed the role of teacher, presenting ideas and questions, allowing us to draw our own conclusions. If he felt that we were missing the point, he might insert a little more direction. I have a clear memory of one long, late-night discussion while driving in the car with Sterling and his daughter Laurie when she and I were in high school. She was recounting a recent seminary lesson about the devil. Sterling simply asked questions of us about evil and the devil. By the time we reached home, the literal existence of a devil tempting people to do evil made no sense to me.

I was a freshman in college when I found out from my mother that all of the parents had an agreement not to criticize the church around the children. Months later, several of our parents were talking with Sterling. When I walked into the room, the conversation stopped. I figured out what was going on. Green, and feeling bold, I said, "Don't you think it's time you gave up this silly idea that you can't criticize the church around the kids? After all, I am in college." Sterling smiled and said, "I think you are right," and they continued the conversation. After that they were less concerned with keeping their views under wraps, and all of my cousins benefited.

There are many things Sterling said to me that have stuck. I can hear him saying, "The idea that religions are true or false is silly. Religions are not true or false; they can be better or worse, but not true or false." Once when I complained about something having to do with the church, Sterling chuckled and said, "Listen, any thoughtful, thinking person could be upset with the church all the time if it wasn't just so damn funny."

Even when we were very young, we knew Sterling was a man of stature, but not until we were older, perhaps in college, did we have a better understanding of what that meant. I'll give an example. Our families had gathered at the cabins just after I finished graduate school. My youngest cousin Jennifer, who was about to be a junior in high school, and I were talking. She asked, "If you could have anybody up here with you to talk with for the summer, who would it be?" I thought for a kid her age, that was an insightful question. I answered, "You know, Jenny, I think he's here." She said, "What do you mean?" I replied, "Well I think its Uncle Sterling." She said, "I don't mean *him*; he's our *uncle!*"

Sterling and Natalie were good grandparents. They traveled all over the world, and like most people, brought back mementos. They had a collection of dolls from various countries. These dolls fascinated their granddaughter, Robbie. When she was in third grade, she asked Sterling to go to school with her and take some of the dolls for show and tell. So he went with her. He started to tell stories about each doll, as Robbie later put it, in classic Sterling style. He talked way over the allotted time, and the teacher let him. By the time he finished, the principal and administrators, plus any available teacher, stood in the back of the room listening to his stories about, of all things, *dolls*!

Ellen: Father loved his children and grandchildren, but he didn't have time to dote on us. Perhaps, he felt that we didn't need him as much as others whose lives were harder. I am grateful that he spent the last ten years of his life in my home. Because of that, my children interacted with him in ways that the other grandchildren could not. As a junior in high school, Lindsay took advanced-placement calculus. In one of their after-school talks, her grandfather told her he wanted to learn calculus. He loved learning. He always said that two of the greatest moments in his life occurred in June of 1978—the LDS Church gave black men the priesthood, and my daughter Lindsay was born.

Linda: Bill, Sterling and his four brothers could not have been more different, yet they enjoyed each other immensely.

Bill: I think they preferred each other's company to anyone else. They were very different, and each had his strategy for controlling a conversation. Blaine, the oldest, would talk without pause to allow someone to interject a word. The youngest brother, Hal, had been an actor in New York on Broadway, and had a voice that commanded attention. His strategy was to talk louder than anybody else. Sterling, of course, was a master storyteller, and once he began with "well, hell . . ." everyone turned to listen. Keith sat quietly in the background, listening to his brothers' egos inflate. He would wait for the moment to pop their balloons with something so funny that they had to let him keep going.

Blaine, a very handsome man even in his later life, always had beautiful clothes, and meeting his standards was difficult. Sterling's clothes were usually more casual and could be a bit unkempt. Once when Sterling returned to the cabins after a stay with Blaine in Los Angeles, I asked how Blaine was. Sterling said he was the same as always, then he told a story to illustrate: "We were going out the door to my lecture, and Blaine said to me, 'Haven't you got some decent clothes to wear to something like this?'" The comment did not surprise Sterling. Blaine added, "A man as important as you should have a decent suit." Sterling asked, "What's the matter with my suit?" Blaine just gave a shrug of disapproval. As they were getting in the car, Blaine said, "Well at least you could comb your hair."

Ellen: My father cared little for personal appearance, evidenced by the cars he drove and his clothing. Finally, in exasperation, my mother began shopping for his clothes without him, and he looked a lot better.

Bill: Sterling was probably closest to my dad. When my father was dying, he was staying with my sister Shelley, who is a teacher and lives minutes away from her school. She had set up a small roll-away bed in the room with him so she could be there at night if needed. Between classes, she would run home and check on him. Most days Sterling's car was at the house. He would be on the roll-away bed and Keith on his bed, talking and laughing. Often they were completely unaware that she had come home. Many times she would return a couple of hours later to find them both asleep between stories.

Linda: Did Sterling affect you and your cousins' view of education, Bill?

Bill: Yes, very much. When I was a graduate student I became quite conscious of his emphasis and commitment to academic integrity. I remember many discussions about history, history books, and even family stories where he would point out the need for complete, unbiased honesty. He could be quite critical of Mormon history. I also remember discussions of early Christianity and other world religions that received some of the same scrutiny. He felt there should be no boundaries limiting the freedom of ideas. With Sterling learning was a lifelong pursuit.

He also had real love and respect for the idea of a university—the history of universities, how they should function, and the role universities play in societies. He wrote that the liberal education found at a

university "frees a person from the bondage of ignorance, incompe-
tence, bigotry, superstition, habit, and irrationality."⁴ He believed that
the future of society relies on human freedom, and that freedom can
come from the idea of a university. Despite offers from many other
institutions, Sterling devoted most of his academic career to the University of Utah—that is where his love was, where he felt he could make
a difference. Indeed, he did make a difference to the university and to
his culture.

Linda: The Tanners and Bennions were next-door neighbors in Millcreek.
How did their friendship manifest itself?

Carolyn: Lowell and Merle were enormously comforting to my parents
in their time of sorrow. As kids, we played a lot together. I was a fan of the
Bennion sons. I witnessed a lot of interesting things on their farm that I
would not otherwise have known about. When a calf was born, or they
would slaughter a cow, Merle would call my mother and say, "Carolyn is
over here, fascinated with what she is seeing, Is it okay if she stays?" They
were always so kind to me.

Ellen: When my parents moved to their Millcreek home, Grace and
Obert would ride up on their golf cart to visit. You could see how much
they enjoyed each other. After Carolyn's dad passed away, she would bring
Grace by to see Mother. They didn't do as much socially, but were good
neighborhood friends. Their youngest son Dave and I had so much fun.
He was bright, and he was such a gentleman. It was something to see a
teenage boy be so kind. I think he learned it from his father.

Linda: Sterling maintained his sense of humor to the end. Bill, you were
with him often in those last days.

Bill: Over the years I have come to realize the profound influence Sterling
had on so many people. On one of my visits with him in the hospital, a

doctor came into his room. He wasn't Sterling's doctor but he had heard he was there and was checking to make sure he was being well taken care of. He had been one of Sterling's students and wanted to thank him for the impact he had on him. Before I left, another doctor stuck his head in the room with essentially the same comment. I said how nice that was, and Sterling replied, "Hell, this has been going on every day." It was clear, however, that he was very pleased. He led a life that mattered to many.

Another time I went to the hospital to see Sterling, he said, "Bill, I'm not concerned about dying—I don't need to hang around here any longer—but I am concerned about pain. I never liked pain. I'm not looking forward to having pitchforks stuck in me and being roasted over the fire." I have to agree with Jack Newell who said, "I don't know anyone who enjoyed life more than Sterling."

Linda: The bond between these three men and their families is a testament to their friendship, common values, and basic goodness. They were all scholars, writers, teachers and mentors, but they each developed unique gifts that defined them individually. Sterling grew up basically happy, secure, and celebrated. He gave the gift of his mind. Lowell also had a secure childhood and willingly shouldered the burdens of those in need. He gave the gift of his heart. Obert knew poverty and strove to overcome it by elevating others through his gift of beauty. We are all richer for knowing them and allowing them to instruct our lives.

NOTES

1. These included: Katherine and Lynn Bennion, who was the former superintendent of the Salt Lake School District; Richard Condie, retired director of the Mormon Tabernacle Choir; Ruth Cannon, widow of Air Force General John Kenneth Cannon; Shelley and Paul Hodson, retired vice president of special projects and international relations at the University of Utah; Peggy Adamson; and Roald F. Campbell, a distinguished professor of education at the University of Chicago, the Ohio State University, and the University of Utah.

2. Eventually, others were invited into the group including Sylvia and John Bennion (son of Katherine and Lynn) and Julie and Dick Cummings. All of the original Monday Nighters are gone now. Paul Hodson, who lived to be 101 years of age, was the last. But the Monday Nighters group continues in the same spirit of open friendship with twenty members, now including Carolyn Tanner Irish and her husband Fred Quinn.

3. At that time, the LDS Church youth program was called the Mutual Improvement Association, shortened to Mutual or MIA.

4. Sterling McMurrin, ed., *On the Meaning of the University* (Salt Lake City: University of Utah Press, 1976), 9.

13

SUMMING UP

Poised Fortuitously in Place and Time

L. JACKSON NEWELL

I had to laugh when I sat down in the spring of 2017 to write the conclusion to a book about three privileged white men who died at the end of the last century. What were we thinking when we conceived this project? Their time has passed. We now grapple with issues they could hardly have fathomed—transgender rights, marriage equality, fundamentalism in politics, and resurgent racial violence in America's cities. Why consider their ideas or recount the turning points in their lives? Why revisit their struggles with faith and church in an era of growing secularism and diminishing respect for institutional religion among those in the rising generation?

The lives of Sterling McMurrin, Obert Tanner, and Lowell Bennion, however, do bear on us and our time in many ways. The quest to reconcile institutional loyalties with personal conscience pertains not just to religious affiliations, but also to our twenty-first-century immersion in the myriad organizations that seek to limit the freedom of our minds. Governments require compliance with their decisions to wage war and refuse to make amends for past breaches of justice. Corporations exact pledges of silence regarding trade secrets or business practices as conditions of employment. Political parties increasingly require tests of ideological purity before backing candidates for election. Modern living requires a perpetual balancing act between institutional demands and individual needs, between affiliation and personal freedom. Membership may have its privileges, but those advantages often exact great costs.

McMurrin, Tanner, and Bennion knew these issues well, took them more seriously than most people do, and arrived at contrasting conclusions. We celebrate their lives precisely because each fought to live with integrity while serving the highest values of their common membership. Mormonism was their culture as well as their religion, and it imbued them with humane ideals, a passion for education, and a penchant for acting on their best thinking. It thereby saddled them with the burden of living consciously with both community loyalty and personal integrity.

Sterling McMurrin chose to define his own membership, denying his church that privilege. Declaring himself publically to be outside the boundaries of its core beliefs on matters of doctrine, he revealed no anxiety about any action its authorities might take to eject him officially.[1] He lived Mormon standards of personal ethics, embraced the culture's optimistic outlook, and admired genuine religiosity—as a sensibility or experience, but not as a set of beliefs about the unknown. As threatening as his ideas were to church orthodoxy, the goodness of his own life—and the prominence of his secular positions—enabled him to live and die as the ultimate independent spirit within the Mormon Church.

Obert Tanner differed little from his lifelong friend McMurrin on matters of belief/disbelief or doctrine, but for him religion was a private matter.[2] He, too, lived the Latter-day Saint code without fanfare or reluctance, and found inspiration in his religion's ideals, which were amplified by his study of Greek philosophy. Tanner did not allow theological issues to impair the effectiveness of his many initiatives to enrich public life in his city, state, and nation. Unlike McMurrin, whose funeral took place in a Mormon meetinghouse, Tanner's life was celebrated in a secular cathedral—Abravanel Hall—which his generous financial gifts and leadership had helped to create.

Lowell Bennion, similar in outlook and ideals to his two friends, plied yet another course. He prized his membership, publically and privately, while devoting his life to teaching what he understood to be his church's essential precepts: justice, mercy, and humility. Even when church authorities forced his resignation from his much-loved job as founding director of the LDS Institute of Religion at the University of Utah—because of his refusal to teach what he did not believe regarding racial policies—he remained faithful to his church. But neither did he violate his conscience. As bishop of his local congregation in his declining years, he continued to fight for racial equality. When asked near the end of his long battle with Parkinson's disease if he believed there was an afterlife, he responded: "I hope there is but, if not, I will welcome the long sleep. I am very tired."[3]

As different as they were, these three men are robust examples of taking the best from one's culture, living those values authentically, and dedicating oneself to high moral purpose. What accounts for their notable attitudes toward life and their insistence on trusting themselves to live by their hard-won conclusions despite the risks?

Like Ralph Waldo Emerson, Henry David Thoreau, Emily Dickinson, and other distinguished literary figures in the Concord circle of the 1840s, they fed off of each other's energy and inspired one another to reach new heights. And our three also savored a larger sphere of unusual contemporaries. In and around their high-achieving Utah circle were nationally prominent intellectuals who had spent important years in Mormon country: Wallace Stegner, Bernard DeVoto, Fawn Brodie, Vardis Fisher, and Mountain Meadows Massacre chronicler Juanita Brooks. The warmth and admiration McMurrin, Tanner, and Bennion felt for these friends dotted their stories in later life. Their sense of kinship, of sharing an important moment in time and place, was palpable.

It is also true, especially for Bennion and McMurrin that they inspired a generation of younger men and women who carried their ideas, alive and vibrant, into a new era. Emma Lou Thayne, Boyer Jarvis, Alene Clyde, Eugene England, Irene Fisher, Dean May, Carlisle Hunsaker, and LDS leaders Gordon Hinckley, Marion Hanks, Paul Dunn, and Jeffery Holland are among the many leaders whose lives and careers were deeply affected not just by one of these men but often by all three of them. Similarly, their influence spawned *Dialogue: A Journal of Mormon Thought* in 1966, *Sunstone Magazine* in 1974, and Signature Books in 1980—all of which continue to flourish as independent voices within Mormon culture.

During the early adult lives of our three subjects, the existentialist movement, precipitated by the Holocaust and two World Wars, exerted a strong influence on European and American philosophy and literature. Its impact was especially evident in McMurrin's belief that we live in a universe that is indifferent to human life, a conclusion that drove his earnest search to find meaning in history. Obert Tanner shared McMurrin's "doubt that the universe is on our side." Lowell Bennion may have wondered privately about this too. The distinctive thing about all three, however, is that they came away with existentialism's most positive conclusions—namely, that remaining conscious of human suffering (rather than being numbed by it) is essential to living an ethical life and, further, that we must each do everything within our powers to alleviate others' pain. Reflecting their heritage too, Tanner, Bennion, and McMurrin were clearly of the family of Christian existentialists, believing that Jesus's teachings and example were their best guides to living a good and just life. Mormon acculturation dictated the positive outlooks of these men, but their keen understanding of the larger Judeo-Christian tradition gave them a grasp of history and theology that Latter-day Saints rarely glimpse.

McMurrin, Tanner, and Bennion all wrote books that placed Mormon teachings in a much larger framework of philosophy, literature, and religion. Earlier in this volume, Bob Goldberg described Obert Tanner's 1955 publication *Christ's Ideals for Living*.[4] Thumbing through this impressive 440-page book, the eye catches the names Benjamin Disraeli, Thomas Carlyle, Emmanuel Kant, John Milton, Reinhold Niebuhr, Elizabeth Barrett Browning, George Bernard Shaw, John Greenleaf Whittier, Shakespeare, and Socrates. What a surprise to find this range in a book "written for the Sunday Schools of the [LDS] Church... at the request of President David O. McKay."

Sterling McMurrin's enduring *The Philosophical Foundations of Mormon Theology* and his other works on Mormonism, described earlier by Brian Birch and me, were also anchored within the larger stream of Western and, sometimes, Eastern religious thought. His remarkable memory for detail made great philosophers and theologians seem like personal friends when he spoke and wrote about them. His intellectual world was large and richly appointed.

Within the last year an unpublished manuscript written by Lowell Bennion came to light.[5] Entitled, "Selected Wisdom from World Religions," this seventy-four-page typescript was apparently intended as part of his series of "little books of wisdom." Emma Lou Thayne and other colleagues vetted and praised the text, but it got lost in the flurry of Bennion's busy later years. This undated work, probably written in the early 1980s, contains separate chapters on nine major religions from Hinduism to Islam, highlighting what Mormons can learn from each. Unfinished though it was, this manuscript presented the most direct attempt of the three men to relate LDS teachings to the sacred wisdom traditions of history.

The strength these men drew from each other is revealed in one of Lowell Bennion's last wishes: "I would just like to visit with Sterling one more time," he said shortly before his death in February 1996; "do you think we could invite him over?"[6] But McMurrin was in St. George, Utah, approaching his own passing, which occurred six weeks later. Obert Tanner had died two-and-a-half years earlier.

Professor Jane Shaw, dean of religious life at Stanford University (a post akin to one that Obert Tanner held on that campus seventy-five years earlier), began her recent book, *A Practical Christianity*, by describing the questions asked of the earliest Christian converts before they were baptized.[7] The key question, she writes, was not, "What do you believe?" but, rather, "How has your life been transformed?" Good works were the test—comforting the lonely, attending those who suffer, speaking and living the truth, and caring about the overall well-being of others, not just their spiritual health. In an era and in a church that increasingly emphasized the importance of what members believed, from the divine origins of the Book of Mormon to the age of the Earth, Sterling McMurrin, Obert Tanner, and Lowell Bennion championed a different understanding of their religion and of the worthy life. Each spoke and acted, in his distinctive way, for the supremacy of that "practical Christianity"—of simple compassion, authenticity, and service—over doctrinal tests of any kind.

From the Hindu Bhagavad Gita to the Platonists of classical Greece, goodness, truth, and beauty were celebrated as universal human values.[8] They transcend Mormonism and every other religion, yet constitute the loftiest ends of a truly religious life. While all three men embraced these ideals, each of their lives seemed especially to resonate with one in particular.

Bennion's consuming quest was to serve those in need by advancing both mercy and justice. His lifelong compassionate works highlighted his goodness above every other laudable quality of his character. His test for every idea was threefold: Is it reasonable? Is it probable? Is it good? He taught caring and love. He practiced humility and kindness.

For Sterling McMurrin, truth seeking and truth-speaking dominated his consciousness and defined his public persona. Settling for nothing short of truth, he believed, is the best way to raise our awareness and advance justice. Knowing the truth about the world around us is the best defense against apathy and callousness. Above all else, McMurrin spoke, wrote, and lived the truth about religion, education, and society even as he sought continually to understand it.

Obert Tanner, while living compassionately and with high respect for truth, found greatest satisfaction in bringing beauty into others' lives, whether through the creation of magnificent jewelry or by filling public spaces with fountains, great music, or fine architecture. It was the beauty of ideas that drove his final effort to found the Tanner Lectures on Human Values. "The most beautiful thing on earth," he said, "is a genuinely free person who is committed to the common good."

Do the lives and ideas of Sterling McMurrin, Obert Tanner, and Lowell Bennion speak to us today? Can any of us do better than to draw from our religious or philosophical roots the universal values that can lift a society or culture toward goodness, truth, and beauty?

NOTES

1. If church authorities proceeded to try him for his membership, he said on several occasions, he certainly wouldn't defend himself, but he would

want to be there for the trial. "I have never objected to questions about my religious beliefs," he told Apostles Joseph Fielding Smith and Harold B. Lee back in 1952, "if they're within a decent context." McMurrin, Sterling and L. Jackson Newell, *Matters of Conscience: Conversations with Sterling McMurrin on Philosophy, Education, and Religion* (Salt Lake City: Signature Books, 1996), 202.

2. Obert and Grace Tanner were never reticent about sharing their views with friends in the "Monday Nighter" discussion group, of which Sterling and Natalie McMurrin, the Newells, and about eight other couples were members. Obert comfortably stated his disbelief in supernatural explanations of religion and religious experience. But he also expressed his admiration for Jesus as the supreme teacher as well as his respect for sincere religious leaders who used their influence for good.

3. The author and his wife were present when Lowell Bennion gave this frank response to the question posed by Maureen Ursenbach Beecher.

4. From the preface to the second edition of *Christ's Ideals for Living*. The manual remained in use by the church's Sunday School Union Board from 1955 until McKay's death in 1970.

5. Lowell Bennion's papers have not yet been given to an archive, but "Selected Wisdom from World Religions" may be found in the L. Jackson Newell Papers, account 2342, Special Collections Dept., J. Willard Marriott Library, University of Utah, Salt Lake City.

6. Lowell Bennion expressed this wish when meeting with friends on December 26, 1993. I wrote in my journal, "Lowell ended [our conversation] by suggesting that we invite Sterling McMurrin to our next gathering, and ask him to talk about God and Truth." From: "Journal, L. Jackson Newell "Twelve Days in December, 1993," Newell Papers.

7. Jane Shaw, *A Practical Christianity: Meditations on the Season of Lent* (Harrisburg: Morehouse Publishing, 2012), n.p.

8. Bhagavad Gita 17:15, describes "words which are good, and beautiful, and true" as the ultimate source of wisdom. The *Catechism of the Catholic Church* references these three qualities as characteristics of God (section 41).

SELECT BIBLIOGRAPHY

LOWELL L. BENNION

Alder, Douglas D. "Lowell L. Bennion: The Things That Matter Most." In *Teachers Who Touch Lives: Methods of the Masters*, compiled by Philip L. Barlow, 23–27. Bountiful, UT: Horizon Publishers, 1988.

Bennion, Lowell L. *Religion and the Pursuit of Truth.* Salt Lake City: Deseret Book, 1959.

———. "Religion and Social Responsibility." *The Instructor* (October 1965): 388–91.

Bradford, Mary Lythgoe. *Lowell L. Bennion: Teacher, Counselor, Humanitarian.* Salt Lake City: Dialogue Foundation, 1995.

Bush Jr., Lester E. "Mormonism's Negro Doctrine: An Historical Overview." *Dialogue: A Journal of Mormon Thought* 8 (1973): 11–68.

DiPadova, Laurie Newman, and Ralph S. Browe. "A Piece of Lost History: Max Weber and Lowell L. Bennion." *The American Sociologist* 23 (Brower. September 1992): 37–56.

DiPadova-Stocks, Laurie Newman. "Lesson for Today from Lowell Bennion's Journey with Max Weber." *Sunstone* 159 (June, 2010), 57–61.

England, Eugene L., ed., *The Best of Lowell L. Bennion: Selected Writings, 1928–1988.* Salt Lake City: Deseret Book, 1988.

Prince, Gregory A., and William. Robert Wright. *David O. McKay and the Rise of Modern Mormonism.* Salt Lake City: University of Utah Press, 2005.

STERLING MCMURRIN

Madsen, Brigham D. "Sterling M. McMurrin: A Heretic but Not an Apostate." In *Mormon Mavericks: Essays on Dissenters*, edited by John Sillitoe and Susan Staker, 285–303. Salt Lake City: Signature Books, 2001.

McMurrin, Jean Ann. *The Deseret Land and Live Stock Company: A Brief History, 1891–1991.* Woodruff, UT: Deseret Land and Live Stock Company, 1991.

McMurrin, Sterling, *The Philosophical Foundations of Mormon Theology.* Salt Lake City: University of Utah Press, 1959.

———.*Religion, Reason, and Truth: Historical Essays in the Philosophy of Religion.* Salt Lake City: University of Utah Press, 1982.

———. *The Theological Foundations of the Mormon Religion.* 2nd ed. Salt Lake City: University of Utah Press 1965; repr., Signature Books, 2000.

McMurrin, Sterling M. and L. Jackson Newell. *Matters of Conscience: Conversations with Sterling McMurrin on Philosophy, Education, and Religion,* Salt Lake City: Signature Books, 1996.

Ostler, Blake. "An Interview with Sterling McMurrin." *Dialogue: A Journal of Mormon Thought* 17 (Spring 1984): 18–43.

OBERT C. TANNER

Tanner, Annie Clark. *A Mormon Mother: An Autobiography.* Rev. ed. Salt Lake City: Tanner Trust Fund, University of Utah Library, 1973.

Tanner, Obert C. *Christ's Ideals for Living.* Salt Lake City: Deseret Sunday School Union Board, 1955.

———. *One Man's Journey: In Search of Freedom.* Salt Lake City: University of Utah Press, 1994.

———. *One Man's Search: Addresses by Obert C. Tanner* (Salt Lake City: University of Utah Press, 1989).

Ward, Margery W. *A Life Divided: The Biography of Joseph Marion Tanner, 1859–1927.* Salt Lake City: Publishers Press, 1980.

ACKNOWLEDGMENTS

The three editors of this volume are indebted to many whose good efforts helped to make it a reality. this book began as an idea, to commemorate two milestones: the twenty-fifth anniversary of the founding of the Obert C. and Grace A. Tanner Humanities Center at the University of Utah and the one-hundredth anniversary of Sterling McMurrin's birth. The first step was a two-day conference, "Faith and Reason, Conscience and Conflict: The Paths of Lowell Bennion, Sterling McMurrin, and Obert Tanner" sponsored by the Tanner Humanities Center in April 2014. Conference sessions considered each of the three notable Mormon intellectuals with several scholarly papers, followed by a final session in which family members engaged in a discussion (guided by Linda Newell) of the personal lives of Bennion, McMurrin, and Tanner and the close bonds they enjoyed with their families.

Some of the papers offered at the conference became chapters in this book. Their authors appear in the table of contents, and their biographical sketches conclude this volume. We thank them for their determination in converting papers to chapters. We also want to thank conference contributors whose work could not be included. With gratitude we acknowledge Sam Allen, James Clayton, Tony Morgan, Grethe Peterson, and Charlotte Hansen Terry.

Tanner Humanities Center staff members were essential to the success of this project. John Boyack repeatedly and patiently worked through the technical glitches to birth a sound manuscript. Beth Tracy orchestrated the conference with great finesse, insuring that we stayed on budget and made the needs of participants a priority. Katlyn Klein checked sources and polished footnotes while working her magic to transform an important historical document into a workable transcript.

Although not on center staff, Annie Freed Goldberg not only engaged extensively at the conference but also helped move the manuscript from draft to publication.

Additional family members who took a special interest in supporting our project and scholarship included Lowell C. "Ben" Bennion, John Bennion, Laurie McMurrin, and Jim McMurrin. Pat Jarvis deserves mention here, too.

We must certainly express special appreciation for the notable lifelong partners of our three subjects: Merle Bennion, Natalie McMurrin, and Grace Tanner. Lowell, Sterling, and Obert would not have been who they were without these women.

We very much appreciated the early encouragement we received from John Alley and Glenda Cotter at the University of Utah Press to turn our collection of conference papers into an integrated scholarly work. They not only inspired our coauthors but also gave us heart to prepare the manuscript.

For all the able support we received in preparing the conference and producing this book, we know it is not a flawless work. The imperfections are wholly our own.

ABOUT THE CONTRIBUTORS

Brian D. Birch received his PhD in philosophy of religion and theology from Claremont Graduate University in 1998. He is director of the religious studies program and the Center for the Study of Ethics at Utah Valley University. In 2003, he cofounded the society for Mormon Philosophy and Theology and served as editor of the Society's journal *Element*. He is editor of the *Perspectives on Mormon Theology* series and is the founding editor of *Teaching Ethics: The Journal of the Society for Ethics across the Curriculum*. In 2011, he was appointed as a senior research fellow at the Foundation for Religious Diplomacy and is currently completing a book project entitled *Mormonism among Christian Theologies* for Oxford University Press.

Mary Lythgoe Bradford is the author of *Lowell L. Bennion: Teacher, Counselor, Humanitarian*, winner of the Ellen Turner Biography Award and the Evans Biography Award. She has also published *Leaving Home: Personal Essays, Mormon Letters*, and *Purple*. In addition, she was editor of *Mormon Women Speak, Personal Voices*, and *Dialogue, A Journal of Mormon Thought*. Her latest publication is *Mr. Mustard Plaster and Other Mormon Essays*.

Kathleen Flake is the Richard L. Bushman Professor in Mormon studies at the University of Virginia. Appointed to the religious studies faculty, she teaches courses in American religious history, with an emphasis on religious adaptation and the interaction of American religion and law. She is the author of *The Politics of Religious Identity: The Seating of Senator Reed Smoot, Mormon Apostle*. She has published in several scholarly journals and is on the editorial board of *Religion and American Culture: A Journal of Interpretation* and the *Journal of Mormon Studies*. Before becoming an academic, she litigated cases on behalf of the Department of Education's Office for Civil Rights and the Federal Deposit Insurance Corporation.

Bob Goldberg is professor of history and director of the Tanner Humanities Center at the University of Utah. He is the author of eight books with his last two, *Barry Goldwater* and *Enemies Within: The Culture of Conspiracy in Modern America,* published by Yale University Press. He has won twelve teaching honors including the Graduate Student and Postdoctoral Scholar Distinguished Mentor Award, Presidential Teaching Scholar Award, and University of Utah Distinguished Teaching Award. In 2003, he held the Fulbright Distinguished Chair in American studies, at the Swedish Institute for North American Studies, Uppsala University. He was awarded the University of Utah's Rosenblatt Prize for Excellence in 2008.

Carolyn Tanner Irish attended Stanford University and then the University of Michigan, where she received her BA in philosophy. She earned a master of letters degree in moral philosophy from Oxford University. After joining the Episcopal Church in 1975, she enrolled at the Virginia Theological Seminary where she earned a master of divinity degree, graduating cum laude in 1984. Carolyn was ordained to the priesthood of the Episcopal Diocese of Washington, D.C. She served congregations in that diocese as well as in Virginia and Michigan. Later she served on the staff of the Washington National Cathedral. In December 1995, Carolyn was elected bishop of the Episcopal Diocese of Utah. She serves as chair of the board of the O. C. Tanner Company.

J. Boyer Jarvis is a University of Utah emeritus professor of communication. He served the University of Utah in several administrative assignments—including associate program director of KUED Channel 7 when it began broadcasting in 1958, assistant to the president and administrator of the University Theatre from 1962 to 1964, and associate vice president for Academic Affairs from 1967 to 1988. In 1961-1962 he was special assistant to the United States commissioner of education in Washington, D.C. He received his PhD from Northwestern University. In 1989, he was awarded an honorary doctor of humanities degree by the University of Utah.

Mark Matheson teaches English at the University of Utah. He was educated in Utah public schools and universities, and he received his doctorate in English from Oxford in 1990. He directs the University of Utah MUSE Project, an office dedicated to enriching undergraduate education. He has served since 2011 as the director of the Tanner Lectures on Human Values.

William McMurrin attended California State University at Northridge where he received a degree in geography. He later taught geography at Dixie College, now Dixie State University. He holds a graduate degree in architecture from the University of California, Los Angeles, and worked as an architect in Berlin, Germany, and Los Angeles before settling in St. George. A founder of the Virgin River Land Protection Association, he currently teaches at the Applied Technical College in St. George and is a principal in the architectural firm of Mesa Consulting, Architects, Engineers and Planners.

Kent Murdock is a University of Utah graduate in history (BA 1972) and law (JD 1975). He was awarded an honorary doctorate of humanities by the University of Utah in 2008. After practicing law in Salt Lake City, he joined the O. C. Tanner Company as president in 1991, and became CEO in February 1997. He retired in 2009. He has served the Church of Jesus Christ of Latter-day Saints in many leadership positions.

L. Jackson Newell earned an MA degree in history and theology at Duke University, and a PhD in the history and philosophy of universities at The Ohio State University. He has been a professor (and dean for sixteen years) at the University of Utah since 1974, but took leave to serve as president of Deep Springs College from 1995 to 2004. His books include *The Electric Edge of Academe: The Saga of Lucien L. Nunn and Deep Springs College* (2015) and *Matters of Conscience: Conversations with Sterling M. McMurrin on Philosophy, Education, and Religion* (1996). Honored as university professor, Jack has also received of the Hatch Prize for Teaching, the national Joseph Katz Award for the Advancement of Liberal Education, and the Deep Springs Medal for Leadership and Service to Humanity.

Linda King Newell is a writer, editor, independent historian, and artist. She is the author of four books, including *Mormon Enigma: Emma Hale Smith*, (coauthored with Valeen Tippetts Avery). Linda has a number of essays in other edited works and has published more than two-dozen articles. She has been a series editor for the University of Utah Press, development director for the Utah Humanities Council, director of special projects at Deep Springs College, and coeditor of *Dialogue: A Journal of Mormon Thought*.

Gregory A. Prince earned doctorate degrees in dentistry (DDS) and pathology (PhD) at UCLA, and then pursued a four-decade career in pediatric infectious disease research. Exploiting discoveries made during his doctorate research, he pioneered the prevention of respiratory syncytial virus (RSV) pneumonia in high-risk infants. His avocation in history led to several dozen articles and chapters, and three books: *Power from on High: The Development of Mormon Priesthood* (1995), *David O. McKay and the Rise of Modern Mormonism* (2005), and *Leonard Arrington and the Writing of Mormon History* (2016).

Ellen Bennion Stone earned her BA degree in elementary education from the University of Utah and a masters from the University of Phoenix. She has also earned teaching endorsements in mathematics and English as a second language. Ellen taught elementary school for eleven years in the Murray School District, and was the district teacher of the year in 1990. She is a reading specialist and works as an instructor-coach for teachers. She runs the reading intervention programs in the district, and has taught classes for teachers through Southern Utah University.

Emma Lou Thayne died at the age of ninety, only months after writing this tribute to her teacher, mentor, and friend, Lowell Bennion. She was much honored and anthologized as the writer of fourteen books of poetry, essays, and fiction. A leader for women in the education, business, and the arts, she taught English and tennis at the University of Utah for many years. Her last book, published in her late eighties, was *A Place of Knowing: A Spiritual Autobiography*.

INDEX

124–26, 217–18; *A Mormon Mother* introductions, 116–18; *New Testament Studies,* 99; personal qualities, 135–36, 139–40, 143, 217, 230; philanthropy of, 137, 143, 226; and philosophy, 96–97, 134, 226; photographs of, *104–6;* as "pragmatic" Christian, 97, 99, 145n28; *Problems of Youth,* 98–99; on religion, 18, 22, 96–97, 133–34; as selfless, 140–41; spiritual quest of, 89, 96–97, 104; and temple, 218; and truths *versus* ideals, 121–22, 125; values of, 134–35, 140–41, 226. *See also* O. C. Tanner Company

Tanner and universities: appeal of, 113, 129; business supporting, 126; graduate education, influence of, 122, 125; perceptions shaped by Annie, 115–16, 118; and religion, 22; social aspects, 125, 127, 129

Tanner Lectures on Human Values, 126–27, 129, 230

Tanner on Mormonism: criticism of, 104; dualistic relationship with, 89–90, 102–3, 129; epiphanies regarding, 96–99; "eternal progression," doctrine of, 135; *versus* home life, 111–12; influence of, early,

111–12, 132–33; liberal movement in, 112, 123; love for, 135, 141–42, 226

Tanner's education: graduate, 10, 120–22, 125, 127, 130n23; in law, 114, 120; undergraduate, 118–19

Tanner's teaching: importance of, 123–24, 135; philosophy of, 124–25; seminary school, 97–98, 119; Stanford, 122–23; University of Utah, 124, 137

The Theological Foundations of the Mormon Religion, 42, 51, 63–65, 70n38

Thomas, George, 34–35, 37

The Truth, the Way, and the Life, 56–57

Udall, Stewart, 39, 73

University of Chicago Divinity School, 56–57

University of Utah: academic freedom investigation, 32–34; Bennion at, 161, 164–65; Bennion Community Service Center, 167; expansion, 1950s, 157; Kingsbury's presidency, 33–34; LDS Institute of Religion, 153–55, 157, 161, 177, 194; McMurrin at, 35, 41, 222; Mormon leadership, clashes with, 36; Olpin's offer to Lowell Bennion, 160–61; student